FUTURE OFFICE

Developments in Information Technology and the resulting knowledge-based economy, as well as the 2001 collapse of the World Trade Centre in Lower Manhattan, New York, have challenged traditional concepts of office design together with many larger precepts of architecture and urbanism. This book examines some of the implications of this revolution and identifies potential new trends in office design and changing patterns of urbanism from an international perspective.

Within a wide range of topics two themes are key: *Place Making* and *Technological Integration*. *Place Making* deals with issues at various scales, from master planning and development of neighbourhoods, to mixed-use building design and the internal environment of the office itself. *Technological Integration* examines the implementation of issues as diverse as sustainable design technologies, moisture permeable building envelopes and Voice Over Internet Protocols. These themes have very definite architectural implications and manifestations.

Practitioners and academics from a broad spectrum of interests contribute essays to this book, which will appeal to people from a range of professions and disciplines, including architects, urban designers, facilities managers and furniture designers to financiers, developers, and IT specialists.

Chris Grech, RIBA, is an Associate Professor at The School of Architecture and Planning at The Catholic University of America in Washington DC, USA.

David Walters, RIBA, is a Professor at The College of Architecture at The University of North Carolina at Charlotte, USA.

FUTURE OFFICE:
DESIGN, PRACTICE
AND APPLIED RESEARCH

Edited by Chris Grech and David Walters

Routledge
Taylor & Francis Group

LONDON AND NEW YORK

First published 2008 by Taylor & Francis
2 Park Square, Milton Park, Abingdon, Oxon, OX14 4RN

Simultaneously published in the USA and Canada by Taylor & Francis
270 Madison Avenue, New York, NY10016

Taylor & Francis is an imprint of the Taylor & Francis Group, an informa business

© 2008 Chris Grech and David Walters, selection and editorial matter; individual chapters, the contributors

Typeset in Avenir by
Keystroke, 28 High Street, Tettenhall, Wolverhampton

Printed and bound in Great Britain by
The Cromwell Press, Trowbridge, Wiltshire

British Library Cataloguing in Publication Data
A catalogue record for this book is available from the British Library

Library of Congress Cataloging- in-Publication Data
A catalog record for this book has been requested

ISBN10 0–415–38590–3 (hbk)
ISBN10 0–415–38591–1 (pbk)
ISBN10 0–203–08595–7 (ebk)

ISBN13 978–0–415–38590–9 (hbk)
ISBN13 978–0–415–38591–6 (pbk)
ISBN13 978–0–203–08595–0 (ebk)

Contents

CONTENTS

Notes on contributors

G.B. Arrington, Principal Practice Leader for Parsons Brinckerhoff PlaceMaking.

John Breshears, Associate Partner at the Zimmer Gunsul Frasca Partnership in Portland, Oregon, USA.

Craig Briner, Cherokee Investment Partners, Raleigh, North Carolina, USA.

Francis Duffy, Founding Partner of DEGW plc., London, UK.

Jupp Gauchel, RaumComputer, Karlstühe, Germany.

Chris Grech, RIBA, Associate Professor, School of Architecture and Planning, The Catholic University of America, Washington DC, USA.

Michael Harrison, Senior Vice President at Hines in Atlanta/Florida, Atlanta, Georgia, USA.

Chris Hays, Director of Hays & Ewing Design Studio, Charlottesville, Virginia, USA.

Judith Heerwagen, Director of J.H. Heerwagen & Associates; Seattle, Washington, USA.

Christoph Ingenhoven, Dipl.-Ing. Architekt BDA, RIBA, Ingenhoven Architects, Düsseldorf, Germany.

Kevin Kampschroer, Director of Research and Expert Services for the United States General Services Administration's public building service, Washington DC, USA.

Dan Kohlhepp, Resident Commercial Division, Crescent Resources, LLC, Arlington, Virginia, USA.

Eugene Kohn, Director of Kohn Pedersen Fox Associates, New York, USA.

Philip Kuttner, Chief Executive Officer, Little Diversified Architectural Consulting, Charlotte, North Carolina, USA.

Vivian Loftness, FAIA, Professor of Architecture, Carnegie Mellon University School of Architecture, Pittsburgh, Pennsylvania, USA.

Steven Ott, John Crosland, Sr., Distinguished Professor of Real Estate and Development at the Department of Finance and Business Law at the University of North Carolina at Charlotte, North Carolina, USA.

Brad Smith, National Sales Performance Executive for Commercial Real Estate Banking at Bank of America, Charlotte, North Carolina, USA.

Matthew Spathas, a Partner at Sentre Partners, San Diego, California, USA.

Jack Tanis, Director of Applied Research and A&D Sales for Steelcase Inc., Grand Rapids, Michigan, USA.

James H. Thompson, Director of Design, Interior Architecture, Little Diversified Architectural Consulting, Charlotte, North Carolina, USA.

Jacqueline Vischer, Professor, University of Montreal, Director, New Work Environments Research Group, Montreal, Canada.

Wolfgang Wagener, Global Head of Real Estate and Construction Practice, Cisco Systems, San José, California, USA.

David Walters, RIBA Professor of Architecture and Urban Design, The University of North Carolina at Charlotte, North Carolina, USA, and Senior Urban Designer, The Lawrence Group St. Louis, Missouri and Davidson, North Carolina, USA.

Scott Wilson, Principal, Gresham Smith and Partners, Charlotte, North Carolina, USA.

Kenneth Yeang, T. R. Hamzah & Yeang International, Kuala Lumpur, Malaysia.

Acknowledgments

An event such as a conference and the resulting publication must by necessity be a group endeavor; the editors are especially grateful to the contributors for their generosity in participating in the Future Office Conference and their continued involvement in the production of this volume. The conference organizers were grateful for the time and resources that the speakers devoted to the success of the event; their reward is manifest in the pages that follow. Special thanks are due to Francis Duffy whose wise counsel led to a comprehensive agenda and a cast of distinguished speakers.

Thanks are also due to the many hands that worked behind the scenes to make the conference a success: the Board Members of the Charlotte Chapter of the American Institute of Architects and the members of the Conference Steering Committee who included Wayne Camas, David Crawford, Rebecca Fant, Rob Johnson, Alan McGuinn, Barbara Price, Terry Shook, and last but not least Scott Wilson who participated in the earliest brainstorming sessions with the editors. We also benefited greatly from the advice of Christy Norcross and the indefatigable energy of Kay Clark of TH Management. Special mention is also due to Professor Ken Lambla, Dean of the College of Architecture at the University of North Carolina at Charlotte for his support, both moral and financial, of the conference and this publication.

We are also indebted to session moderators Philip Kuttner of Little Diversified Architectural Consulting and Professor Steven Ott of the University of North Carolina at Charlotte who valiantly stepped into the breach when circumstances required.

The editors are also grateful to the following students who rendered essential services: Sara Murray, Leslie Phipps and Lara Reeve who forged the link between the spoken and written words by diligently transcribing many hours of audiocassette recordings; Ryan Clark for performing the seemingly impossible task of videotaping concurrent presentations; Adam Wilson, Andrew Craven and Amber Bowman for assisting with the drafting of illustrations.

Finally, we acknowledge the support and assistance provided by our colleagues at the College of Architecture at The University of North Carolina at Charlotte and we offer our sincere apologies to anyone who provided valuable assistance whose name we may have accidentally omitted.

Chris Grech
David Walters

Introduction

The Future Office: Design, Practice and Applied Research

Chris Grech and David Walters

When United Airlines flight 175 slammed into the South Tower of the World Trade Center at 9.05 a.m. on September 11, 2001, many people, architects and office users alike, thought that tall buildings would quickly go the way of the luckless dodo. Some critics used the tragic deaths of the office workers to predict the death of the skyscraper office tower. After all, safety aspects aside, why should a seemingly intelligent species gather willingly in concentrations known only to battery chicken farmers, for eight, ten or even twelve hours a day, five days a week? We were then, and still are, bombarded every day by dozens of images extolling the virtues of information technology and the alleged freedom it brings for us to work how, where and when we choose. The life of every person living today in the developed world has been transformed by the ubiquitous computer; mobile phones facilitate communication practically anywhere and any time, electronic banking allows us to complete financial transactions online whenever and from wherever we like, wireless networks provide access to worldwide information from our corner coffee bar, and iPods provide us with entertainment "on the hoof." When one can work comfortably from home, the bar, or the beach, why do we need to spend hours traveling to congested city centers, wasting valuable time and polluting the air in order to work for several hours in sterile environments?

The events of 9/11 prompted many such questions but the messy aftermath of the disaster hinted that answers would be a long time in coming. As part of this reappraisal, and starting from the belief that the education of architects is closely linked to the practice of architecture, The Future Office Conference Steering Committee in Charlotte, North Carolina, started considering some of the larger issues that faced the designers of office buildings in these fast-changing times. It was clear that, like all areas of architectural endeavor, these issues were not isolated but involved the synthesis of diverse factors. If the collapse of the Twin Towers was to generate a debate about the future of office buildings, then that discussion would need to be framed by a variety of considerations ranging from urban design at one end of the scale to details such as raised floors and furniture design at the other. Within this broad spectrum of topics two themes developed: the first was the idea of *Place Making* which in itself ranged from large-scale issues related to the master planning and development of whole neighborhoods, to mixed-use building design, and down to the internal environment of the office itself. The second theme was *Technological Integration*; while the technologies discussed in this volume vary from the tangible (moisture-permeable building envelopes) to the intangible (Voice Over Internet Protocols), the implementation of these technologies has very definite architectural implications and manifestations. With this broad spectrum of issues in mind, the Conference Steering Committee set about assembling a line-up of speakers whose national and/or international expertise would introduce these themes to practicing professionals in North Carolina and beyond, and initiate a discussion that would help the audience to integrate these ideas into their own practice of office design and development.

One particular ambition of the Steering Committee was that even though this conference was primarily aimed at architects, it should also reach out to a wider audience; a sure way of initiating change in the design and construction industries is to educate the entire multidisciplinary team. The conference thus attempted to address many of the concerns raised by developers, financiers, tenants, and engineers; survey results showed some measure of success in this endeavor by the fact that roughly 40 per cent of the attendees came from disciplines outside architecture.

This breadth of interest and audience has been maintained in the selection of papers and presentations developed for this book, organized under the two main themes. Within this diversity, the section on *Place Making* begins with tightly focused discussions that concentrate on the workplace itself, and these expand into the wider realm of the urban community.

Place Making

The first two chapters, "Organizational Change" and "The Interior Environment" clearly demonstrate one of the underlying themes of this book: the importance of multidisciplinary research and the completion of the feedback loop that is so important to the design professions if they are to serve their clients diligently. It is therefore no coincidence that all the contributors to these discussions are engaged in both research and practice. Three common themes emerge from these two groups: (1) the use of cultural anthropology as a tool for the analysis, implementation and measurement of change; (2) the provision of a variety of environments to suit particular activities and tasks; and (3) the participation of all levels of management to generate a sense of empowerment throughout the workforce. The general consensus also emerges among the contributors in these discussions that while it is erroneous to think that organizational change can only happen with parallel architectural change, it is undoubtedly true that the presence of architectural change can accelerate and reinforce organizational change.

Jacqueline Vischer takes up a variety of related issues in the third chapter, "Towards a Psychology of the Work Environment," where she sets out her thoughts on worker productivity and comfort and suggests ways in which physical, psychological and functional well-being can be evaluated. Next, James H. Thompson, in "The Cultural and Physical Environment as Drivers of Workplace Design," argues that while the most common approach to workplace design has been through functional and aesthetic considerations, these may not be the most effective methods of engaging the user. As an option, Thompson advocates a design approach that considers a number of additional factors, such as management structure, social networks and human capital, which, taken together, define an organization's culture. In this way, Thompson also reinforces the idea that the physical environment can facilitate the realignment of an organization's objectives.

The remaining chapters in Part I explore the larger-scale *Place Making* relationships between new trends in office design and changes in the urban form of mixed-use communities and neighborhoods within which new types of office space are becoming integral elements. David Walters expands on this theme in his chapter, pointing out cultural trends (with some unlikely precedents for our revived love affair with cities), and discusses opportunities for more sustainable urban design. Scott Wilson extends this latter topic into new marketing opportunities for developers, capitalizing on Americans' changing expectations for their suburban environments. Both chapters point to new ways of integrating the workplace into mixed-use, walkable and transit supportive communities. G.B. Arrington and Craig Briner emphasize the importance of *Place Making* in their practice-based discussions on how public transit technologies are changing the form of the city and thus the physical and social context for the workplace. Of particular relevance are ways in which previously polluted sites in strategic locations can be remediated and brought back into productive economic and social use through mixed-use development where different types of workplace are important social and economic components.

Theory and practice meet hard realities in Dan Kohlhepp's chapter "Challenges and Lessons Learned at Arlington Potomac Yard," where Kohlhepp recounts some of the many challenges faced (and successes achieved) by progressive developers who are trying to capitalize on these trends and opportunities to produce profitable construction projects.

Technological Integration

The wider realms of practice in the larger community link neatly to the opening series of chapters in Part II, *Technological Integration*. Christoph Ingenhoven and Eugene Kohn share a common desire for the understatement that is often the hallmark of confident and consummate designers. In his chapter, "Enthusiastic Pragmatism," Ingenhoven articulates his concern for a sustainable approach to all facets of human activity and he illustrates through his built work the ability to integrate technology and form seamlessly in the creation of buildings that are admired for their transparency and clarity. Ingenhoven's work has consistently embraced both themes identified by the conference organizers: Place Making and Technological Integration. "Enthusiastic Pragmatism" is a personal manifesto that will inspire architects and students alike to create buildings that provide real, tangible benefits for our environment.

Despite the increased terrorist threat posed to tall buildings, this building type still retains popularity. As Eugene Kohn demonstrates in "Form, Function and Aesthetics in the Design of Tall Buildings," the title of World's Tallest Building holds a symbolism all its own. While for many years this moniker was linked primarily to the technical prowess of the host city or nation, the title has gradually come to symbolize instead the economic strength of a global region. It is astonishing to realize that while the Empire State Building held the title of World's

Tallest Building for 43 years, and the Sears Tower enjoyed this accolade for 24 years, only six years later the new leader, the Petronas Towers in Kuala Lumpur, was itself overtaken by the Taipei Financial Center. The rapidity with which this title has recently changed hands demonstrates that tall buildings still hold a tight grip on the symbolism of economic strength. As such, it is no surprise to see this competition being played out against the backdrop of the economically successful countries of the Western Pacific Basin.

If the title of World's Tallest Building is of necessity unique, one potential consolation for not winning appears to be the desire to outshine one's neighbors through extravagant form. The results of this secondary competition can sometimes lead to uncomfortable juxtapositions, but Kohn demonstrates, through the example of his practice's design for the Shanghai World Financial Center, that there is always a place for simple elegance. Kohn Pedersen Fox's shard-like structure shows with exemplary skill how a multiplicity of uses can be appropriately accommodated within the subtly changing profile of this impressive tall building.

Kenneth Yeang's vision in "Green Design" is closely related to the natural ecosystems that once dominated our planet. Humankind's activities in the past two centuries have threatened nature's delicate balance; inorganic artifacts are replacing organic materials. Yeang believes that architects, as responsible people, must engage in the creation of a society that follows nature's example by recycling, reusing and reabsorbing the buildings and systems that our consumer society creates.

Michael Harrison, Senior Vice President at Hines, with special responsibilities for the Atlanta and Florida regions in the south-eastern USA, flies the flag for enlightened developers. The firm's founder, Gerald Hines, has always recognized the value of architectural design in the marketing of office space, and Harrison, through his early exposure to architecture, shares similar interests. Harrison explains from his personal experience how current best practices in office design and development can usefully employ ideas of sustainability to create a market lead over the competition. In doing so, he stresses how the dogged investigation of seemingly trivial details, like swirl pattern air diffusers, can allay unfounded fears and overcome client and user resistance to the introduction of new technologies.

The discussions in "The Added Value of Sustainable Design" bring to the fore issues that find echoes elsewhere in these pages. The most pressing questions for many people with regard to sustainable design are: first, how best to quantify its benefits, and second, how to persuade financiers and developers to adopt sustainable practices. The conclusion one inevitably draws from this discussion is that these two questions are closely related. Chris Hays informs us that his method of dealing with sustainability involves the consideration of strategies rather than concepts; how, for example, the maximization of natural lighting can reduce a building's reliance on demand-side energy, leading to annual cost savings that can result in estimated payback periods as short as six years. While Brad Smith applauds the sustainable approach, he also warns that intangible benefits do not satisfy investors. In his view, the "commoditization" of sustainable technologies will make them desirable; such a process can be provided by effective post-occupation evaluation where performance data can be analyzed to prove (or deny) predicted benefits. Such valuable research will help to fine-tune prediction models and should assist the design community in speeding up the slow evolutionary process of converting risk-averse capital investors to appreciate the many advantages of sustainable design. As Michael Harrison points out in his chapter, developers are becoming increasingly aware of the growing demand from potential clients for facilities that will enhance the well-being and comfort of their employees. Fortunately pressure from the grassroots is also creating a demand for sustainable practices.

In "High Performance Building Envelopes," Christoph Ingenhoven and colleagues offer some strategies for dealing with the issues that confront architects in the South-east region of the USA. Here he brings to bear his experience in Germany and his pragmatism with regard to fuel prices, passive technologies, and annual holidays. Kenneth Yeang, no stranger to hot humid climates, tackles the same challenges, while John Breshears uses his perspective as mechanical engineer turned architect to inform us about his research into building skins that filter the moisture out of hot humid air.

Most office users either take for granted or are happily oblivious of the detailed technical innovations that have transformed the workplace in recent years. In "Information Technology and Building Infrastructure," Wolfgang Wagener, Jupp Gauchel and Matthew Spathas give readers a technology-friendly view "under the hood" of state-of-the-art digitally integrated buildings. Without baffling the digitally challenged reader, they outline the benefits of web-accessed Building Operating Systems and demonstrate the need for user-friendly interfaces that our grandparents would feel comfortable using. As we become increasingly reliant on digital technologies, the efficiency of buildings will depend on the degree to which all technologies are integrated into the building infrastructure. The long-term implications for developers will be the automatic inclusion of many systems that are today viewed as add-ons, while the implications for architects will lead to a greater degree of integration during the design process.

If the content so far gives the impression that the design professions have defined the challenges ahead and are coming to terms with the new digital paradigm, then Wolfgang Wagener, in his chapter "Connected Buildings," demolishes any reason for complacency. By looking back at significant technological innovations, such as the invention and distribution of electricity, the invention of the motorcar or the introduction of air conditioning, he shows that the new technologies forced new types of buildings to emerge. Therefore he suggests convincingly that as we head for digital convergence, where ceilings turn into antennas and walls evolve into media-rich surfaces, we should prepare ourselves for a new architecture where time rather than space becomes the principal organizing factor.

The Future . . .

The last word on the future of office design has been left to Francis Duffy, whom many readers will recognize as one of the foremost voices in the design and analysis of office space. In the concluding chapter, "Measurement: The Key to Reinventing the Office," he reminds us of the promise held by early twentieth-century buildings such as the Larkin office building designed by Frank Lloyd Wright. However, Duffy is quick to point out that the wholesale adoption of Frederick Taylor's theory of Scientific Management through the subdivision of labor has had drastic effects on the practice of business and architecture; in business, it has resulted in the banal and depersonalized office layouts with which most people are familiar, and in architecture it has reduced a holistic profession once rich in sub-disciplines to one where the architect often works only as an external decorator, a designer of façades seemingly influenced largely by personal whim. The solution, Duffy argues, lies in architects reclaiming their position of knowledgeable authority and regaining the confidence of clients by engaging in systematic research that will enable them accurately to assess their designs against their clients' business goals.

Although our twin themes of *Place Making* and *Technological Integration* may at first seem unrelated, it becomes apparent throughout the book that the gap between these strands narrows until they converge. Surely no workplace designer can neglect either theme if he or she wishes to offer users a comfortable, effective and sustainable environment? There is no doubt that as the pace of change quickens and the built environment is forced to transform itself, clients will demand greater levels of assurance from designers that their buildings will prove efficient and effective. Thorough research into client demands and design solutions will undoubtedly provide the most effective learning tool for designers, and the dissemination of this research into the public domain will prove beneficial to allied disciplines. The issues at hand cannot be resolved by practitioners alone; academic institutions, whose very essence is the discovery and dissemination of knowledge, have an equally important part to play in this evolutionary process. As Wolfgang Wagener asks at the end of his provocative chapter: "Can the profession" – and here we have to add, the academic community – "rise to the challenge?"

Part I

Place
Making

Organizational Change

Philip Kuttner, Jack Tanis,
Kevin Kampschroer, Judith Heerwagen
and Francis Duffy

1

Editor's Introduction

Philip Kuttner

In Chapter 17, "Measurement: The Key to Reinventing the Office," Francis Duffy describes how the fabric of late nineteenth- and early twentieth-century office buildings were the architectural embodiment of Taylorist principles. Twenty-first-century business practices, impacted by the liberating and democratizing influence of Information Technology, are in a state of flux. How can the design professions, in dialog with the business community, develop a new architectural paradigm?

The authors of this chapter all have one thing in common: they have each committed their careers to advancing the knowledge required to transform the workplace into a powerful and competitive environment for organizations and their employees. My hope is that after reading this chapter, we will all be in a position to go forth into our own as well as our clients' organizations and make an effective case for the argument that truly effective organizational change can only be achieved with parallel change in the design of the workplace. Jack Tanis is the Director of Applied Research at Steelcase Inc. and has been deeply involved in workplace research and design for many years. Jack leads the Steelcase research teams to develop and implement advanced office concepts. Kevin Kampschroer is the Director of Research and Expert Services for the United States General Services Administration's public building service. As a result of his work with facility disciplines, leading companies and national universities, Kevin has been widely recognized for his leadership role in examining and measuring the important relationship between space and productivity. Judith Heerwagen leads her own research and consulting firm in Seattle, J.H. Heerwagen & Associates; she is widely respected for her unique perspective as an environmental psychologist and for her extensive research and writing which is focused on workplace ecology, the psychosocial value of space and the human factors of sustainable design. Finally, Francis Duffy is recognized internationally for his research and writing on the design and analysis of office space; he is probably best known for his pioneering work in helping corporations use space more effectively over time.

Workspace and Behavior

Jack Tanis

My perspective is a business perspective since my formal education was in Business and Economics. I would like to start with a question that our Chief Executive Officer, Jim Hackett, would typically ask CEOs in other businesses. His question gives us some idea of how business people talk to each other about "space." I will start out with this provoking thought: "Why bother with space at all?" If I really start to dig deep into a CEO's mindset, I would want to know if there is the desire not only to minimize space, but possibly to get by without space at all. In many cases space is viewed as a necessary evil and many business leaders do not understand space and its role in helping to facilitate their organizational change. To illustrate this point further, I refer to the concept of User Center Design as practiced by IDEO, one of Steelcase's sister companies. Their studies start out with the observation of people; however, they go beyond observation and into the realm of analysis of the data gleaned through observation. We learn from cultural anthropologists that most people engage in observation to confirm concepts they already hold. The disciplined science of observation enables cultural anthropologists to discover patterns of behavior. They see users in the context of what they do; the key is to be able to improve profitability by creating a new experience. Therefore, we should ask ourselves exactly what that pleasurable experience is and how we can best support it. The solution therefore lies in observing, discovering and co-creating space with the same attention that we devote to the product development cycle. At Steelcase we have been attempting to utilize this User Center Research method to help create space. A relevant analogy would be with Amish barn raising; the delightful aspects of Amish barn raising are, first, that it all happens in one day and, second, that it is a combination of individual and community collaboration. The idea of community participation in the creation of the built environment is what I would like to focus on; the creation of space is one particular kind of experience and the use of space also creates a shared experience.

The history of the office as a workplace illustrates that there is a close correlation between the way people are governed and the layout of offices: rigid organizational structures that are manifested in conventional office layouts. However, this bears little relationship with the way more and more people are working nowadays. Business practices today are far more complex than they used to be and behavioral change is the key to innovation. Hierarchies are giving way to human networks and the networks are acting as catalysts to behavior. The key is to understand people's behavior and to develop ways of changing behavior over time.

Hierarchies are bound by the shape of the corporation and the hierarchy is limited to what's inside the four walls of an office. However, networks know no boundaries; they spread, they connect and they are based on trust. Peter Drucker said a few years ago: "Old organizations are based on force and new organizations are based on trust." The emerging networks are expressions of trust between people. It would therefore make sense to look at workspace as an opportunity to provide proximity and relationships in the network; such spaces can be dedicated to individuals or groups.

If buildings can shape behavior, then how can we design buildings to assist in behavioral change? We found that our own User Center Research showed us a number of things that we were able to verify through observation. Historically, in a typical office configuration 70–80 percent of the space is dedicated to individuals. We will call this "I" space. Therefore the remaining 20–30 percent is "we" space. We started by looking at our own leadership community and we found that we needed a ratio of 30–40 percent of "I" space and 60–70 percent of "we" space. Not everyone goes that far but encouragingly we see many examples of a 50:50 split where the collaboration space is really the key to supporting the knowledge-based culture. The convergence of proportions demonstrates an enormous shift.

At this point I would like to examine the definitions of *efficiency* and *effectiveness*. In 1963, Peter Drucker defined efficiency and effectiveness as follows: "Efficiency is doing things right, effectiveness is doing the right things."[1] He also said: "Businesses are dominated by efficiency measures and need an equal imbalance of effectiveness measures." Forty years later we still have the same need. We still do not have an equal imbalanced set of effectiveness measures. The following are some of the more common efficiency measures which will be familiar to anyone in the world of architecture and design: efficient use of space, square footage, churn, asset management, accommodation technology, procurement process, and satisfying environmental issues. The measures of effectiveness relate to helping people be more effective; they are about fostering innovation, enhancing communication, encouraging learning, improving work process, expediting decision-making, and so on. It should be obvious that management uses the former more frequently than the latter.

So how can we all facilitate the changes I describe? We should use the principle of applied research. The key is to learn experientially; we get the user involved in the experience of what really needs to happen. So we structure this using "ask first" questions just like those used in surveys. We use cultural anthropology techniques to get deeper into observation and interpretation; we then make a new experience by prototyping it and we follow this by asking and observing all over again. We offer this service in the form of three-day workshops where we go through an *ask*, *observe* and *make* sequence. We have carried out a number of these workshops at leading corporations; the outcome frequently inspires our clients to adopt a completely different way of thinking about themselves. The teams that engage in these workshops generally include architects, facilities managers and all levels of management, i.e. top management, middle management and users. The main objective is to go on observation safaris that allow them to gather information about their own organization. When this information is collated and analyzed, it is quite obvious that this process is very different from a traditional programming exercise.

One of the most important parts of this process is to close the gap between the language used by the design and the business disciplines. Design professionals sometimes have a difficult time speaking the language of business and the business community is quite frightened of design language because they don't understand it. Our hypothesis is that the language of people and culture is the best way to bridge this gap (Figure 1.1). In other words don't leave your people (i.e. the users) at the kids' table. If users become engaged, they will understand a new process; they will be more creative and most importantly they will buy in to something new. The idea is to get users to participate. Where necessary, the idea is to "irritate the

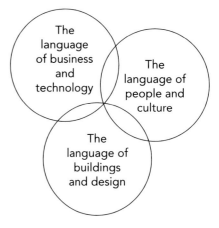

1.1 The Language Bridge

oyster" by disrupting commonly held assumptions in a clear and visible way so that people "get it," i.e. they start to understand the reason why the change in the process is necessary.

There are many different levels of change. We can illustrate this by using the concept of Joe Pine's pyramid from the *Experience Economy*[2] and we can put a little different spin on it (Figure 1.2). The lower level is "As Is"; it is about first costs, standards, status quo and also possibly about the introduction of new products. This is a new engagement or the recognition that something needs to change. The next level is "Refine"; it is about moderate changes in space, technology, work processes and culture. The third level offers to "Redefine" any one of the four categories in the previous level. The fourth level is "Transform" which is about fundamental breakthroughs and new discoveries.

Conclusion

One of the things that we like to say is that space does not necessarily lead to transformation but it needs to *support* transformation. Therefore, in any kind of cultural transformation we really need to focus on space in order to support change. Over the years we have advised a number of corporations and in each case we have helped them to build a prototype site at

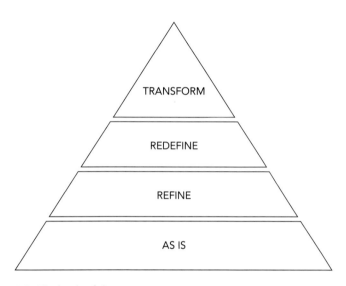

1.2 The levels of change

either the "Redefine" or at the "Transform" level where they have changed their technology and their work processes. They did this by observing and engaging their own users, implementing a User Center Design pilot site and validating it before embarking on a large-scale implementation. All these clients believed that they had a fundamental need for organizational change in the way that they operated in order to survive and go forward. Our goal at Steelcase is to help people work more effectively and to help organizations work more efficiently, we believe it is important to consider both of these issues together and not separately.

Cultural Alignment

Kevin Kampschroer

The General Services Administration has a unique opportunity to influence the work environment because our mission is to "help federal agencies better serve the public by offering, at best value, superior workplaces, expert solutions, acquisition services and management policies."[3] The most significant aspect of that mission statement is that it says "at best value"

not the cheapest way possible. We are responsible for 31 million square meters of space around the country, 8,300 facilities and 1.1 million tenants. We operate on a business footing: we collect rent from our tenants, we generate $8 billion in revenue and we produce about $800 million in net income which we give back to our board of directors.

Ironically both the federal government and the space it uses have grown pretty dramatically over the past 35–40 years; almost all of this increase has been in leased property due to the changes in the way space is being used over time in the federal government (Figure 1.3). One must also remember that for most organizations during this period the nature of work itself has been changing; outsourcing in both the private and public sector is probably the principal cause of this change. Another critical generator of change has been the gradual recognition of what the core values and the core competencies of a company might be. We are not doing the same kind of repetitive work any more; we're not facing the same kind of problems day after day. Work is becoming more strategic; the new approach creates greater value for organizations. As the nature of each task has become more individual, much more collaboration occurs; work is much more improvisational. It is these new circumstances that we need to tackle in the design of the workplace.

So where do we start? What do organizations care about? They only care about cultural alignment. All the research that's been done in the behavioral and business worlds over the past 40 years has shown that cultural alignment, i.e. the quality of work-life, allies itself with high performance; if you don't have cultural alignment, your organization doesn't perform well. Our research has shown that there is the potential for space, buildings, or the physical environment to affect and improve organizational change. The basic thesis of all the contributors in this chapter is that for organizations to change dramatically, they have to have a corresponding component of architectural change. Now, I propose that this is *not* true; organizations can change without architectural change, however, without architectural change you miss the opportunity to accelerate or reinforce the change. Failure to integrate spatial changes with organizational changes presents missed opportunities. Therefore we begin and end every project in which we are involved with a focus on organizational performance. We do this

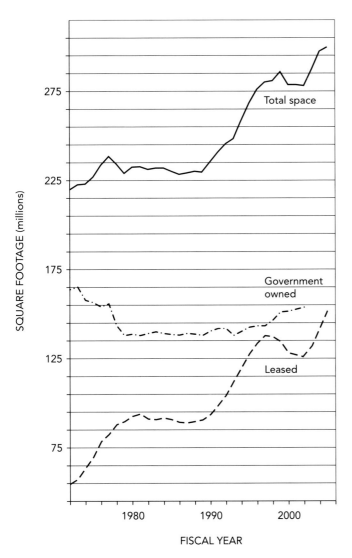

1.3 Trends in owned, leased and total space, 1972–2003

Behavior and Business (Figure 1.4). Business leaders understand the link between individual behavior, group behavior and organizational performance; what we have to do is talk about the mediating value of architecture and space in reinforcing those interactions. Remember that it is not enough to go through a process of making sure that you have efficiency, effectiveness and expressive measures; you should have some method of measuring that collaboration is beneficial in both financial and human capital terms. Only then can you start to develop a hypothesis that says: "If I remove doors and make accessibility greater, I'm going to increase the ability of people to get next to each other and that should have an effect on collaboration." Then you can go back and measure the results to determine whether the desired results have been achieved. The ideal method for measuring the results is by using that organization's own criteria; as a second best option you could use some other measure derived from a similar area of research. The greatest value of this kind of research is not just to throw these ideas out there, and say: "Well, I guess they've worked, I'm on to the next job" but to analyze whether the hypothesis has actually achieved the desired results.

by carrying out our own research since there's not enough data available to draw on. We say forget about productivity measurement and enhancements; if you address organizational performance, then productivity will take care of itself. Once again it comes back to the integration of three arenas: Building,

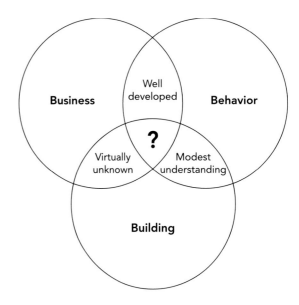

1.4 The integration of Building, Behavior and Business

The great benefit of the work we are engaged in at the GSA is that we can analyze the results of what we do. The application of these tools we have developed also brings a richness to the design process because we can create something that is new. This new process comes from a true understanding of the value that people put on what they do and why they care about space at all. In many cases, you can even create an understanding that space does in fact matter. This is a new process and we feel proud that we are helping to create it.

Transformative Change

Judith Heerwagen

Organizational change can involve two vastly different processes. The first is *focused change* that is concerned with making adjustments to an existing system. This usually means that an organization may have strayed from its original purpose and desires to realign itself with its primary mission by making itself more efficient or by supporting new kinds of relationships. In this case, the organization is willing to accept existing work processes and just desires to do things better. The second category of organizational change is far more radical; it is *transformative change* which means doing new things, i.e. setting new missions. The first is low risk, the second is high risk. The high risk associated with transformative change comes from wanting to change everything, to enter a new realm where the very survival of the organization may be placed in jeopardy.

Transformative change often occurs during periods of disequilibrium. The notion of disequilibrium comes from chaos theory. There has been some very interesting research recently on the topic of chaos theory and organizational change which suggests that periods of drastic change can cause disequilibrium. The change can be externally driven by things like market forces or it can be internally driven as in the case of the workforce. For example, there is going to be an enormous change in the workforce in the USA over the next few years as the baby boomer generation retires and makes way for a younger generation with different skills and expectations. As a result there is going to be a major transformation that the government is very concerned about. There is generally a great deal of tension related to this transitional phase. According to chaos theory, learning, creativity and innovation occur during this period of tension or disequilibrium. In fact, we need the disequilibrium to generate the pressures for change. The optimal stage of disequilibrium is the point just before chaos; what is called "the edge of chaos." If there is too much perturbation in the system, it can lead to the destruction of an organization. Therefore the line between chaos and progress needs to be managed carefully. If this is done successfully an organization can end up generating a new equilibrium at regular intervals. I can illustrate the requirement for balance with a case that I have direct experience of; in a former organization where I was a senior scientist, we went through organizational change, i.e. major change, every two years. However, after a while, the workforce got so used to the idea of periodic change that they failed to understand why things were being changed. This attitude indicated that change was no longer valid, and they basically paid little attention and grew very cynical.

I agree with my fellow contributors in saying that we are talking about linking people, process, place and also technology, when we address transformative change. We know that there have been many experiments on the workplace; there has been the free address, no address, the mobile office, the non-territorial office, work anywhere, anytime, etc. As a result these changes have prompted us to do new things: new ways of working, new ways of thinking, new ways of behaving, and I think it makes many of us feel like experimental rats. I think people are being asked to change too much, without reason and without understanding what they are doing. Therefore, I think the key issue we face is that of articulating clearly the value of the desired change. The person who is doing the work needs to understand what this change means to them, how it's going to help them and how they will be able to carry out work they could not do before. In many cases people feel like things are being done *to* them, not *with* them; obviously there is a very big difference between the two. What is actually required is the generation of solutions from below, not from the top down as is commonly the case. There is always a problem with overcoming adaptation to the current state. I often hear people say: "Why do we need to change? It works fine now." Encouraging people to imagine a future state, a future way of working, is a major challenge and new techniques are required to achieve these changes effectively. It is sometimes necessary to ask people to forget what they're doing now and to imagine doing things differently. I think that many of the suggested changes require experimentation; we will not know what the benefits and costs of these new workplaces will be until we carry out the experiments and analyze their results.

If we look at transformative change processes we can see that since the 1940s psychologists have carried out a great deal of research into the issues related to problem solving. A couple of key issues have been determined from this research: one is that solutions and directions have been generated from both the top and the bottom levels of management. If we examine this phenomenon organizationally, we can conclude that the higher-level management should set the vision and the goals and should provide a rationale for the change in a way that articulates its value. However, the solution should be generated from below; it should come from the people who will be working in the new environment; this will allow them to understand what needs to be done and should enable them to look together at how things could be done differently. These are two different processes and all too frequently projects become top-down decisions rather than solutions where the linkage between the mission setting, the vision setting and the solutions come from below and go in both directions.

I will illustrate some of these ideas by describing two case studies. The first is an example of the GSA Office of the Future and second is an experiment currently under way at Cisco Systems. As Kevin Kampschroer pointed out, the GSA now has to compete with the private sector in terms of the quality of the work environment. This means there is a tangible external pressure on the GSA to support change within its client organizations. We all know that the nature of work is changing; it is much more mobile, much more flexible, much more technology enabled. In addition, we need to take account of the demographic shifts that I mentioned earlier. The goals of the GSA Office of the Future project were to experiment with new ways of working, to increase collaboration across units and to focus on strategic issues in a way that would also showcase the GSA's capabilities. This particular office belonged to a GSA leadership team in Washington State. Their work environment was typically hierarchical with large corner offices and beautiful views of Mount Rainier. The senior management had worked for

20 years to get to these offices. As a result of the changes implemented in the Office of the Future design, these managers were pulled out of their separate offices and were grouped together in an open plan environment with 8×10 ft (2.44×3.14 m) spaces. It was these people who experienced a major shift in how they were working. This was actually dictated from the top because the senior officials realized that all three units within that organization went out individually to their customers. Therefore, the management said "We all ought to be talking to one another and integrating our approach to the customer." The workspace solution that they came up with pulled the leadership out of their enclosed office spaces and placed them in open plan areas on the ground floor rather than on the upper floors, thus providing centralized areas for large group meetings and informal work as well as many different sized meeting rooms and some very small closed rooms for focused work.

As part of my research I carried out extensive interviews with Bob Hunt of Hellmuth, Obata + Kassabaum to assess the results of the changes described above. We found that there was indeed increased communication within the groups but not necessarily across the groups in the way that was intended. The leaders interacted more because they were forced to share a workspace. However, there were some conflicting values about the space itself; many felt forced into this space and those who did not believe in the change were still complaining about it two years after the changes. Nonetheless, they did recognize that seeing other group leaders probably did have some value, they just were not working together. We found that the reason for this was that there was no way for them to do so; they had different cultures and different business models. In fact, the groups often found themselves in competition with each other. So the changes carried out in this organization had mixed success. Part of the problem was the top-down decision making where visionary leaders said: "This is what we'll do" rather than providing the vision and allowing others to ask: "How are we going to reach it?" In this case there was a lack of problem solving at the bottom. I think that in the case of organizations with a rigid hierarchy, it is very hard to get individuals to collaborate unless major organizational changes, like changes in reward structure, changes in how people do business etc., are introduced at the same time.

The second case study is the Connected Workplace at the Cisco Headquarters in San Jose, California, that Wolfgang

Wagener refers to in Chapter 15. Wolfgang and his colleagues are working on some experimental workplaces (see Figures 15.1 and 15.2); they are trying to demonstrate how new technologies can enable mobile work by using internet phones, wireless, and so forth which are built into the building fabric. What this means is that nobody has an assigned workspace; the idea is that you move around to where you need to be or near whomever you want to work with. Obviously, there is an economic value in this concept; you don't have to have an individual workspace for everyone. Some of the design solutions are to move away from cubicles to very open environments that have no visual barriers or very limited visual barriers so that the sense of awareness is very high; you can see and hear what's going on and you can talk with people more easily. The entire work environment has wireless support, many small, enclosed rooms and informal, den-like spaces and a central café that both is a meeting space and provides food and beverages. This type of office is very different from the typical cube grid; there is a multiplicity of spaces, different kinds of meeting rooms with the idea that people will go where they feel most comfortable. Cisco's early research shows that even after just a couple of weeks of moving into these new work environments people are responding positively to these spaces. I think that in time we will find that there are going to be major developments in this direction. However, just as some organizations will adopt these more flexible plans some other organizations will not find them conducive to the way they work. It is for these reasons that more research is required.

Some of the preliminary findings at the Connected Workplace show a number of unexpected benefits; the most important being increased communication. Typically, one can see whether a colleague is present and walk over to ask a question rather than telephoning or emailing and waiting for a response. There is also the notion of the 5-minute meeting, where you do not need to reserve a meeting room, you meet at the workspace, settle an issue and move on. However, the biggest problem is the potential for distractions; this is a very difficult problem to solve because there are the benefits of social engagement and the problems that arise with work that requires either focused attention or complex cognitive functions which are difficult to carry out in a noisy environment. I think that with further research we will begin to know more about what works under these kinds of circumstances.

Transformative change is not easy and I think we need to draw on new models to understand how to think about transformative change. I like to think of the zoo as a metaphor. If we look at the old model for the zoo, it was about survival – keeping the animals happy. I equate this with the cube environment; the animals are isolated, they can't see or interact with one another or with different species. The second model is where you adjust the system by letting the animals share the cube. The third model involves changing the system completely by putting animals in natural habitats. If we look at the old zoo, the animals were very restricted, they couldn't do much at all; they were highly controlled and were meant to be on display so that the people could see them. This environment led to a great deal of dysfunctional behavior. What is the new zoo about? It's about behavioral choice. The animal can go where it wants, when it wants and it can interact with who ever it wants to at any time of the day. Sometimes the animals aren't around when the people go to the zoo, and the visitors get irritated because they can't find the kangaroo, or the giraffe but that's what the animals want: not to be seen all the time. Zoo designers have done their research; they have looked at what the animals need to thrive. They have asked themselves what the animals do in their natural habitats and how do they use their habitat, how do they interact with other species? How do they interact with their con-specifics? As a result of this research, zoo designers have taken the central features of the animals' requirements and have put them together to provide a more pleasing environment for the animals. So now we see giraffes interacting with zebras instead of being separated in different parts of the zoo; this is more natural and has had an incredibly positive impact on the animals themselves. There is less dysfunction, there's less aggression and there is improved well-being among the animals and they reproduce more, which is the animals' natural productivity. The other consequence was that it actually increased zoo attendance. Previously zoos were doing poorly financially, so by transforming the zoo experience for the visitor as well as the animals they have transformed everything including the financial outcome. This is a typical systems change and a model we should think about when we're designing space because it has the essential elements we also need: the zoo designers actually listened to the animal – and we are all animals too.

Professional Change

Francis Duffy

It struck me that there is a huge contrast between what the other contributors to this chapter are proposing and the stock of office buildings we have inherited. Many of these buildings were actually designed at the beginning of the twentieth century when the office building began to be important; a time when ideas about office behavior were imported directly from Taylorism. Fredrick Taylor believed in the scientific management of work, i.e. breaking work down into manageable parts. He assumed that because his management system was scientific, it was actually getting rid of people's bad habits and training them to work in a way that was beneficial to the employer. His ideas fundamentally meant "divide and rule." By employing these principles you ultimately break organizations down and disempower people.

I think there is a direct parallel with the history of the architectural profession in the twentieth century. I feel that I am allowed to say this because I was for a time in the early 1990s, the President of the Royal Institute of British Architects and was deeply involved in the politics of our profession. At a particularly difficult time in the UK during the early 1990s, architects suffered rather badly because of an economic recession. At this time, the government was also on the attack by wanting to deregulate all the professions and architecture being the weakest profession was the first on the list. Then, of course, there were the comments from the Prince of Wales about modern architecture; so the architectural professionals were really beaten about the head. This led to bad behavior by architects; to things like fee cutting. In that context, I carried out a study on the structure of the architecture profession in the UK called the "Strategic Study,"[4] which diagnosed various problems. In fact, there was a section in that document called Architectural Knowledge that may well have led me to be thinking about these issues.

The point I want to make is that architecture, too, suffered from Taylorist division; there was a separation of functions in a hierarchical way but there was also a separation horizontally. The history of the architecture profession since the end of the nineteenth century shows that, in the United Kingdom at least, architects behaved like drunken sailors by getting rid of things

that they could not cope with; cost control became a separate profession quite early on; the discipline of surveying went out the door with chunks of engineering that used to be part of architecture; landscaping also went quite early; interior design lingered into the 1940s and 1950s. These separations of function left us with pure architecture on its own. Therefore, in a very precarious economic situation, architecture, as it was then practiced, was very vulnerable as it had few allies; we did not help ourselves at all by these changes. Other professions, notably medicine and surveying, have developed in a federal way, easily incorporating emerging sub disciplines. Not architects – we have preferred the myth of pure architecture. The economic consequences of this tendency have made architects peculiarly vulnerable.

That is the background to the reflection I want to make about another kind of change. It is vitally important that for architects to be successful they should engage beyond architecture and use non-architectural skills. Jack Tanis, Kevin Kampschroer and Judith Heerwagen have all alluded to this idea. This is the most appropriate way for architects to help transform the culture of organizations; this is something I have been closely involved with for many years and am enormously excited by this potential. The price for architects to get involved in this use of the leverage of design is that we have to embrace a wider range of skills than are currently taught in schools of architecture. It is important for architects to realize that when engaging in the kind of transformational situations that Judith Heerwagen was describing, that it is impossible to effect a design change without parallel change management within the client organization.

These are the new rules of engagement: the understanding of how organizations work, the willingness to embrace new tools and new techniques to understand the culture and to help them embrace it and change it. The commitment, that is necessary in order to achieve this, has huge implications for the way in which we operate as designers in the early twenty-first century. That is my strongest message. Not only should we talk about changing our times; we should talk about the implications of change on changing ourselves as professionals.

Notes and References

1 Brech, E. and Robertson, A. (eds) (1964) *The Effective Business, The Effective Executive*, London: British Institute of Management.
2 Pine, B.J. and Gilmore, J.H. (1999) *The Experience Economy: Work Is Theatre and Every Business a Stage*. Boston: Harvard Business School Press.
3 GSA Strategic Plan, April 2002.
4 *Strategic Study of the Profession – Phases 1–5, 1992–1995*, London: Royal Institute of British Architects.

The Interior Environment

Vivian Loftness, Jacqueline Vischer and Jack Tanis

Editor's Introduction

Chris Grech

Rapid developments in Information Technology are forcing enormous change in our work environments. We can think of these environments in terms of the technological infrastructure and the physical surroundings (lighting, acoustics) that support work. Both environments affect comfort and performance; the first case relates primarily to the hardware infrastructure and is arguably simpler to quantify than the second environment that relates to psychosocial aspects of human behavior.

The authors of this chapter will inform us about their research into the office environment and will touch on various aspects of the issues mentioned above. Vivian Loftness has been a key player in the development of the Intelligent Workplace, a living laboratory of commercial building innovations for performance at the Carnegie Mellon University School of Architecture. She will outline various aspects of her research at the Intelligent Workplace. Next, Jacqueline Vischer is an environmental psychologist and Director of the Interior Design program at the University of Montreal. She will examine how comfort, performance and control affect productivity. Finally, Jack Tanis, Director of Applied Research and A&D Sales for Steelcase Inc., addresses issues of worker effectiveness.

Future Office Environments

Vivian Loftness

I believe that the four most important points related to future office environments are: (1) infrastructures for dynamic work environments; (2) collaboration and concentration as related to open versus closed workplaces; (3) layers of closure; and (4) design for sustainability.

The first issue has to do with the misplaced notion that as a design profession we can predict the kinds of office layout that an organization will need for its present as well as future needs. The dynamic nature of contemporary work mandates that we develop multiple workplace scenarios for the lifetime of each project. We should proceed by designing infrastructure and furniture systems that support change. With this brief in mind, it is evident that we can no longer live with the embedded HVAC, lighting and networking solutions of the past; flexible infrastructures are critical to future office environments. These new systems need to facilitate change with minimum disruption.

A few years ago, Steelcase's *Workstage* project introduced workplace systems that established an identifiable grid of service; however, the nodes of service were totally idiosyncratic. This allowed the user to move outlet boxes, air diffusers, task lights and controls with a continuous choice of location and density of infrastructure. With this "grid and node" strategy for infrastructures for dynamic workplaces, it is possible to separate ambient from the task air conditioning, lighting and network capabilities. It is vital to be able to move those nodes of service with ease and to avoid obsolescence.

The average churn rate in American organizations is close to 40 percent, and the average cost of churn ranges between $400 and $2,000 per move per workstation, depending on whether it is a simple office content move or a full rebuild. The ability to quickly reconfigure the infrastructures that support the workstation ensures significant "churn cost" savings. For example, when the Hines Partnership completed a "build to suit" for Owens Corning they achieved an average drop in churn costs from $450 to $150 per move. This magnitude of savings generated a payback period for the installed cost of the raised floor and its infrastructures of less than one year.

Second, "layers of collaboration" and the tools needed to support shared work processes are key. Obviously, conference rooms support one form of collaboration. Yet, "project places" which are dedicated to a team for a duration of time may be even more effective since they provide a location for residual information and asynchronous exchange.

The electronic collaborative environment is a developing area that has significant potential. The General Services Administration's *20.20* projects are supporting research that should help us to understand the various kinds of collaboration. Social network analysis, e.g. whether you have your best friend at work and how often interact with the people around you, provides the first level of insight into the effect of workplaces on collaboration. The highest level of collaboration is ideation and creative development that crosses disciplinary boundaries. Researchers at the Center for Building Performance have a

theory, which we hope to quantify over the next few years, that the shared equipment space, meaning the service hub (Figure 2.1), will support networking and knowledge transfer, and even some coordinated work, if you have the right tools there. However, dedicated project rooms are necessary for the move into ideation and creative development.

The third issue is the "layers of closure" required for privacy and interaction. We have found that people spend a great deal of time doing collaborative work and meeting, but they also spend a lot of time doing heads-down work like reading and writing. In examining the links between acoustics and performance, research reveals that acoustic privacy is still important. Quieter environments are definitely more conducive to the execution of complex tasks, including memory and recall. Therefore, it is important to provide environments in which you can create visually, spatially, and possibly acoustically closed spaces.

Finally, I would like to mention the importance of access to the natural environment and its contribution to a healthy, sustainable work place. Daylight, views and natural ventilation will become increasingly important factors in the office of the

2.1 The Intelligent Workplace Laboratory at the Center for Building Performance and Diagnostics, School of Architecture, Carnegie Mellon University

future. We need to reduce the size of office floor plates to increase the amount of natural light that enters offices. Research shows that performance gains of 10–25 percent of output can be achieved by access to daylight and views. At the same time, a 5–10 percent reduction in sick building syndrome and over 30 percent energy savings can also be achieved. Natural ventilation can provide 40–70 percent reduction in cooling loads and potentially increase productivity by 0.4–18 percent. Even high-rise buildings can be naturally ventilated, as demonstrated by the recently completed Commerzbank by Foster and Partners in Frankfurt and the RWE Tower in Essen by Christoph Ingenhoven (Figure 9.3).

In conclusion, the visionary Office of the Future will depend on the design of flexible infrastructures to support ever changing patterns of open and closed individual and collaborative spaces, each with access to the natural environment, for individual health and productivity, organizational effectiveness, and long term sustainability.

Comfort, Performance and Control

Jacqueline Vischer

My perspective on these issues is a little different from Vivian Loftness's because I am a social scientist. I look at the same issues from the point of view of a psychologist.

My work concentrates on the three areas that I think are relevant to productivity. The first is *comfort*: what does comfort mean, and how can we use that concept? The second is *performance* as a measure of productivity. Third is the topic of *control*.

Many of the studies I have carried out have tended to focus on satisfaction, i.e. do you like what you have? In terms of the physical environment, we are looking, at the bare minimum, at two definitions of productivity: we can look at the performances of the individual and the team. There is also a third area that we call organizational effectiveness; this increasingly relates to being competitive or having an advantage over competitors.

Individual productivity is tied to the performance of the person in the environment. In other words: are they working better? Are they working faster? Are they making fewer errors? When we look at how effective the lighting or the acoustic environments are, we are looking at whether the person's performance has slowed down or speeded up, and whether the output of that performance is better or not. With regard to the importance of creativity and ideation, i.e. are more ideas being generated? Are people being more creative? These are all questions that relate to the performance of the individual.

I would argue that the group productivity or the measure of team effectiveness is closely linked to the product. When an organization puts a team together, it is generally because they want an end product that is better than that already available on the market.

Linking psychological considerations to the ambient environmental conditions, i.e. lighting, ventilation and thermal comfort, we see that they have a direct effect on performance. The layout of the space, the furniture configuration, the placement of equipment, the configuration of the meeting places, etc. will all affect how a team functions. So right there we have two different definitions of how the environment affects productivity, and both of them lead to different ways of measuring.

The psychosocial aspects of this research topic affect our definition of the measurement paradigm. There are two existing models that we use and refer to on a daily basis that are part of the way we think about this whole area; one is the adaptation model, i.e. adaptation control. This model has a long history in psychology, in terms of measuring how human beings adapt to different situations. What interests me is how human beings adapt to environmental situations. There are psychological and physiological aspects of this adaptation behavior, and we also know that in a situation that requires excessive effort to adapt to the environment both discomfort and stress are being created. So we can make a theoretical link between an existing area of psychological research and the effectiveness of the work environment. The other model is "motivation mental hygiene," where the most important element in the workplace is worker motivation. Therefore, anything that improves worker motivation is above the neutral line, and anything that demotivates the worker goes below the neutral line. The environment is included in the list of influences, although the environment is usually only noticed when it is so dysfunctional that it demotivates people. This brings me to the question of comfort: we generally talk about comfort in rather broad terms. I suggest that there are at least three ways of looking at comfort.

Physical comfort is what we think of first when we think of comfort. There are, for example, the American Society of Heating, Refrigerating and Air-Conditioning Engineers (ASHRAE) standards, which set out comfort criteria. If we follow these guidelines, ASHRAE informs us that 80 percent of the population should be within their comfort zone. We know also that there are basic levels of habitability. If people are physically uncomfortable, i.e. if they're really cold, or if rain is pouring in, they just will not remain in that building. So we must ensure a basic level of physical comfort. I would like to make a distinction between physical and psychological comfort. I have just dealt with physical comfort; psychological comfort is something that we in the design professions are meant to know about and recognize, and so I believe that we should start taking it into consideration as an entity meriting objective investigation and incorporation into our projects.

We come now to issues of territoriality. The component behaviors related to territoriality are privacy, status and control relative to our co-workers. I would suggest that privacy as it concerns us has two meanings: the privacy that I am referring to is the privacy of being able to control one's accessibility from other people and thereby maintaining indications and signs of status. I consider this to be a psychological aspect of privacy related to status, which is not quite the same as the functional privacy which I'm going to talk about next.

We can look at empowerment, first, as access to information about one's environment and, second, as the ability to change one's environment. The less one is made to feel like a passive victim, and more like an actual user, i.e. a consumer, the more empowered and therefore the more psychologically comfortable one will feel. Therefore, any strategy that actively involves users can contribute to psychological comfort.

There is a third area of comfort that is linked to the performance of a task; it relates to the definition of productivity in terms of individual performance. To assess the criteria by which the environment enhances productivity at this level of functional comfort we must analyze: (1) the requirements of the task; and (2) whether the environment is designed to meet those criteria. Once more I refer back to the issue of user likes and dislikes; it is not always what users like and dislike that is important in the performance of tasks, it is what can help people work better that is significant. One has to take a step back from the evaluation of environment, and try instead to measure whether people are working faster, harder, and with a reduced level of absenteeism.

Needs analysis in this situation is focused on tasks, and the issue of control is also raised here. Control, like privacy, is a psychological as well as a functional concept. Typical issues of control might be: can I close a door when I need to? Can I concentrate when I need to? In these cases the idea is that control is determined by knowledge of the environment; the user probably had some say in the manifestation of the environment and therefore has some control of how it can be changed to meet his/her needs. We therefore end up with a conclusion which indicates that in order to design a work-supporting environment, one needs to look at all three areas: you look at *physical comfort* by respecting standards, you look at *psychological comfort* by the process that you use to engage people and for gauging users in decision making. We look at *functional comfort* by analyzing tasks. As a result, we can influence not only the effectiveness of workers, but also their morale. A functional comfort model is useful to illustrate the idea of measuring how task performance is affected by the elements in the environment. The influences that support work are the "energy in" part of the equation; when the environment supports work, the person's energy is totally concentrated on their work.

In summary, I would like to stress that as designers and researchers we should be examining aspects of comfort more closely by breaking it down objectively into its component parts and by establishing a theoretical framework that links it to performance. Many of us are heading in this direction and a comparison of our results should prove extremely useful in establishing some common criteria.

Worker Effectiveness

Jack Tanis

At Steelcase, we consider office environments as inter-related systems of people, process, technology and space. Wolfgang Wagener presents a model that demonstrates the convergence of technology and space in Chapter 16. We share that perspective also. In this chapter I would like to concentrate on the results of our research into worker effectiveness rather than worker efficiency.

When effecting change it is important to consider culture, process, technology, and space as elements in an interrelated holistic system. It is the dynamic of the relationship between all these factors that is critical. We like to consider space as a tool for the development of social networks. The social networks I refer to are particular to our human condition; they relate to the interaction between individuals and groups and they inform us how the knowledge/work relationships are generated and maintained.

Traditional hierarchies still persist in corporate governance, and it is the hierarchical model that has dominated our image of office space. Developing technologies have made information ubiquitous and have therefore given it a new strategic value. Human networks have thrived on the availability of information and have gained ground over hierarchies as catalysts for changes in behavior and work patterns. One of our primary research areas has involved mapping the strength of these emergent networks as they affect space.

Whereas traditionally there has been an approximately 3:1 ratio of "I" to "we" spaces, today we are experiencing a greater investment in collaborative, i.e. "we" spaces. By monitoring test sites we have found that the most commonly sized collaborative group is a meeting of two individuals. There is, however, an interesting dynamic because a group of two can quickly become a group of three, four or more and that group may then split into smaller groups; these new groups may not have been working on the same task and so the network will have been extended. However, a meeting of two people generally generates the deepest dialogue and requires the most concentration, therefore the "I" spaces which can support a meeting of two or possibly three people should not be obliterated.

Recent developments in WiFi have attracted a great deal of attention due to the fact that they have enabled a greater degree of worker mobility as well as providing additional ways to achieve privacy. These are both issues that address the "I" space. Our organization has been conducting much research into the use of "we" spaces; these are the collaborative spaces or team rooms that are dedicated to specific groups working on specific projects. One of the best documented examples of research in this area was the work done at the University

of Michigan with Ford iTek that demonstrated a significant increase in productivity as a result of the strong linkage between business process change, productivity change and space. The outcome of this research was published in *Science Daily* in December 2000 and so the results have been around for people to see. This project identified the fact that people working together in a dedicated room achieved a significant increase in productivity. This result was significant as it proved that group work and group computing achieved improved results. When we look at group work we usually find that there are many instances of productivity loss; 15 seconds wasted here and there eventually add up to a significant amount of time. One must also consider the productivity losses generated in gathering a group of people for a meeting. A few people generally arrive early, some late; some will need to be brought up to date; a few more minutes are lost finding the minutes of the last meeting and distributing them. Now imagine that the team members walk into a room where the lights come on automatically and all the relevant project information is instantly available and displayed on the walls. This is all technically feasible today. In fact, it is already being done. This is where technology can bring productivity gains to team work.

I believe that one very useful tool in the analysis of workplaces is cultural anthropology since it tells us a great deal about those things that fit worker beliefs and customs and how office design can support work patterns and user behavior. However, the gathering of suitable information for analysis in this way can be problematic since response to questions can be biased in such a way that it is of little relevance. For example, one's impression of the time taken to perform a task may not be accurate. Cultural anthropology techniques teach us that observation and measurement are more reliable. When we study results from surveys we find that there are actually six patterns of how we manage information and objects in our own personal workspace. So we have now embedded all six of those categories in a tool set that we employ in our analysis and programming. When we use these more sophisticated analysis tools, we can always confirm our findings through direct observation.

One of the things that we have found very powerful in our observation activities is to get a cross-section of senior management, middle management, and the user level involved in carrying out these observation activities. We were not very sure we could engage all three levels at once but we found that it was very successful. We sent them out with cameras on "safari" in their offices and they come back with many pictures; they got very engaged in the process and did a very good job of identifying barriers to work and characteristics they wanted to eliminate.

Finally, I would like to mention best practice models which are the way real estate executives look at the business. A business needs phases: a contract phase, a design phase, a bid, and so on and so forth, in the same way that architects and designers split projects into work stages. Business professionals tend to look at projects from a macro perspective which essentially arrives at the same point: they ask how they can explore, plan, provide and manage a project. However, we have learned that the best practice model requires the whole team of consultants and designers to enter a project together at the earliest stage possible; entering the project in a sequential basis really bogs down the process and leads to lost value. Maybe one reason why the process is currently fragmented is because the business and design languages do not share much common ground. However, both professions understand the common human factors and cultural needs and, in fact, our work has concentrated on bridging the communication gap between the business and design professions. My vision is that there really is a greater opportunity for programming to become a much richer, more consultative process focused on the issues of business and human factors than is typically practiced today and that the results of this new process should provide richer, more efficient workplaces.

Towards a Psychology of the Work Environment*
Comfort, Satisfaction and Performance

Jacqueline Vischer

Changing Trends in Workspace Occupancy

Over the past ten years, major changes in office work, technology and environmental design have generated a growing number of questions about links with worker productivity. What have we learned about the ways in which workers in offices are affected by features of the building in which they work? A number of recent studies of environmental conditions in office buildings suggest that features of the office environment have effects not only on how people feel – their level of satisfaction – but also on their perception of their jobs, their levels of stress, and, ultimately, their physical and mental health.

Perhaps the first major study to link environmental design to worker performance in a systematic way was the BOSTI study, in which a large number of white-collar workers completed an exhaustive questionnaire survey before and after moving into a new office building.[1] More recently, the same authors concluded that the trend toward more open work environments had a measurably adverse effect on office workers, such that the investment in individual private offices could be shown to pay off in terms of increasing workers' productivity.[2]

Do we know this to be true? And if it were the case, how many international companies in this day and age would be willing to reconsider their considerable investment in flexible systems furniture and the open plan workspace to replace it with immovable walls and doors in the hopes of increasing the productivity of their employees? In fact, if anything, the trend appears to be going in the reverse direction, with companies increasingly concerned to reduce occupancy costs and to get as many people into as small a space as possible. This being the case, what can we say about the effects of workspace decisions on the quality of people's work, on their morale, on their health, and on the likelihood of their choosing to stay in or leave a job?

Office Worker Productivity

Many studies have looked at the effects of indoor air quality and ventilation system performance on workers' productivity.[3] Others address various types and levels of lighting, spatial comfort, density, personalization and furniture layout.[4, 5] In addition, the effects of acoustic conditions have been investigated.[6] Two basic categories of office worker productivity have emerged, each of which has a slightly different relationship to the environmental design of workspace. These are Individual Task Performance (ITP) productivity, and Collaborative and Team Work (CTW) productivity.

Studies that examine ITP productivity measure the effects of varying environmental conditions on tasks performed by the individual. Do people type faster, read more quickly, make fewer errors, solve customers' problems, or perform any other of numerous individual tasks better or worse as a function of a varying environmental condition, such as temperature, lighting levels or background noise? Traditional experimental designs measure the effects of different lighting levels, for example, on speed and accuracy of individual task performance. Surveys of indoor air quality (IAQ) and thermal comfort in office buildings ask individuals to rate their comfort, satisfaction and health levels. Ergonomic studies that focus on features of furniture layout and the performance of tasks are oriented to the comfort and functioning of the individual in a given furniture configuration or workstation.

Fewer studies have looked systematically at CTW productivity.[7] This is defined in terms of how people communicate, where and how they transfer needed information to co-workers, how long these exchanges take, and how useful the information is that is being transmitted. Sociological studies of small group communication and decision-making are well established in the psychological literature, and address issues of group configuration, individual distance, and the impact of communications tools.[8] In recent years, companies deciding to redefine work in terms of projects performed by teams, rather than a series of individual assembly-line functions, have often been motivated to open up workspace, substituting clusters of workstations and low partitions for offices lined up down hallways, each with its own door and window. However, data on whether or not teams were actually more effective as a result are hard to come by. Some companies, for example, Amoco Oil and Gas in Denver and Hypertherm in New Hampshire, consider group productivity to be improved as a result of designing team workspace. But other companies install team workspace without reorganizing the work into project-based work, and then wonder why the space functions so badly and people are so discontented![9]

Each of these two broad categories of productivity can be measured in similar but different ways. Both ITP and CTW productivity can be assessed according to positive and negative criteria. Positive measures of productivity include *faster, more accurate output, faster and more effective employee recruitment and retention, better quality products/services to clients, faster and better quality decision-making*. The argument states that a supportive environment increases the rate or the magnitude of these outcomes to a measurable extent. Negative measures of productivity include *rate of absenteeism and illness, employee turnover, product and services returns,* and *error and complaint rates*. According to this argument, an effective work environment counters these effects, reducing their incidence and prevalence, often comparing favorably to some previously calculated error rate or quality indicator. In many studies, some mixture of both positive and negative outcome measures is used, as summarized in Figure 3.1.

Depending on whether ITP or CTW is the focus of the research and how data can be applied to outcome measures in each situation, environmental influences on, and support for,

	POSITIVE MEASURES	NEGATIVE MEASURES
ITP Individual Task Performance	Faster, more accurate output; employee recruitment and retention	Absenteeism and illness; employee turnover; reduced task speed
CTW Collaborative and Team Work	Better quality output; lower costs; better ideas and decisions	Error rate; shrinking group size; customer complaints

3.1 Positive and negative outcome measures for individual and group productivity

productivity are defined differently. For example, light levels, thermal comfort, and other types of ambient environmental condition affect individual performance. On the other hand, furniture layout and configuration, acoustic conditions and the convenience and adequacy of group workspace in a building affect team performance, communication, and collaborative tasks.

Measuring Worker Comfort

However, employees themselves may have a differing definition of productivity. For workers, improved productivity may result in less staff being hired to perform the same amount of work, or more, thus having an overall negative effect. To engage users in discussion of the environmental effects on productivity, therefore, it is more useful to talk about comfort. In 2000, the New Work Environments Research Group was formed at the University of Montreal to study human comfort in the workplace. One of the questions to be tackled is determining the distinction between user *satisfaction* and user *comfort* at work.

People are always ready to let you know whether they like something or not (their furniture, the air quality, the lighting, the quality of FM services in their building) – but what are we actually learning, other than the general orientation of people's likes and dislikes? For example, we know that people "like" high partitions and enclosed offices better than they "like" low partitions and systems furniture. We know that people "like" as much file storage as they can squeeze into their workstation,

that they "like" privacy; and that they "like" sitting near the people they work with. Other than providing predictable lists of workers' likes and dislikes, these studies yield little in the way of a working knowledge of effects on individual and group performance, individual morale and effective teamwork. In research language, we need new and better outcome measures – for example, can the concept of comfort be systematically related to worker performance?

The idea of human comfort has a long history, having guided historical research in architecture and interior design to enable scholars to understand the functionality of architectural decisions in the homes and buildings of older and remote cultures. Comfort has more recently been applied to defining norms and standards for interior environmental conditions in public spaces such as office buildings. Comfort as a basis for setting environmental standards developed out of recognition of people's need to be more than simply healthy and safe in the buildings they occupy. Once health and safety are assured, users need environmental support for their work, that is, comfort. Comfort links the psychological aspects of workers' likes and dislikes with concrete outcome measures such as improved task performance and worker productivity. In understanding comfort, how it works and how building users judge it, we find out more than people's preferences, and we are in a better position to apply this knowledge to building design and operation.

The concept of comfort is complex, and in applying it to human comfort at work, we have established three levels of comfort to be measured (see Figure 3.2): physical comfort; psychological comfort; and functional comfort.

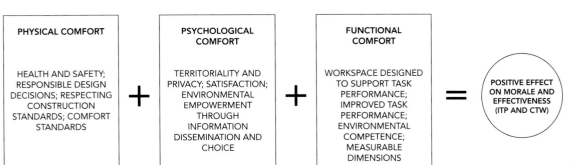

3.2 Levels of comfort

Physical comfort

Physical comfort is what most of us think of as comfort. It is assured by responsible building design and operation, setting and meeting standards of health and safety, as well as ASHRAE-type comfort standards. These standards mostly address extremes, such as too much heat, cold or noise. They exist to ensure that people at work are not placed under undue stress through having to adapt to extreme environmental conditions. Relatively few modern office buildings fail to be physically comfortable. Examples of physically uncomfortable workspace occurred, for example, during the indoor air quality crisis of the 1980s, when older buildings with undersized ventilation systems failed to exhaust enough heat or to bring in enough fresh air, and people reported illness and fatigue. Another example occurred when the incidence of repetitive strain injuries (RSI) increased after the large-scale introduction of computer screens and keyboards without adapting furniture, lighting or the way tasks were performed. Again, extensive and vociferous complaints from building occupants (employees and their unions) drew attention to these comfort problems. They are seen less in modern office buildings, although they do occur: the odor that cannot be traced or eliminated; the noisy, drafty ventilation system; the increasing number of screen-based workers needing corrective lenses.

In terms of its effects on worker performance, users' physical comfort must be assured. Lack of basic physical comfort prevents work from being done. As well as interior office conditions, interruptions or deficiencies in basic building services, such as elevators, bathrooms, parking (if appropriate), and cleaning and maintenance, also affect workers negatively. In previous work I have characterized this basic level of building habitability as "building convenience".[10] Our research indicates that a building that scores low on building convenience is not likely to be acceptable at any other level of comfort. When workers identify a physical comfort problem, it tends to have a negative effect on their judgment of all other workspace features.

Psychological comfort

In spite of the influence of industrial and occupational psychology, psychological comfort is only beginning to be measured in the office environment.[11] Many of these studies indicate that psychosocial aspects – such as the scale and structure of social networks at work, employer–employee relations, the demands of the job, and the type and extent of rewards and recognition for work performed – have an important effect on environmental perception and work performance. So what are the implications for the effects of the physical environment on users?

A primary component of psychological comfort is sense of territory, both individual territory (office, workstation) and group territory (team workspace). The concept of territory can be applied equally to ITP and CTW productivity assessment, in that individuals define individual territory and teams define group territory. Sense of privacy, social status and individual control are fundamental components of territoriality, and most people perceive and judge workspace, in part, according to these criteria.[12] Studies have found that people moving out of private enclosed offices into open workstations judge their environment more negatively, citing lack of privacy, acoustic conditions, and confidentiality problems. These reasons are given irrespective of whether or not their work is confidential, and whether or not they need to be alone to perform tasks effectively.

A recent study found a significant relationship to job rank, with more negative assessments of privacy, status and control by senior staff as compared to lower-level employees. This seems to be independent of the actual physical features of the workspace, such as furniture configuration and partition height. The study also found that workers at different job levels have different perceptions of their territorial boundaries, with more senior workers (professionals and managers) having more physical boundary markers over a wider area than clerical and technical workers. Moreover, measures of office personalization indicate that differences depend on people's longevity with the company and the type of work they do, rather than on any physical characteristic of the office or workstation.[13]

Recent accounts of major office redesign and renovation projects that have attempted to replace traditional enclosed office concepts with more "dynamic" open environments indicate slow acceptance by workers, and in some cases, out-right rejection.[14] Evidence from industrial psychology research on decision latitude suggests that providing opportunities for employees to participate in decision-making may be a constructive response to the need for psychological comfort. Decision latitude indicates the degree of autonomy or control a worker has over the performance of their work. More control is positive in several ways: it helps people cope with psychological demands, and it encourages people to find new ways of solving problems, such that growth and learning occur.[15] The equivalent of decision latitude in our world might be called environmental empowerment. It means keeping people informed about workspace-related decisions, providing opportunities for participation in decisions about their own space, and giving them some say in how they define their territory.

Functional comfort

The notion of functional comfort has been discussed at length elsewhere.[16] This aspect of comfort addresses how effective workspace is in helping users perform their tasks. It is therefore independent of individual preferences and needs. It is anchored in generic human requirements for tools to perform work, and therefore forces us to define the physical environment as a tool for getting work done. It speaks to the need to invest in good workspace design and management in order to add value to the work performed by workers. As the range and types of tasks performed in offices grow and become more complex, so the concept of functional comfort becomes more important. Today's workspace has to facilitate a wider variety of tasks without becoming complex and costly to build. As a result, users' assessment of their functional comfort provides an important indicator to managers and designers of how well workers feel they are functioning in their workspace, and whether or not improvements need to be made to help people perform their tasks better and more quickly.

Our research has yielded a number of key dimensions of functional comfort that tend to be standardized across different types and locations of office building. These include air quality, thermal comfort, spatial comfort, privacy, lighting quality, office noise control and building noise control. Other less commonly present dimensions include collaborative or team workspace, visual comfort, and security. These can be measured by asking occupants to evaluate a standardized number of environmental conditions on a 5-point scale. Data from some 6,000 respondents to date have contributed to the establishment of normative scores on each of the functional comfort dimensions, to which results from new surveys can be compared. Deviations from the norm in either a positive or a negative direction indicate either adequate functional comfort for users, or problems in performing tasks.

Figure 3.3 indicates how adequate functional comfort (deviation in a positive direction) allows the worker to concentrate all her energy on her work, whereas a lack of functional comfort (deviation in a negative direction) requires the worker to expend her energy on solving workspace problems in order to perform work. The results of the user survey indicate whether work is supported (energy in) or slowed down (energy out) on each of the functional comfort dimensions.

Workspace that supports task performance boosts the energy of the worker, who can concentrate on the task without needing to struggle against environmental elements. This is "environment as a tool for work." Workspace that is inimical to task performance draws energy out of the worker, as he/she grapples with environmental barriers in order to perform the task, and therefore has less energy to expend on performing work. It should be said that most workspace environments have a little of each built into them!

In addition, the quantified difference between a building's score and the baseline norm on each of the dimensions establish priorities for follow-up actions. The survey results can be directly applied to maintenance planning, priority-setting on repairs and renovations, and budgetary planning.

FUNCTIONAL COMFORT

LACKING ← Energy out | Energy in ← SUPPORTIVE

3.3 Functional comfort model of user–space interaction

In order to ensure that workspace meets functional comfort criteria, ways must be found to integrate task requirements with environmental design decisions. This means that users are valuable measuring tools, as they can, if asked appropriately, define features that are or are not comfortable related to task performance. For example, a task performed on an oversized computer screen requiring excellent visual conditions for colors and graphics will have precise environmental requirements, no matter who is using the computer. Thus, standardizing workspace design around task performance means bypassing individual tastes and preferences ("satisfaction") and creating the tools for any and all workers to use ("comfort").

To sum up, users require physical comfort as well as psychological and functional comfort in order to use their environment to perform their tasks well. An effective and supportive environment provides comfort at all three levels. These different experiences of comfort are amenable to objective measurement and can be integrated to provide a reliable outcome measure of environmental effectiveness.

Comfort and Productivity

Many companies are satisfied that standard office layouts in generic office buildings are adequate to support their employees' work. In view of the fact that most of what is known about worker psychology in the office environment concerns worker satisfaction (people's likes and dislikes), hard-nosed corporate executives concerned with the bottom line fail to see an advantage to investing additional effort in workspace design simply in order to make people feel happier. However, current research is evolving to take into account more complex definitions of user behavior, such as task performance and user comfort. Numerous attempts to quantify that proportion of worker productivity that can be said to depend on support from the physical environment suggest a range of productivity increases that are sustained over time of between 5 and 25 or even 30 percent, depending on whether new technology or new business processes are introduced at the same time as environmental change.

The analysis of task requirements and the relationship between environmental design and task performance (effec-

tiveness at work) can increasingly be linked empirically to environmental measures. For example, people working at screens all day long require low background light levels and preferably indirect lighting sources. People who spend a lot of time in meetings need small, functional meeting spaces nearby that can be used informally and do not require reservations in advance. People who have special equipment or large documents may need larger-sized work surfaces or higher partitions. These environmental items are necessary tools for the performance of work. Thus, regardless of people's individual preferences, combining physical, psychological and functional comfort links directly into people's productivity, that is, how fast and well they work. Replacing the simple concept of individual satisfaction with the complex idea of comfort increases the validity of user-environment interaction studies and can be applied to measuring both ITP and CTW productivity.

Environments that fail to respond to users' needs at one or more level of comfort risk creating a stressful situation that may have long-term negative consequences. Physical comfort problems lead directly to dangerous, unsafe and unhealthy conditions. They prevent the effective performance of tasks and generate stress conditions that, over time, cause illness. Psychological comfort problems occur when there is a mismatch between the demands placed on users and the control they have over the environment. Concerns with privacy, status and control arise when people are not psychologically comfortable, their territoriality is threatened, and they are therefore under stress. Functional comfort problems mean that people are expending more energy than necessary to perform their tasks. In each of these cases, the non-supportive workspace generates worker stress (or "strain") whether this is at a physical, functional or psychological level. Sustained stress leads to health problems, absenteeism and employee turnover. Comfort and stress are at the extreme opposite ends of a continuum along which almost any workspace can be placed – more stress in some environments, more comfort in others.

Feedback from office workers in each of the three areas of comfort can be analyzed in terms of building habitability (physical comfort), territoriality (psychological comfort) and task performance (functional comfort). Research results to date suggest that user feedback does not always indicate whether their comfort assessments refer to psychological, functional or physical categories, as people tend to criticize physical conditions, for example, when they are psychologically uncomfortable. The researcher's job therefore is to identify and classify the pattern of comfort that characterizes each user evaluation of the work environment.

Future research will focus on before and after measures of environmental effectiveness and links to changes in worker performance, as well as on additional parameters of psychological comfort. To date, our limited knowledge of how people define territorial boundaries and how they defend them, of the complex notions of privacy in offices, as well as of environmental empowerment and strategies of user participation, is not fully integrated into space design and management practices. Ultimately, the three-pronged approach to comfort will help office workers become more productive through making better use of the environments they occupy.

Notes and References

*This chapter is based on a paper given at a conference, IDEACTION 2004: "Spheres of Influence", Brisbane, Australia, 12–14 May, 2004.

1 Brill, M., Margulis, S. and Konar, E. (1985) "The Impact of the Office Environment on Productivity and the Quality of Working Life," 2 vols, Buffalo: Westinghouse Furniture Systems.
2 Brill, M. and Weideman, S. (2001) *Disproving Widespread Myths about Workplace Design*, Jasper, IN: Kimball International.
3 Wyon, D.P. (2000) "Individual Control at Each Workplace: The Means and the Potential Benefits," in D. Clements-Croome (ed.) *Creating the Productive Workplace*, London: E & FN Spon, p. 192.
4 Vischer, J.C. (1989) *Environmental Quality in Offices*, New York: Van Nostrand Reinhold, and Vischer, J.C. (1995) *Workspace Strategies: Environment as a Tool for Work*, New York: Chapman and Hall.
5 Churchman, A., Stokols, D., Scharf, A., Nishimoto, K. and Wright, R. (1990) "Effects of Physical Environmental Conditions in Offices on Employee Stress and Well Being," paper presented at 22nd International Congress of Applied Psychology, Kyoto, Japan. Also Wells, M.M. (2000) "Office Clutter or Meaningful Personal Displays: The Role of Office Personalization in Employee and Organizational Well-Being," *Journal of Environmental Psychology*, 20: 239–255.
6 Cohen, A.J., Campanelle, A., Marshall, L. and Grant, C. (1987) "Perspectives on Acoustics in Environmental Design," *Journal of Architectural and Planning Research*, 4(2): 162–179. Also Kupritz, V. (1998) "Privacy in the Workplace: The Impact of Building Design," *Journal of Environmental Psychology*, 18(4): 341–356.
7 Some experts consider designing workspace for workgroups one of the major neglected contributions of workspace to productivity. See Leaman, A. and Bordass, B. (2000) "Productivity in Buildings: The Killer Variables," in D. Clements-Croome (ed.) *Creating the Productive Workplace*, London: E & FN Spon.
8 For example, Allen, T. (1977) *Managing the Flow of Technology*, Cambridge, MA: MIT Press.
9 Vischer, J. (2003) "Work Environment and Well-being: Beyond Working Space," paper given at Art and Synergy in Design Conference, Sydney, Australia, February.
10 Vischer, J.G. (1996) *Workspace strategies: environment as a tool for work*, New York, Chapman & Hall.
11 Fischer, G-N., Tarquinio, C. and Vischer, J.C. (2004) "Effects of the Self-Schema on Perception of Space at Work," *Journal of Environmental Psychology*, 24(1): 131–140.
12 Vischer, J.C., McCuaig, A., Nadeau, N., Melillo, M. and Castonguay-Vien, S. (2003) *Mission impossible ou mission accomplie? Résultats d'une étude d'évaluation du mobilier universel dans les édifices à bureau*, final report, Montréal: Groupe de recherche sur les environnements de travail, Université de Montréal.
13 Ibid.
14 Berger, W. (1999) "Lost in Space," Wired Magazine, February.
15 Karasek, R. and Theorell, T. (1990) *Healthy Work: Stress, Productivity and the Reconstruction of Working Life*, New York: Basic Books.
16 See note 4, above.

The Cultural and Physical Environment as Drivers of Workplace Design

James H. Thompson

4

Introduction

Traditionally, architects and designers have worked with clients to develop and implement design solutions from both a functional and an aesthetic approach. The functional approach is justifiable from user needs and activities assessment studies as well as programming data. Aesthetic approaches to the built environment are typically realized through the thoughtful selection of materials, color, pattern and textures. Yet a lingering question exists as to how the cultural environment might be harnessed and shaped by the user and how one, in turn, "engages" space. How one realizes the benefits of effective and thoughtful design through the careful and meaningful creation of the new workplace remains an often elusive, yet important area of exploration.

The Culture-Driven Workplace

The cultural environment has a significant impact on the physical workplace and its ability to influence the social relationships of those who work within a space. By definition, a cultural environment is the overall attitude, beliefs, expectations and habits of the workforce. One of the most important facets of workplace culture is the development of social relationships. A 1999 Gallup poll named employee satisfaction and retention, praise and recognition as the main building blocks of a profitable, productive work environment.

Corporations can harness the power of workplace culture by cultivating the individuals who play key cultural catalyst roles in an organization. These individuals need to be formally recognized and rewarded for their actions and sense of personal responsibility for their work environment. Doing so reinvigorates the workplace with a positive focus on personal initiative which becomes not only a self-perpetuating marker of the health of workplace morale, but also improves overall employee satisfaction and retention. Aligning a company's entire organization – the structure, social networks, culture, and human capital – with knowledge workplace principles requires a proactive change management program.

As an example, Tivoli Partners, a marketing firm, was looking at the design of their new environment as an opportunity to

4.1 Tivoli Partners, interior view

re-invent their company and create a space that would support it. Towards this goal, the design team worked closely with the company's leadership and employees to understand where there might be disconnects between the culture of the environment and how employees engaged each other and directed their collective efforts. During this process, the team discovered a disconnect in their existing facility between team structures and professional disciplines (creative teams vs. technical teams). The physical environment was such that teams lived and performed their jobs in "cells" (i.e., divisional physical space organization). This disjointed allocation of space was organized around creative teams or highly technical teams, resulting in distinct disconnects between the groups and a level of anxiety related to how they engaged each other – if at all. In communicating with Tivoli Partners, the design team realized the potential of the physical environment to overcome this sense of angst and to leverage group activity within the organization towards a common goal (Figures 4.1, 4.2).

A knowledge workplace, such as Tivoli Partners, puts value on the diverse experience, creativity and innovation provided by employees. Furthermore, employees need to be united by the unique attributes of their company's values and goals, belief systems and cultural environment.

Companies must first recognize that a people-centered culture is a holistic culture. Within organizations, workers are no longer expected to be obsessed with their work. Employees today feel significantly less loyal than those of the previous century because they "own" the company's means of production – essentially, their knowledge and expertise. Consequently, the actions of a workforce are motivated by their own values and belief systems along with that of the organization. This includes how the group approaches life and work, which values take precedence and under what circumstances, how behavior is situational rather than stereotypical and the best practices that bridge cultures effectively.

As outlined above, the power of any organization is its workforce, the people-centered culture that makes it unique and the physical environment that supports it. But it is important that *the individual* – that employee who brings a level of diversity and uniqueness to an organization – is not overlooked. This same individual *profile* can be the source for dramatic cultural change that is unexpected, unwanted and, unfortunately, at times unavoidable.

Cultural diversity is the uniqueness each employee brings to fulfilling these values and achieving these goals. Diversity covers a broad range of personal attributes and characteristics such as race, gender, age, cultural heritage, personal background and sexual orientation. By recognizing common values and goals, employers are better positioned to create an advantage from employee differences. People whose work is fairly routine and repetitive perform better when they are in a stimulating environment with easy access to other people. Social interaction helps them through days that might otherwise be boring and anonymous. On the other hand, this type of setting is a relative disaster for people whose role requires intense thinking and analytical work for which they have to constantly draw upon their memory and unique, creative thoughts. These people need quiet time, but must eventually re-engage with their community and external stimulation.

The Physical Environment: Place Making

The relationship between the designed environment and the development of social and cultural networks (the flow of information throughout an organization, tracing how ideas expand, diffuse and turn into innovations and cognitive realization) is complicated yet highlights a unique way of thinking about issues that are of value to organizations.

4.2 Tivoli Partners, interior view

Corporations can begin by determining what is of value to an organization and its workforce and then uncovering what they do and how they do it, what determines quality from their perspective, what differentiates a high quality product from a low quality product, what they want to achieve that they can't do now, what innovation means to them, and what would it mean to do things differently. Identifying these factors that determine quality and backing into what is known about the physical environment helps determine the final outcome. It is about having the right kind of spaces that actually build upon cognitive, social, psychological, physical and, most importantly, cultural needs.

Admittedly, business leaders are skeptical about the psychological, social and cultural impacts on the workplace. When they look at their workforce, they see the quality of their work as determined by ability, effort, motivation and results. What is often overlooked, however, is the power of the environment to shape the overall attitude, beliefs, expectations and habits of a workforce, and in turn, productivity and profitability. In the effort to convince business leaders of the power of thoughtful, well-executed designs for the workplace, try not to ask them to make

a "leap of faith." Instead, share "success stories" from previous clients and bodies of work with them, and use a series of surveys to measure progress toward specific business goals outlined at the inception of the project. These surveys monitor not only the conviction and attitudes of leadership, individually and collectively, regarding their workforce and the environment, but also the attitudes and beliefs of a workforce. This helps identify disconnects between leadership and the workforce, and potential areas of concern with respect to how social networks might be leveraged to realize strategic corporate goals (Figure 4.3).

Employees are well aware of the power of the physical environment to influence social relationships simply because they are experiencing them daily through the cultural environment. Measurement through simple, articulate surveys and questionnaires is an easy way to gather quantifiable data to substantiate to leadership, objectively and proactively, how space design directly relates back to the people who use it.

The synthesis of the cultural and physical environment encompasses a company's own internal knowledge of strategy and processes, and its ingrained values and business practices. In considering the development of new workspace, designers

Workplace Environment Survey

Thank you for completing this survey, which should take less than five minutes of your time. When providing your ratings, please think about <u>all</u> of the spaces in the building that you use throughout your typical workday. Click the "Submit by Email" button to submit your completed survey. Please note that your responses will be kept confidential.

	Poor	Below Average	Average	Good	Excellent
	1	2	3	4	5
1. Rate our current space on its:.					
a) acoustical privacy	○	○	○	○	○
b) lighting	○	○	○	○	○
c) cleanliness	○	○	○	○	⦿
d) thermal comfort	○	○	○	○	○
e) security (during work hours)	○	○	○	○	○
f) security (after hours)	○	○	○	○	○
g) ergonomics	○	○	○	○	○
2. Rate our current space on how well it accommodates your daily responsibilities.	○	○	○	○	○
3. Rate our current space on how well it promotes collaboration.	○	○	○	○	○
4. Rate our current space on how well it promotes creative problem solving.	○	○	○	○	○
5. Rate our current space on how well it represents the kind of company we are today.	○	○	○	○	○
6. Rate our current space on how well it represents the kind of company we want to be.	○	○	○	○	○
7. Rate our current space on how well it *fosters* our brand attributes:					
a) creative	○	○	○	○	○
b) trustworthy	○	○	○	○	○
c) expert	○	○	○	○	○
d) innovative	○	○	○	○	○
e) passionate	○	○	○	○	○
f) dynamic	○	○	○	○	○
8. Rate our current space on how well it *represents* our brand attributes:					
a) creative	○	○	○	○	○
b) trustworthy	○	○	○	○	○
c) expert	○	○	○	○	○
d) innovative	○	○	○	○	○
e) passionate	○	○	○	○	○
f) dynamic	○	○	○	○	○

9. Comments:

> _____

Submit by Email

are able to create a design that is an explicit, detailed and ultimately a strategic map for supporting the culture and corporate strategy.

Constructing this *design/pattern language* for an organization (a set of spatial strategies from a broad scale to the highest level of detail) allows a design team to implement a corporate strategy and vision for cultural change through the design of the workplace. The discourse between individual needs and collective interests can give birth to a *new* cultural dimension that enables the individual. A primary objective is to ensure that these individuals feel comfortable within the organizational environment and, therefore, motivated to deliver expected results.

The success and outcome of thoroughly knowing and understanding a client and their workforce are seen in how programmatic requirements are married with cultural goals. A strong architectural vocabulary and visual language are at the core of successfully realizing the power of the workplace as an enabler. In a project for the Muzak headquarters, one sees the strength of applying urban planning principles to the organization of a very large environment (125,00 sq ft/11,600 sq m). The thoughtful integration of these principles created a level of clarity regarding how space might be organized around spontaneous company gatherings and how these same spaces can communicate to a prospective client the power of a unified organization. From large-scale planning to navigating within

4.4 (left) Muzak Headquarters, internal view

4.5 (below) Muzak Headquarters, internal view

such a large facility, deliberate consideration was paid to the choice of materials. Metals, woods, plastics, masonry and other materials are incorporated as way-finding tools to communicate "boroughs" or neighborhoods within the space. Thoughtful attention was paid to every detail; even the music playing in the parking lot that one hears upon arrival speaks to the total experience that is Muzak and the culture that lives it (Figures 4.4, 4.5, 4.6 and 4.7).

The design of Accenture's Charlotte office, as another example, called for a number of different types of workspaces to accommodate various work styles and needs, one of which was a series of spaces that were highly private and in turn inwardly focused. These spaces allowed for concentrated work and were historically placed away and visually disconnected from the remainder of the work environment. In considering these spaces for their new office, the approach was to make these very private rooms the most dynamic formally and, in turn, the most visible in the office. Clustered in groups of four and placed in public spaces where major circulation occurs, these rooms became landmarks within the environment that people move towards and around. What was formerly seen as highly private, tucked-away space became the most public, formally recognizable space within the environment while still meeting the functional programmatic needs of Accenture (Figures 4.8, 4.9).

In the design and development of an organizational culture, *pattern language* can address several dimensions of size and quantifiable measurements. Employees need a sense of

4.6 Muzak Headquarters, internal view

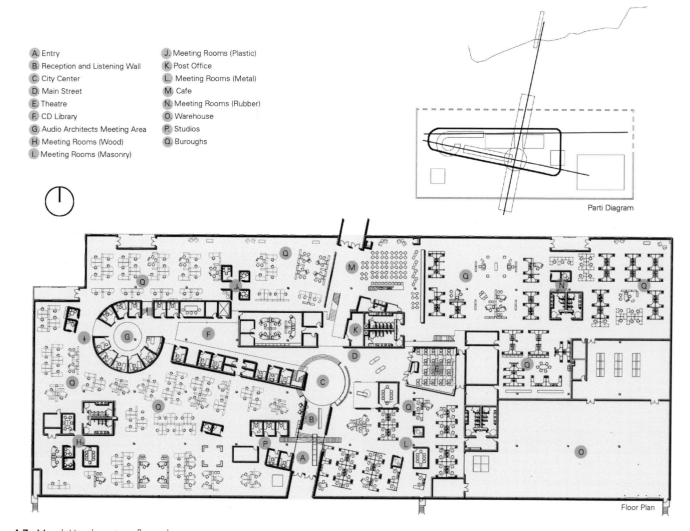

A. Entry
B. Reception and Listening Wall
C. City Center
D. Main Street
E. Theatre
F. CD Library
G. Audio Architects Meeting Area
H. Meeting Rooms (Wood)
I. Meeting Rooms (Masonry)
J. Meeting Rooms (Plastic)
K. Post Office
L. Meeting Rooms (Metal)
M. Cafe
N. Meeting Rooms (Rubber)
O. Warehouse
P. Studios
Q. Buroughs

Parti Diagram

Floor Plan

4.7 Muzak Headquarters, floor plan

comfort that might be otherwise ambiguous. (That is to say that, spatially, the physical workplace should communicate at many different levels.) The sense of empowerment that is so critical to individual achievement and effectiveness is tied to the myriad of spaces and inherent flexibility of today's workplace. Evaluation of the orientation of space is necessary to determine if the physical layout is public, private or a mix of both. This extends to the posturing of space as well; the extent to which one sees doors closed versus open and the extent to which employees are protective of their space/territory.

With the variety of workspaces in many organizations comes a condition that is similarly dependent on the shaping of "space" in relationship to the cultural organization. These spaces resonate with the inherent power born from process – spaces that allow for and make brainstorming a religion practiced every day – where it weaves itself into the cultural fabric of an organization. These spaces create the competitive advantage so elusive to many organizations, but one that is dependent and all-embracing of the cultural body.

4.8 Accenture, internal view

Core Space   Technology   Community Space

Service Areas   Meeting Space

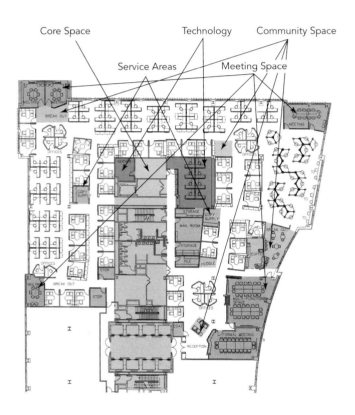

4.9 Accenture, floor plan

When space is attuned with the cultural environment, the insightful observation of the "right people" – those who accomplish what is needed but go beyond and likely do things differently – is encouraged and expected. This passive and active engagement encourages and reinforces both corporate and organization culture, and activates a very integral cultural "cross-pollination." From this, an organization sparks its workforce to think beyond the norm, to naturally take chances and solve problems. A workplace that drives the cultural environment is one that enables individuals while leveraging the collective body of an organization. The best solutions embrace people's differences. By keeping close to the action and embracing diversity in the workplace, employees are inspired from seeing, hearing and feeling – in effect, being there and immersing themselves in the environment.

Moving forward with the design of workplaces that directly respond to cultural and physical drivers, ongoing change must be anticipated and speculation to what causes change should be studied. For example, it is critical that the leadership of any organization seeking to consolidate offices and locations understands the underlying factors outside of their immediate control. The fact that businesses compete in an ever more competitive, sophisticated and changing world is proof that consolidation of resources and personnel is more important than ever. The obvious reduction of real estate cost, redundancy of efforts and the like create an undeniable business case. More importantly, the cultural significance of this as a business strategy is a critical measure of an organization's success. Workplace design can help a company realize many goals, perhaps the most elusive of which is the social relationship that bears the people-centered cultural environment.

Bringing potentially diverse work groups together through consolidation, either through individual work style, education or geography, can be alarming. Relocating an urban presence, for example, to a vastly different geographic location under the same guise and culture as before might be an elusive, if not impossible task. The power of a culture is built upon the diversity of the individuals that make it up, yet the cultural implications of a workplace are more than the drivers that create the design.

Organizations can have finite goals, cultural initiatives and facilities to support them, but are ultimately dependent on the people capable of understanding and embracing their cultural significance. Unforeseen hurdles, such as a rural versus an urban workforce to recruit from, can influence the corporate culture and in turn alter the physical significance and outcome of space. What would otherwise be a powerful, comprehensive and holistic culture can be less than so if an organization is not aware of the implications regarding a workplace location and the surrounding demographic from which individuals will be recruited and ultimately comprise the social and cultural fabric of the workforce.

Conclusion

Companies need to be aware of the many factors that come together to ultimately create a workplace culture. Though difficult, the ability to quantify these environmental factors will encourage organizations to consider the ways in which both their cultural and physical workplace is established. A careful and continued observance of these factors will enable designers to move towards the creation of the new workplace. In the design and realization of a client's environment, designers look for quantifiable results that help them make judgments about the success and shortcomings of their work. As discussed earlier, solving for programmatic and aesthetic needs has been the compelling driver of architecture and design. By example and by design, one can see how the careful consideration of the workplace aids in the cultural significance of an organization. Though each company has unique needs, the lessons that may be considered are those where a dialogue is established early on with business leaders and the workforce. By aligning the ideology and mindset of any workplace, leverage and thoughtful, articulate and knowledgeable experience can be applied towards realizing the goals of a workplace that is aligned physically and culturally. Working with and experiencing environments that have embraced this awareness, such as Muzak, Accenture, Tivoli Partners and others, have allowed for the drivers of design – culture and physical space – to be catalysts for fundamental and powerful change in the workforce and, by consequence, a company that is more profitable, competitive and internally aligned in the marketplace.

Further Reading

Buckingham, M. and Coffman, C. (1999) *First Break All the Rules: What the World's Greatest Managers Do Differently*, New York: Simon & Schuster.

Hagenbaugh, B. (2004) "Muzak Thinks Outside the Box," *USA Today*, August 6.

Holt, N. (2001) "Workspaces: A Look at Where People Work," *The Wall Street Journal*, July 25.

Kelly, T. (2001) *The Art of Innovation*, London: HarperCollins.

Milshtein, A. (2001) "See the Music," *Contract*, June.

Salingaros, N.A. (2000) "The Structure of Pattern Languages", *arq (Architectural Research Quarterly)*, 4.

Week, D. (2002) *The Culture Driven Workplace*, Canberra, Australia: Royal Australian Institute of Architects.

Workplace and the New American Community

David Walters

As we read elsewhere in this book, significant changes are occurring in the meaning and content of office work in America, ones that will change radically the lives of the workers, the form of the buildings they work in, and the urban settings within which the new workplaces are located. Importantly, these changes in office design affect not only the office interior, but go beyond even the design of the building itself. They will affect the form of American cities; skyscrapers, America's urban hallmark for over a century, are most vulnerable to this revolution in the design and management of corporate real estate, and the generic suburban office park is next in line. The leasing agents of new towers and generic low-rise suburban buildings may not know it, but it's likely they're dealing in dinosaurs.

The changes in office work in the next few decades will transform the city landscape as surely as the changes of the Industrial Revolution did 200 years ago. It's a complex story involving information technology, global competition, increasing energy costs, higher expectations by workers of their building environments, and fundamental changes to the concept of real estate, where time becomes more important than space. This makes it an issue of the bottom line. And that's why this change is inevitable.

"All that is solid melts into air," was Karl Marx's poetic metaphor about social change in the nineteenth-century industrial world, and it still fits the transformations of our post-industrial age, especially those having to do with firm phenomena like buildings and cities. Years before September 11, 2001, altered forever the way we think of skyscrapers, an unprecedented convergence of global economics and information technology forced companies to rethink working methods and organizations in radical ways. Mundane tasks were outsourced to back offices in rural America or developing countries, all linked by the Internet. Information technology makes it possible to use time and space in ways that we barely understood even a decade ago: for example, the workplace now follows the sun. At the close of their working day, architects in cities all across the USA email sketches to offices in India or China and have them back on their PCs or laptops the next morning, developed and rendered. By using time in this way, the offices use less space and save money. Good news for the firms, but bad news for the larger world of corporate real estate.

In *The New Office,* Francis Duffy, an international expert on office design and a major contributor to this book, relates a story that's become well known – about an epiphany that came to him some years ago as he gazed over the skyscraper skyline in Dallas, Texas.[1] Earlier in the day, he'd been advising the senior partners of a large international corporation how they could use their office space more effectively; in their passionate pursuit of profits, the partners wanted to reduce their occupancy costs, cutting rent, property taxes, service charges and energy bills. Duffy explained how the company could shrink its office space almost by half by using technology more effectively, and by reducing and reshaping its work areas to fit the new work patterns. In short, they could vacate a lot of space in the downtown towers of Dallas and other cities, saving big bucks in the process. The executives were ecstatic.

But Duffy relates how his mind was troubled. Many of the glittering towers he was looking at were less than 10 years old – and his expert advice was already making them obsolete. Not only that, these towering buildings, from which Dallas derived its identity, and from which Duffy had just eliminated a major tenant (and presumably, several more companies that would follow this cost-cutting example) were parts of his clients' pension fund portfolios. Suddenly, real estate didn't seem so real any more.

Duffy's epiphany pointed to a sharp reversal of trends in American office work and office design, trends that had become institutionalized during the twentieth century. Today, more than 50 percent of North American employees work in offices, up from a mere 5 percent in 1900. But for most of the last century, office work was seen as dull, or worse: in the early decades of the century Franz Kafka depicted the office as a nightmare; during the 1950s, William Whyte's "Organization Man" revealed a culture of conformity where employees sacrificed their own individuality for the good of an organization; and in the 1980s, director Terry Gilliam's movie *Brazil* resurrected Kafkaesque themes and projected a surreal and ghoulish vision of a giant, faceless, and malign bureaucracy controlling the lives of workers and citizens alike. While this last example was a dramatic fictional exaggeration of office work, it was certainly true that as the twentieth century progressed, more and more people were required to process more and more information, often by means of tedious, repetitive clerical tasks undertaken in dull and dreary office environments. This debilitating ethos and its dismal surroundings were well captured by cartoonist Scott Adams in his long-running "Dilbert" comic cartoon and by the hilarious BBC TV series, *The Office.*

The dominant model of corporate order and conformity on which all these dystopias are based stems from the work of Frederick Taylor (1856–1915) whose great contribution to the twentieth century was "scientific management," or, treating people as if they were simply units of production, extensions of machines. Taylorism, as it became known, dehumanized work, first in the factory, then in the office. From a company's point of view, employees were managed best if they were treated as automatons, required to come and go at fixed hours and to follow set procedures. Innovative thinking was the last thing expected from rank and file office workers.

Taylorism was the dominant management philosophy when the large urban office building was developed in America over a century ago, and Taylor's values – order, hierarchy, supervision, depersonalization – became integral principles for American office design. When combined with technological innovations such as the steel frame, the elevator, electric light, the telephone, and with new patterns of downtown real estate – very tall buildings on small sites – this once radical mixture became so successful that the model of clustered skyscrapers has proved remarkably resistant to change. It's still a basic premise of much American real estate planning (Figure 5.1).

Even when new management theories evolved in the 1960s, and technological innovation blossomed in the 1990s, these changes made little impact on the way designers and real estate professionals thought about office environments. Until now.

While much of this change comes from new technologies, other factors derive from the influence of continental European office design that has been shaped by very different values. European cities are older, and achieved their identities before the modern office building was invented; hence such buildings have not been granted the same prestigious place in the urban environment as their American counterparts. Employees' rights and opinions also play a larger role in Europe than in America: in the social democratic climate of northern Europe, "Workers' Councils" in Germany, Holland and Scandinavia have the right to negotiate the working environment with employers. No one

5.1 Downtown towers, Charlotte, North Carolina

in a Dutch office sits further than 16 ft (5 m) from an openable window; to do otherwise would be illegal. Most European workers have direct external views, and control over their own heating and lighting. Many workers have their own cellular offices, regardless of rank. This leads to longer, shallower, and more energy-efficient buildings. Contrast that with the common American practice of windowless offices buried deep inside buildings where no natural light or air ever penetrates.

European countries take energy more seriously. Americans waste energy at work the same way they squander it in their SUVs despite rising fuel costs. Until very recently Americans have taken cheap energy for granted, despite global conflicts and climate disasters; hackneyed designs for energy-hungry buildings save the developer money in upfront costs but increase energy consumption and push other, indirect costs onto society – in the form of pollution, noise and waste.

Similar simplistic and short-term thinking has determined the type and location of offices for the past several decades, either in downtown central business districts or in separated pods of low-rise suburban office parks. Wherever they're situated, conventional offices can work only if everyone is at his or her place at the same time. The standard nine-to-five working day, the clear separation between home and work, the bedroom suburb, the uptown core, the suburban office park, and the vast apparatus of commuting which still characterizes American life, all derive from this simple premise of simultaneity (Figure 5.2).

As clearly shown by other contributors to this volume, office locations now, and in the future, will be increasingly affected by trends toward smaller core operations, more networking, and more people working on the move. These tendencies reduce the need for large buildings, and place more emphasis on the recycling of existing ones, for example, turning mills,

5.2 Suburban office parking lot, University City, Charlotte, North Carolina

5.3 Converted mill buildings in SouthEnd, Charlotte, North Carolina

warehouses and other building types into flexible office space, or live–work units (Figure 5.3). The majority of office organizations are small and getting smaller as static bureaucracies dissolve through continual outsourcing and the development of a more mobile workforce where more people work away from the office for longer periods.

Thinking about the office as a special, separate building type might soon be out of date. The practice of spending vast amounts of money on buildings used for only a fraction of the working week is almost certainly doomed. Once viewed as assets on a balance sheet, corporate real estate in the global economy is now a cost, and something that must be minimized to enhance profitability, as exemplified in Duffy's Dallas consultancy. In this context, property is more often the rock on which a business can founder than the foundation for future growth.

Corporate real estate will need to respond to this world of dissolving bureaucracies. Many experts think it will be more economical to utilize the less attractive, lower-cost sites, and sell off the "jewels" – usually the downtown towers – of the portfolio. Skyscrapers are inherently less flexible with large amounts of space being taken up on all floors by rows of expensive elevators, clusters of escape stairs and mechanical ductwork, none of which can be easily modified. This leads to some older downtown office buildings being converted into housing as the center city residential boom continues in many American cities, fueled by patterns of working and living that are characteristic of the new American demographics – more and smaller households, fewer suburban nuclear families, and disparate age groups (baby-boomers and their children, the "echo-boomers") – all of whom demonstrate a marked tendency to live once again in the city. Members of these groups predominantly grew up in the suburbs and now tend to find them boring and unsatisfying (Figure 5.4).

These specific, but large demographic groups crave something else: the synchronicity and serendipity of city living, where unrelated events can come together to provide meaning and

5.4 Downtown building conversion from offices to housing, Charlotte, North Carolina

richness to life without the artificial simultaneity of culturally encoded routines so common in earlier suburban lifestyles. This lifestyle choice was itself prefigured by the cultural shift notable during the 1980s and 1990s in – of all things – TV sitcoms, such as *Friends*, *Seinfeld*, and *Sex and the City*. These and other TV shows charted the shift in cultural perception from the city as a dark, scary place to one that was hip and cool, particularly as a place to live and work in a flexible rhythm.

The relationship between popular TV shows and the changing pattern of work in the urban environment is the subject for a much deeper investigation than can be undertaken here. However, a brief review of some major trends can illustrate the shift in popular attitudes to urban living and working that helps explain these recent, significant shifts in demographics, taste, and lifestyle preference.

In the late 1950s and early 1960s, American TV was host to sitcoms such as *The Dick Van Dyke Show*, *Father Knows Best*, *Leave it to Beaver*, and *The Donna Read Show*. Shows like these were set around parents in their thirties with young kids, living in the suburbs, usually with the father commuting to work while the mother stayed home to raise the children.

During the 1970s, the emphasis shifted with programs like *The Mary Tyler Moore Show*, where workplace issues began to emerge as major script material with the main character a single woman in her thirties trying to make it on her own without the traditional support of a man. In the newsroom of a fictional television station the heroine found an ultimately supportive "workplace family" among her co-workers.

The 1980s saw the development of this trend into a new genre of workplace sitcoms, such as *Murphy Brown*, where the office itself became the major setting for action and theme of the program. Cultural norms for women were again challenged by the main female character, who this time chose to have a baby out of wedlock (to the great displeasure of conservative politicians such as American Vice-President Dan Quayle).

Most pertinent to the cultural shift towards urban living and working in close proximity to home and recreational pursuits were two massive hit series, *Seinfeld* and *Friends*, developed later in the 1980s and continuing through the 1990s. These shows featured characters who were the "30-something" children of the 1960s suburban generation: the parents still resided in the suburbs but their offspring, having become bored with the 'burbs, had moved into the city. The main characters lived a cool urban lifestyle, inhabiting trendy loft apartments and mixing together home, work and recreation all in the same urban environment. The city itself was now an important player in such shows, a trend exemplified in the late 1990s hit *Sex AND the City*, (author's emphasis) where the urban environment itself is a personality on a par with the human protagonists and their sex lives. The city has now become the location of choice for the cool, hip characters featured in these and other series.

With the great success and popularity of *Seinfeld*, *Friends*, and other trendy programs across a wide spectrum of American TV audiences, it is no surprise that the lifestyle and surroundings depicted in the TV shows should affect the living and working preferences of the younger adult audiences at whom it was aimed.

While many of us will work from a number of different places – home, the car, the hotel, the airport – several American downtowns, far from decaying, are regenerating themselves as the settings for this new, more integrated lifestyle. More surprisingly, oases of new urbanity are springing up in the suburbs with the development of mixed-use "urban villages," often evolving around train stations as part of new, transit-oriented development (TOD) (Figure 5.5). Here, many smaller, state-of-the-art offices are integrated into communities along with housing, shops, schools, churches and other civic uses. These high intensity, mixed-use neighborhoods are becoming destinations in their own right, offering the convenient urban lifestyles required by many office workers, without the car-dependent isolation of the suburbs. As twenty-first-century offices evolve into different forms, the real estate industry will

5.5 Fruitvale Transit-oriented Development, Oakland, California

need to develop new ways of thinking about property management and financing. Technical innovations in management and design will make current conservative practices – such as the isolation of office buildings into a separate category for easy funding – retrogressive and ultimately futile. The resistance to funding innovative mixed-use buildings will dissipate, not because architects wish it, but because the technologically and demographically driven marketplace will demand it. More radical concepts in space leasing, such as paying on the basis of services rented per hour, rather than square footage per year, are becoming increasingly common.

Skilled office workers relish the kind of creative networking arising from the half-accidental, half-planned encounters that only dense, mixed-use urban areas can provide; this serendipitous engagement of people and places prefigured in the plot lines of TV series are an increasingly essential part of our normal, everyday business lives. Even in the electronic age, cities suit networkers, now more than ever.

To understand this apparent paradox, it's worth reviewing the outlines of a larger cultural debate in American urbanism, one that's shaped and reshaped the American city for the past 50 years: the dialectic between propinquity – being near

everything one needed – and accessibility – being able to get to things and places easily. While these concepts may appear synonymous at first glance, they do embody important differences; propinquity is a function of *distance*, while accessibility is usually measured in *time*. Propinquity lends itself to a compact, mixed-use environment where everything is accessible because it's nearby; accessibility uses technology to overcome distance, thus allowing widespread suburban expansion – first, by means of the car in the 1950s; now by means of the Internet.

The first clear statement of the ways in which technology was changing city space in the twentieth century came, not surprisingly, from America, where, in 1963 and 1964, the academic planner Melvin Webber from Berkeley, California, wrote two influential articles entitled "Order in Diversity: Community without Propinquity" and "The Urban Place and the Nonplace Urban Realm"[2,3]. In these writings he rejected models of the city based on traditional spatial patterns of densely arranged streets and squares housing a wide variety of uses. Webber and others argued that it was a mistake to critique the expanding city as shapeless sprawl, and to long for traditional streets and squares, because this missed the point that the car had changed the relationship between space and time in cities. People now conceptualized distance not in miles, but in minutes, based on the time it took to drive to their destination. Propinquity, being near everything one needed, was no longer a necessity for mobile families. Instead of defined physical places in the traditional townscape sense of spatial enclosure and walking distances, the new city was based on accessibility, a pattern of dispersal where individuals and families constructed their sense of the city from a series of physically discontinuous locations, connected only by driving. The city was no longer experienced as an integrated hierarchy of places and neighborhoods. Instead it became a non-hierarchical network where locations were equalized by their accessibility by car.

Webber's argument that the automobile would release people from the ties that bound them to particular places, and open up new possibilities of mobility and connections with a wide variety of locations, coincided with the explosive growth of American suburban development in the 1950s and 1960s. New housing subdivisions, shopping centers and office parks were built on open land with few spatial constraints, and connected by the ubiquitous system of (then) high-speed commuter freeways. The real point of Webber's thesis, however, was not simply that it was possible to move around easily to lots of different places, or that a new architecture could evolve from the technologies of movement, but that at a deep, fundamental level, *place didn't matter any more.* Instead of community being grounded in a particular location, a new pattern of social relationships could be created from weaving together the disparate strands of daily life from a variety of generic locations. In this context, argued Webber and other academic planners, traditional urban forms were simply irrelevant.

In Britain, the Archigram movement of the 1960s and 1970s extended this thesis with inspiring images of "walking cities" that carried everything needed to sustain life and culture in their famously massive tortoise-like forms. A few years later, the same group proposed a contradictory "soft" architecture that placed more emphasis on fast-changing technical systems that could "plug in" to any existing building situation and provide environmental and cultural services that could enrich all locations. The place didn't matter, and the character of the buildings in any location was immaterial. Drawing on a unique blend of science fiction and science fact, Archigram elaborated the theme

that technology can render geographic location unimportant by supplying all necessary support systems without primary recourse to the natural or urban worlds.

This shifting equation between propinquity and accessibility has remained a central issue for architects, planners, geographers and cultural critics.[4, 5, 6, 7, 8, 9, 10, 11, 12, 13, 14] Many have expounded at length on this dilemma, offering various interpretations regarding the urban politics of power and place. For Webber and his colleagues 40 years ago, the issue was originally one of new equations between physical distance and ease of personal travel, but the information technology revolution of the 1990s has radically changed the parameters of the discussion once more.

Webber, Archigram and many other designers, planners, and critics reordered physical space relative to new technologies, but real space was still the medium of human discourse. Proponents of our new digital society have argued that our computer-rich culture, redolent with electronic spaces, has superseded all such discussions.[15, 16, 17] The virtual spaces of the Internet, available to everyone with a computer, have brought Marshall McLuhan's "global village" to fruition.[18] Some even suggest that traditional community life is obsolete, and that virtual space will replace physical space as the primary medium of personal, commercial and cultural dialogue. The "electronic cottage" in the wilderness is now a reality, and information technology, these same critics argue, has rendered traditional urban places obsolete at an even more fundamental level than Webber predicted. Once again, traditional urban places are under attack. One author, Michael Dear goes so far as to say that "the phone and the modem have rendered the street irrelevant"[19].

Despite these dire predictions, traditional urban places have not become irrelevant as witnessed by the revival of many American city centers as places to live and play as well as work. Additionally new urban places are being constructed in the suburbs, as the preferred location for office work – close to housing, transit and retail and recreation facilities. Contrary to the "death of place" scenario, in a society that enables us to live and work anywhere we like, the places we choose to inhabit become *all the more precious* and important. Indeed, the concept of urban place itself is fast becoming the main organizing feature of economic activity (Figure 5.6).

5.6 Worker on laptop on quayside, Dartmouth, UK

Given their flexible and unpredictable work schedules, creative professionals require access to recreational and entertainment opportunities at a moment's notice. They increasingly act "like tourists in their own city"[20, 21] and require amenities close at hand, within walking distance if possible. There is only one kind of urbanism that can meet this need: the traditional public spaces of street and square, park and boulevard.

At an urban design conference in Melbourne, Australia, in 2001, author Joel Garreau, best known for his seminal book *Edge Cities*,[22] reinforced this theme, noting that cities are changing faster today than at any time for 150 years, and that computers are reshaping our urban world to favor places that provide and nourish face-to-face contact. Garreau expressed his belief that the urban future could "look like the eighteenth century, only cooler." Edge cities and downtowns "that are sterile and charmless will die." In common with the observations of Richard Florida, the American expert on economic development whose book *The Creative Class* has provoked so much discussion, Garreau believes the primary purpose of future cities will be to provide optimum conditions for face-to-face contact, an ancient but still primary human need.[23] In this context, good urban design and traditional public space are crucial in providing the appropriate environment for the future office.

As witness to this belief, a symposium entitled "Thinking Creatively for Our Economic Future," featuring Richard Florida, at the University of North Carolina at Charlotte in April 2003, brought together nearly two hundred people from the Charlotte region to brainstorm ideas that would increase the economic competitiveness of the city and surrounding counties in the global marketplace. There were only a handful of design professionals in the audience, but of all the dozens of innovative ideas discussed, the top recommendation of the day by a large margin was the creation of new urban spaces and public places where people could connect with each other and thus spur the creation of ideas. This strategy is called "designing for collisions," best understood by a simple analogy of molecules bumping into each other and creating reactions. The more molecules that bump around in a space, the more creative collisions occur, resulting in yet more innovative encounters.

This creative energy is precisely the opposite of the passive consumer culture portrayed by several critics of traditional urbanism.[24, 25] These critics mock this search for a more walkable urban future as the "café society" and often dub such efforts at community building as "latte towns." These commentators see such urban villages only as the commodification of urban experience, reducing the richness of public life to mere spectacle and entertainment courtesy of Starbucks, The Gap, Victoria's Secret and Williams-Sonoma. However, contrary to this academic critique, urban villages, with their greater density of occupation and more eclectic mixture of uses (including offices) create more energy and a greater potential for economic development than other separated, single use types of development.

Academic critics of the kinds of traditional, mixed-use urbanism that will increasingly be home to the office of the future often assert that somehow, the urban life in these urban villages isn't authentic.[26, 27, 28, 29, 30, 31, 32] Some go further, and argue that the only valid, creative urban activities take place in marginalized neighborhoods amidst nondescript surroundings.[33] While every city needs unloved and unlovely places that can be appropriated cheaply, or at no cost, for non-programmed uses by individuals and groups outside the mainstream, there is a major inconsistency in academic efforts to glorify these acts as somehow more profound or better than actions taken in public space by middle-class residents and office workers. Appropriating urban space for culturally specific activities by individuals and groups of all complexions is a valid endeavor, and needs to be facilitated wherever possible – even at the expense of social discomfort, as in protest rallies and demonstrations. A culturally diverse city needs different places for different activities, but for critics to disparage the business meetings, local commerce, and spontaneous conversations in the new suburban mixed-use centers as a mere "simulation" of urbanism is nonsense. Authentic cultural production can take place in well-designed surroundings as well as in abandoned parking lots.

Two examples may serve to demonstrate the cultural relevance and market potential of these new suburban mixed-use centers as the sites for new offices integrated with other urban activities. Both are chosen from the author's locality, in suburban towns north of Charlotte, North Carolina, and both show the importance of a hitherto unmentioned factor: having in place appropriate municipal master plans and/or zoning codes that facilitate this kind of mixed-use development. The first example, Birkdale Village, in Huntersville, North Carolina, was completed in 2001, and the second, a new development a few miles further north in Mooresville, North Carolina, is planned to start in 2006. Both provide an urban setting in the suburbs as the context for new offices and are symptomatic of new development across America.

Birkdale Village achieves the goal of integrating office development into a mixed-use urban village with meaningful and active public space; it supplies urban amenities to the suburban middle class from Huntersville and beyond. Birkdale has gathered unto itself many aspects of the traditional center, including high quality office space that the tiny town of Huntersville never possessed prior to its evolution from a sleepy farm community of less than 2,000 people in the 1980s into a burgeoning bedroom community of 32,000 in 2002.

Like a traditional town center, the 52-acre (20.8 hectares) Birkdale Village, with its apartments and offices over the stores, and a cinema at the end of Main Street, physically connects via a grid of walkable streets to adjacent housing developments. But beneath this veneer of normality, Huntersville is a town with extraordinary social demographics. The town's population is 86 percent white and its median household income is a whopping $72,000, considerably more than the regional average. Not surprisingly, the stores in Birkdale Village are upmarket, and the rents for the apartments and offices are relatively high, but this prosperity combined with the sense of near-genuine urbanity has bred considerable commercial success for office, retail, and residential uses (Figures 5.7 and 5.8).

The one important element that is missing is a civic presence. There is no Town Hall, no library, police station or post office. The library is isolated on the other side of a nearby freeway, while the other civic functions remain rooted in the small downtown core, three miles away, in the town's brave effort to stabilize and retain that fleeting piece of history.

Despite its positive impact on the community, not everybody can afford to live, work or shop in the new *de facto* town center. It's a fact of development economics that the extra costs and complexity of creating a true mixed-use center of this type can most easily be justified in an area of high demographics and above average disposable personal income, both factors that contribute to an educated and affluent workforce. However, this critique of higher costs can easily be overstated. The construction costs of Birkdale Village averaged out to $75 per square foot. Given the lower land costs for the smaller area required for this more compact development compared to a conventional suburban development that would need a larger site to lay out offices, retail and housing in separate pods, this is not an extravagant figure.

The multiple market opportunities represented by the growing urban desires of increasing numbers of the baby-boom and echo-boom generations have boosted the economic

5.7 Birkdale Village Main Street, Huntersville, North Carolina

5.8 Birkdale Village crowds

profile of urban villages in America considerably, whether on recycled grayfield or new greenfield sites. In May 2003, the Charlotte developers of Birkdale Village announced they had sold the majority share in the development to a national Real Estate Investment Trust (REIT) a very significant purchase because REITs comprise large and powerful investors at the end of the development chain. At the outset of any development process, all developers try to establish their exit strategy, i.e. who will they be able to sell the development on to? Until recently, urban villages were regarded as unproven in the marketplace, and large investors were skittish about their long-term value as investment property. This in turn made the initial developers nervous about making the original investments in these kinds of projects. The decision by the cautious, conservative end of the financial markets to put increasingly large investments into urban village developments does a great deal to establish the credibility of the mixed-use center as a stable development type.

Even with economic success stories like Birkdale Village, it's difficult to create urbanity fully formed in the heart of American suburbia. This is a process that will take some time, and Birkdale is one important stage in an evolutionary process. It has been helped by the fact that the town of Huntersville has operated a sophisticated form-based zoning ordinance since 1996, when the author of this chapter co-wrote the document with town staff. This was one of the first such progressive zoning ordinances in the nation, and in common with its successors, such as the much publicized "Smart Code," the document altered the basis of conventional zoning based exclusively on building uses with no references to building or urban form.

Conventional codes have segregated the American landscape into single-use pods of development, labeled "office," "industrial," "commercial," or "residential." This reduction of community life into separate specialty areas has resulted in American suburbs becoming a collection of monocultures, with no consideration given to the creation of urban and suburban places with real differences and character. By contrast, form-based zoning codes operate from the premise that buildings and urban spaces last far longer than transient building uses, so it makes most sense for regulations to orchestrate a hierarchy of urban and building forms appropriate to the local environment and circumstances that create character from the start, and

which can adapt and respond to changes of use over several generations. In the Huntersville case, the town rejected initial developer demands to construct a standard strip commercial center on the site, and held firm until such time that other, more progressive, developers (Crosland and Pappas Properties) came forward with a vision that matched that of the town officials and the author. This strength of civic will is not always common among American municipalities, but in the case of Birkdale Village, the town's foresight has paid handsome dividends, just as the developers' determination to anticipate change and respond to new patterns of living and working has been generously rewarded in the financial success of the project.

In American suburban culture, real urbanity is not something many citizens have experienced, and in this context Birkdale's Main Street ambience is a novel condition. The development's truly public spaces, the unusual suburban presence of people working and living above the shops – sharing in the public realm of the street from their balconies and windows – is the nearest thing to city life that many Americans have ever experienced.

Surveys and empirical observations clearly show Americans are hungry for an urban experience, and growing numbers of Americans are learning the lessons of history about what it means to be urban dweller and worker. At lunchtimes and during the evening hours Birkdale plays host to plenty of genuine street life and urban activity. Office workers descend into the street for lunch at one of the many restaurants or coffee shops, mingling with other pedestrians going about their business. After work, the wine bars are busy as office workers relax amidst residents, shoppers, and teenagers en route to the cinema – all combining to create a fledgling American version of the European *passegiata*, the evening promenade along Main Street.

The second example comes from Mooresville, North Carolina, a town of some 20,000 people, located 10 miles further north from Huntersville and 25 miles north of the city of Charlotte. The town is likely to be the last stop on a planned commuter rail line connecting to central Charlotte, and in 2000 and 2001 the author was instrumental in developing an urban design master plan and form-based zoning codes for 1200 acres (480 hectares) of predominantly greenfield land 3 miles south of the town center. The master plan, in its various versions, has provided a framework to manage growth around an important regional hospital, a future train station, and an interstate interchange – while maintaining an appropriate urban scale and environmental protections. The new growth fuelled by this large hospital, the extensive suburban expansion of Charlotte around nearby Lake Norman (the largest man-made lake in the Carolinas), and the potential for future transit-oriented development around the train station, all combined to bring considerable development pressure to bear on this area.

The first version of the master plan was completed in 2000, and featured detailed provisions for office, residential, and retail buildings, public parks and areas of preserved landscape, and an interconnected street network, all coming together to create an urban village centered on the future train station and supported by freeway access. The plan recommended in this instance that the village be developed as an "employment-led transit-oriented development (TOD)," with a combination of office and housing rather than retail, which should be limited to smaller neighborhood service stores and restaurants. Included in the study area was a small historic settlement, Mount Mourne, which included a post office, school, fire station, and several churches; this civic fabric provided some of the essential community "glue" missing from the Birkdale Village example, and formed a solid foundation for the master plan.

Most importantly the plan identified this largely flat and easily developed land in large, single ownership tracts as a prime site for a major corporate headquarters adjacent to the village center, easily accessible by road and future rail connections. Shortly after completion of the plan, this prediction came true when the Lowe's corporation (America's No. 2 "do-it-yourself" and home improvement retail chain) relocated their corporate headquarters to this site. This major economic boost to the local economy was brought about in no small measure by the accommodating provisions of the original master plan and its synchronized zoning ordinance that made relocation of this large facility relatively straightforward. A revision of the original plan was necessary in 2001 to incorporate the specifics of Lowe's proposal and in 2003 the plan was again revised to accommodate the influx of a new wave of subsidiary office development to provide space for the host of smaller companies that supply Lowe's with goods and services (Figure 5.9).

In order to implement many of the recommendations of the Mooresville master plan, it was important to establish a new regulatory framework in which appropriate future development could occur. The current zoning regulations were insufficient to enforce many of the recommendations, and the author and his colleagues therefore wrote and drew a new form-based zoning ordinance for the town to cover the master plan area, and which could be extended to other parts of town as needed. This zoning code, another example of the form-based zoning philosophy so successful at Birkdale Village, was adopted by the Mooresville town council in 2001 shortly after the acceptance of the master plan. The whole code for the plan area comprised only 19 pages, of which six were full-page diagrams and drawings.

The importance of the combined urban design master plan and form-based zoning code was illustrated yet again in 2005,

5.9 Mount Mourne, master plan, Mooresville, North Carolina

when a development company announced plans for a 27 acre, 450,000 square foot mixed-use complex on the site of the proposed urban village. The press reports of the development specifically stated that the development will be "consistent with Mooresville's . . . adopted master plan for the Mount Mourne community".[34] The developer's master plan comprises nine new mixed use buildings providing offices, retail space and condominiums arranged around an urban park adjacent to the future train station, just where the author's master plan indicated. The developer expects the urban village to serve Lowe's employees and vendors, the adjacent medical center, and families in the area. Offices will lease for about $20 a square foot annually with retail rates for the specialty stores and restaurants ranging from $22–24 a square foot annually (Figures 5.10 and 5.11).

Effective office work requires new environments not only within the office, but outside in the community as well. People crave human contact of the sort provided by revived central cities and the new suburban mixed-use centers. But real estate professionals and the bankers who finance their projects often view change with suspicion, and tend to fund the future with what's worked in the past. However, this strategy won't suffice when globalization and information technology are rewriting the rulebook faster than we think. Do we have the entrepreneurial spirit to explore new options, and embrace change in time to profit from it? Do we have the clients to commission new, smarter buildings? Do we have the bankers to fund them, and architects to design them and the property managers to run them? Do we have the urban designers who understand the spatial and functional dynamics of new urban villages, and the planners to zone land in ways that encourage them? All these professions have a learning curve; in these challenging times of global competition and changing demographics, it's likely only the most intellectually innovative and progressive professionals will prosper.

The two mixed-use developments described above point the way forward; it's often progressive small towns forming the suburban fringe around major cities that can position themselves most easily to profit from the rapid changes, with good master plans and form-based zoning ordinances. Large cities, with their more complex bureaucracies are slower and more resistant to change, and innovative development is often harder, more time consuming and expensive for developers.

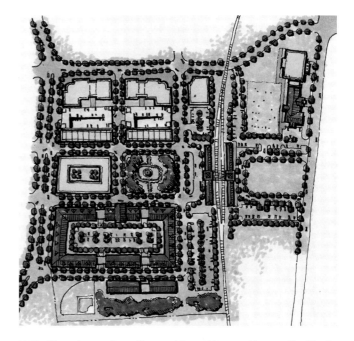

5.10 Plan of new urban village at Mount Mourne, Mooresville, North Carolina

5.11 Aerial perspective of new urban village at Mount Mourne, Mooresville, North Carolina

The challenge of the new office and the new community is one that cannot be met by either the private developers or governments working alone. As both examples indicate, a progressive partnership between public and private sectors provides the basis for future success. In the fractious political climate that characterizes America in the early years of the twenty-first century, this is a tough test. The examples outlined above show we know what to do and how to do it. But do we have the political will to reshape American cities and suburbs to meet the demands of a new age?

Notes and References

1 Duffy, F. (1997) *The New Office*, London: Conran Octopus Ltd.

2 Webber, M.M. (1964a) "Order in Diversity: Community without Propinquity," in L. Wingo Jr. (ed.) *Cities and Space: The Future Use of Urban Land*, Philadelphia, PA: University of Pennsylvania Press.

3 Webber, M.M. (1964b) "The Urban Place and the Nonplace Urban Realm," in M.M. Webber, J.W. Dyckman, D.L. Foley, A.Z. Gutenberg, W.L.C. Wheaton, and C.B. Wurster (eds) *Explorations in Urban Structure*, Philadelphia, PA: University of Pennsylvania Press.

4 Sennett, R. (1971) *The Uses of Disorder: Personal Identity and Communal Life*, London: Allen Lane.

5 Sennett, R. (1974) *The Fall of Public Man*, New York: Alfred A. Knopf.

6 Castells, M. (1989) *The Informational City: Information Technology, Economic Restructuring and the Urban-Regional Process*, Oxford: Blackwell.

7 Castells, M. (1997) *The Information Age: Economy, Society, and Culture*, vol. 1: *The Rise of the Network Society*, Oxford: Blackwell.

8 Harvey, D. (1989) *The Condition of Postmodernity: An Enquiry into the Origins of Cultural Change*, Oxford: Basil Blackwell.

9 Soja, E. (1989) *Postmodern Geographies*, London: Verso.

10 Jameson, F. (1991) *Postmodernism, or the Cultural Logic of Late Capitalism*, Durham, North Carolina: Duke University Press.

11 Howell, P. (1993) "Public Space and the Public Sphere: Political Theory and the Historical Geography of Modernity," *Environment and Planning D: Society and Space*, 11: 303–322.

12 Watson, S. and Gibson, K. (eds) (1995) *Postmodern Cities and Spaces*, Oxford: Blackwell.

13 Mitchell, W.J. (1995) *City of Bits: Space, Place, and the Infobahn*, Cambridge, MA: MIT Press.

14 Mitchell, W.J. (1999) *e-topia: 'Urban Life, Jim – But Not As We Know It,'* Cambridge, MA: MIT Press.

15 Mitchell, W.J. (1995) *City of Bits: Space, Place, and the Infobahn*, Cambridge, MA: MIT Press.

16 Kelly, K. (1998) *New Rules for the New Economy: 10 Radical Strategies for a Connected World*, New York: Viking.

17 Gilder, G. (2000) *Telecosm: How Infinite Bandwidth Will Revolutionize Our World*, New York: Free Press.

18 McLuhan, M. and Fiore, Q. (1967) *The Medium is the Massage*, New York: Bantam, p. 63.

19 Dear, M. (1995) "Prologomena to a Post Modern Urbanism," in P. Healey *et al.* (eds) *Managing Cities: The New Urban Context*, London: Wiley, pp. 27–44.

20 Lloyd, R. and Clark, T.N. (2001) "The City as Entertainment Machine," in K. Fox Gotham (ed.) *Critical Perspectives on Urban Redevelopment: Research in Urban Sociology*, vol. 6, Oxford: JAI Press/Elsevier, pp. 375–378.

21 Florida, R. (2002) *The Rise of the Creative Class: And How It's Transforming Work, Leisure, Community and Everyday Life*, New York: Basic Books, 225.

22 Garreau, J. (1991) *Edge City: Life on the New Frontier*, New York: Doubleday.

23 Garreau, J. (2001) "Face to Face in the Information Age," unpublished conference paper, City Edge 2: Centre vs. Periphery, Melbourne, Australia.

24 Kaliski, J. (1999) "The Present City and the Practice of City Design," in J. Chase, M. Crawford and J. Kaliski (eds) *Everyday Urbanism*, New York: The Monacelli Press.

25 McDougall, I. (1999) "The New Urban Space," in *City Edge Transcripts*, the Proceedings of the City Edge Conference: Private Development vs. Public Realm, City of Melbourne, Australia, pp. 29–35.

26 Sudjic, D. (1992) *The 100 Mile City*, San Diego: Harcourt Brace and Company.

27 Rybczynski, W. (1995) *City Life: Urban Expectations in a New World*, New York: Scribner.

28 Safdie, M. (1997) *The City after the Automobile*, New York: Basic Books.

29 Dovey, K. (1999) "Democracy and Public Space?" *City Edge Transcripts*, the Proceedings of the City Edge Conference: Private Development vs Public Realm, City of Melbourne, Australia, pp. 45–51.

30 McDougall, I. (1999) "The New Urban Space," in *City Edge Transcripts*, the Proceedings of the City Edge Conference: Private Development vs. Public Realm, City of Melbourne, Australia, pp. 29–35.

31 Marshall, A. (2000) *How Cities Work: Suburbs, Sprawl and the Roads Not Taken*, Austin, TX: Austin University Press.

32 Sorkin, M. (2001) *Some Assembly Required*, Minneapolis: University of Minnesota Press.

33 Chase, J., Crawford, M. and Kaliski, J. (1999) *Everyday Urbanism*, New York: The Monacelli Press.

34 Smith, D. (2005) "Growth Area to Get Big Boost in Mooresville," *The Charlotte Observer*, Aug. 19, D1–2.

Reinventing the American Suburban Business Park

Scott Wilson

Suburban office park development in America has cooled considerably from the heady expansion days of the 1980s and 1990s. The bursting of the dot-com bubble and fluctuations within the US economy have led to market saturation in many regions of the country; the suburban office market is now seeing only anemic growth nationally after three years of steady vacancy rate increases. Within this lackluster context, one promising trend within the suburban office market is the rise of office space integrated with a mix of other uses in new suburban "town centers" or walkable "urban villages." This movement reflects a growing demand that office workers be more readily connected to a range of daily activities outside the workplace.

Traditional suburban office parks located off an interstate freeway or outer beltway exit stand inherently alone; they are decidedly car-oriented and disconnected from shopping, entertainment, and residential communities even if these uses are to be found nearby (see Figure 5.2 on p. 44). The design intent of such developments is primarily focused on creating a business address within a cloistered setting emoting gravitas and prestige where well-landscaped drives lead up to over-stated entrances. To this end, the individual office buildings are planned as solitary sentinels set amidst the amenities: beyond the requisite surface parking, walking trails generally thread through park-like landscaping, ponds and outdoor lunch areas. Suburban business parks are inherently designed to give at least the illusion of splendid isolation from the suburban sprawl at their edges, and within this tightly defined typology the usual strategy for leasing success is differentiation from competitors through a small range of variables: convenience of location, efficiency of building floor plate, and the attractiveness of the landscape amenities sprinkled throughout the development.

Many of the lavish amenities built into office parks in the early 1990s are no longer economically viable or offer sufficient differentiators to warrant the additional expense. Swimming pools, fitness clubs and on-site day care are seldom offered now except for the most ambitious office park developments. And while marketing perks may be constantly changing, the design and planning criteria for the developments have not evolved radically.

The typical office park building comprises primarily three or four floors with a mean national average of approximately 25,000 sq ft (2,320 sq m) per floor, and the standard plan layout has central cores of elevator banks, stairs and toilets of no more than 30 percent of total gross building area. This model has worked well for the last quarter century in the sprawling suburbs of the American sunbelt and other fast-growing regions of the country, but with the market now suffering from a saturation of such products and with many of the first-wave 1970s and 1980s office parks getting close to the end of their competitive life cycle, suburban municipalities, as well as the development market, must grapple with how to keep these areas economically vibrant and competitive. Replacing the old developments with new versions of the same outdated model will not significantly impact a slow market or assure vibrant ancillary growth in the immediate surroundings. As evidence of this, recent suburban office developments built during the past three years are showing similar vacancy rates as their more established predecessors built within the past 20 years. Moves in housing starts coupled with new shopping centers and transportation infrastructure are forever putting pressure on the market to create the "next big thing" one off-ramp exit away to where potentially newer and more affluent growth is evolving. Inevitably many older business parks, developed 20 years ago in first tier suburbs, have few options beyond attractive lease packages to make up for their lack of the latest "must have" amenities offered by newer developments. This problem is compounded by the dramatic increases in building and grounds maintenance costs as the older office parks reach their 25- and 30-year milestones. Clearly new thinking in office park design is required to ensure that this cycle of gradual yet assured obsolescence is not replicated *ad infinitum*.

While current market trends are still showing that the most significant office product coming on line is still the traditional corporate office park, the most interesting trend for the future of suburban development is the growing number of office buildings designed as part of ambitious walkable urban villages or town centers. Pioneering town centers designed in the late 1980s and early 1990s are creating impressive, positive data on what may be the best approach to resurrect a moribund market sector and assure sustained economic vitality.

The new urban village or town center follows traditional urban forms, such as town squares, plazas or pedestrian-friendly main streets (see Figure 5.7 on p. 50). They always comprise a blend of uses that may include residential, office, retail and entertainment, as well as occasional civic components. It is this integration of everyday activities within a walkable environment that creates a true 24/7 public realm, or at least an active 18-hour cycle. "Mixed-use" implies buildings in which uses are mixed vertically (offices or apartments above shops being the most common example, following the model of the traditional American downtown), but under some circumstances, "multi-use" developments, projects where the same mix of uses is present, but in a format where each use is in a separate but adjacent building can be considered urban villages if all the components are linked together by a pedestrian-friendly system of streets.

The core of a typical urban village in a suburban location on the edge of a major US city is likely to consist primarily of shopping and entertainment facilities with offices and or residential units designed within close walking distance. It is important to distinguish this more complex typology from the trend in "lifestyle centers," which are often (sometimes intentionally) misinterpreted as town centers or urban villages when they are primarily themed outdoor shopping centers creating the illusion of "Main Street USA." In many instances, these centers offer absolutely no activities other than those related purely to shopping and entertainment.

Many new suburban town centers are reinforcing their potential as true centers of community life by integrating transit stations into their design. Transit-oriented developments of this type are nothing new. Their origins lie in the late nineteenth-century suburban developments built around the pre-industrial urban core of large metropolitan cities such as London; similar transit systems were also introduced around the edges of many American cities during the same period. These transit-oriented developments can be seen in many major US cities, especially in the northern states, the North-east, and parts of the West Coast. The new phenomenon we are seeing today is the way that light rail transit is being embraced by the ever-expanding cities of the American South-east and South-west. In these areas the connection between the suburban developments and the suburban transit stations is still very much in its infancy. The economic advantages of transit-oriented developments are obvious: their connections back to city cores, airports and other satellite communities ensure they have unique market differentiators from non-transit-oriented products. They can greatly assist municipalities in ensuring that growth expands along dedicated corridors, reducing infrastructure costs and saving more open green space. However, they also represent significantly greater challenges in the early planning stages. Incorporating the design of transit stations can disrupt circulation patterns, especially if the rail line bifurcates the center of a development. Much of the infrastructure cost is considerably higher and while this cost is normally borne by the public sector, it often suggests a more ambitious project requiring significantly more investment capital than non-transit-oriented developments. Other issues such as additional coordination with transit authorities and local municipalities can cause delays so that sometimes the development is completed but the transit station is slow to follow. The majority of transit-oriented developments eventually pay the promised dividends, but it may not be in time to ensure critical initial leasing. The complexity, additional bureaucracy and delays in getting the product to market can snuff the life out of many a time-sensitive *pro forma*.

Many of the most prominent town centers developed in the 1990s, such as Reston Town Center, Reston, Virginia; Easton Town Center, Columbus, Ohio, and on a smaller scale, Mockingbird Lane Station in Dallas, Texas, all have differences in their mix of uses as well as unique differentiators, such as hotels, convention centers or transit stations. The great commonality is their performance. They all have out-performed their regional competition in traditional suburban developments and offer attractive precedents for future models.

Reston Town Center opened its first 20 acre (8 hectare) phase in 1990 and will be completed with the final phase of construction in 2006 (Figures 6.1 and 6.2). The initial phase included 530,000 sq ft (49,200 sq m) of office space and 240,000 sq ft (22,300 sq m) of specialty retail and restaurants: the completed development now has 1.5 million sq ft (139,000 sq m) of office and retail and 700 townhouse-style apartments and for sale condominiums. Reston boasts a Hyatt Regency Hotel, urban amities such as outdoor skating rinks, amphitheaters and a recently completed Washington Metro link station. Ancillary development of multi-family residential, offices and hotel accommodation are enjoying a healthy "halo effect," achieving considerably higher rents than the surrounding Dulles market in the Washington, DC, area.

6.1 Reston Town Center, master plan
Image: © Maxwell McKenzie

6.2 Reston Town Center, general view
Image: © Maxwell McKenzie

The massive 1,200 acre (486 hectare) Easton Town Center opened its first phase in 1999 and is scheduled for full build-out in 2010 (Figure 6.3). The development comprises 3.3 million sq ft (307,000 sq m) of retail, 5 million sq ft (465,000 sq m) of office space and 1,000 multi-family residential units. The development also includes many civic features such as a band shell, open-air market, and a library, all centered round an amply sized town square. Last year over 10 million people visited Easton. This commercial space, which has been almost fully leased for six years, enjoys a 98 percent occupancy rate, outpacing downtown Columbus by 30 percent.

Keller Town Center, in Keller, Texas, is a 360 acre (146 hectare) development, started in 1999 with build-out scheduled in 2010 (Figure 6.4). The office component is fully leased and averages 25–35 percent higher rents for comparable properties in the Dallas–Fort Worth suburban market. This is significant achievement considering how quickly the leases were signed up in an over-saturated and rent-competitive suburban market.

Keller Town Center also has significant components of single and multi-family residential units within the overall master plan. Another unique attribute is a linear park that follows a stream running diagonally through the site and connects the residential to office and retail components. The site is also buffered by a large natural preserve allowing for parks, lakes and woodlands in an existing floodplain.

Southlake Town Square in Southlake, Texas, is a 130 acre (52.6 hectare) development begun in 1999 and scheduled for build-out in 2020. The office component enjoys the same successful leasing premiums that the Keller Town Center has achieved. The retail stores are centered round a large town square anchored at one end by Southlake city hall and a band stand at the other. The vernacular style of the development picks up on the "Main Street" architecture of many small Texas towns and the patina of time will only strengthen its sense of place. One unique differentiator in the planning of Southlake is its central square that is activated throughout the year by substantive community concerts and festivals. Such amenities go well beyond the ice cream social at the lone picnic table of traditional office parks and instead give the office employees an instant sense of connection with the greater community. Developers Cooper and Stebbins were quick to promote these

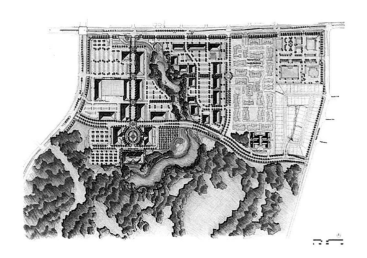

6.3 Easton Town Center, general view

6.4 Keller Town Center, master plan

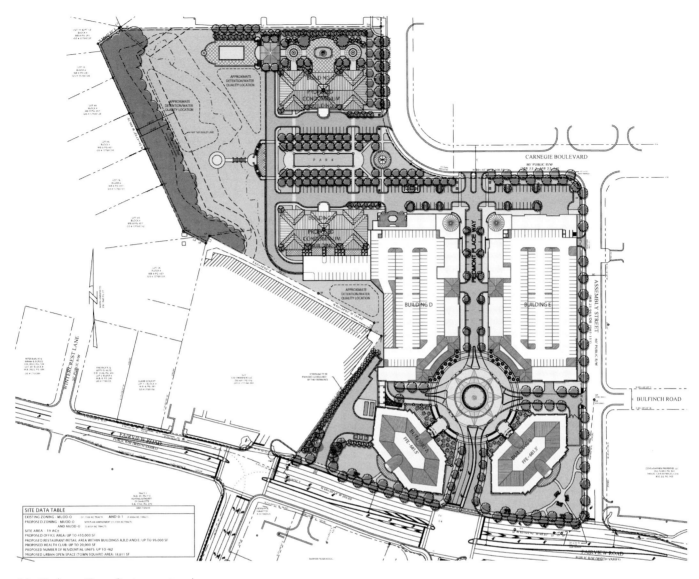

6.5 Piedmont Town Center, master plan

market differentiators and have been rewarded by strong leasing premiums for their initiative.

Piedmont Town Center recently completed in Charlotte, North Carolina, is a 20-acre mixed-use project in immediate proximity to the exclusive SouthPark mall and a mature office market of suburban office buildings and several mid-rise office towers (Figures 6.5 and 6.6). The new urban village development sits in proximity to downtown Charlotte, just five miles away, and is nestled in one of the city's most affluent residential areas; these factors provide a considerable competitive edge over other sub-market developments located several miles further out on Charlotte's outer belt freeway. Piedmont Town Center has approximately 400,000 sq ft (37,200 sq m) of office space in two eight-storey towers flanking a large circular plaza with ground floor retail, and high-end restaurants. A new street, lined on both sides with multi-storey condominiums and ground floor retail, links the plaza to existing major streets in the neighborhood. The first phase of 90 residential units, which ranged from the low $200,000s to million-dollar penthouses, sold in a few days. The assured success of Piedmont Town Center is evident in its leasing rate of $27 per square foot, rivaling center city rents and $4–5 higher than the average SouthPark rate.

With the completion of Piedmont Town Center there now remains little available open space in Charlotte's SouthPark area which currently contains almost 3.8 million sq ft (353,000 sq m) of office space, the second highest concentration of office space in the Carolinas, behind downtown Charlotte and ahead of downtown Raleigh. The logical next phase of development will be likely focused on the suburban office park of three- to five-storey buildings built in the late 1970s and early 1980s directly behind SouthPark mall. These buildings, while enjoying the benefit of inclusion in what is the region's most vibrant sub-market, still have healthy demand but it may not be sufficient to keep the wrecking ball from coming in the not too distant future if pressure for larger, super-class A products in an urban setting remains at current trend levels.

The uniqueness of living and working in Piedmont Town Center is manifested in the lifestyle it affords. Residents and office workers can stroll down the main street of Piedmont Town

6.6 Piedmont Town Center, general view

Center, window shopping or dining in one of the many upscale restaurants that line the street and main plaza, or savor the allure of being within easy walking distance of retailers such as Nordstrom, Neiman Marcus and other high-end stores that have made SouthPark much more than a business address. It is now a significant lifestyle destination.

With the clear success of many new urban villages it is in many ways curious that more are not being built. This may be because the evidence is not all rosy; anecdotal evidence suggests that urban village developments are doing better than the established stand-alone office park but they do not necessarily guarantee higher returns to their investors. The higher than average values or rents that these developments have generated do not guarantee they will out-perform their competition in terms of investment. The greater complexity of the development pushes costs higher and as most town centers or urban villages are targeted towards higher-end markets, this also results in higher priced products, and higher rents but not always higher returns.

Other concerns arise from the complexities of bringing such unique and place specific products to the market. Prominent examples, such as Reston Town Center, have been around for more than 15 years yet they still remain too unique and there-

fore too great a risk for many tradition-bound lenders. The planning and construction investment for mixed-use developments are usually considerably greater than for most single-use projects, and in addition the build-out time can be between 10 and 20 years from initial ground breaking to final phase completion. Such significant requirements of capital and time normally necessitate more than single source financing; the alternative requires multiple lenders with higher equity requirements and more complicated underwriting arrangements. Such complexities and obvious risks to the developer's equity assets can be too great for many players. Other ambitious projects never get beyond the initial conceptual stage because of their dependency on some component of public financing to attract additional private funding; the inability to receive public investment can be the difference between the project's real viability or not. A new development in Charlotte, North Carolina, at Metropolitan Avenue by local developer Pappas Properties is a case in point. This ambitious design, including vertically stacked specialist Home Depot and Target big-box stores integrated into a "Main Street" type of development plan with offices, housing, other retail, and a hotel also involved a major public project to reclaim and open up a substantial creek as an urban water amenity on the site as part of a county-wide greenway link (Figures 6.7 and 6.8). The public–private mix of investment for this extensive and complex project included a request by the developer for a range of tax subsidies totaling several millions of dollars from the City of Charlotte; eventually agreement was reached, but not until after much heated political debate had delayed the project by a couple of years.

The approval process itself can be another significant obstacle. Many zoning and entitlement roadblocks can hinder many desirable mixed-use projects. Fairfax County Virginia did not have the appropriate mixed-use zoning to permit Reston when it was first proposed. City Place in West Palm Beach and Easton Town Center in Columbus experienced equally difficult challenges. These more notable examples were typical in the 1990s and remain a problem in many municipalities years later. Whether the zoning is in place or not, the approval process for mixed-use projects in many jurisdictions are often extremely time-consuming and have the effect of discouraging rather than encouraging developers. By contrast, the example of Birkdale Village, in Huntersville, North Carolina, just north of Charlotte,

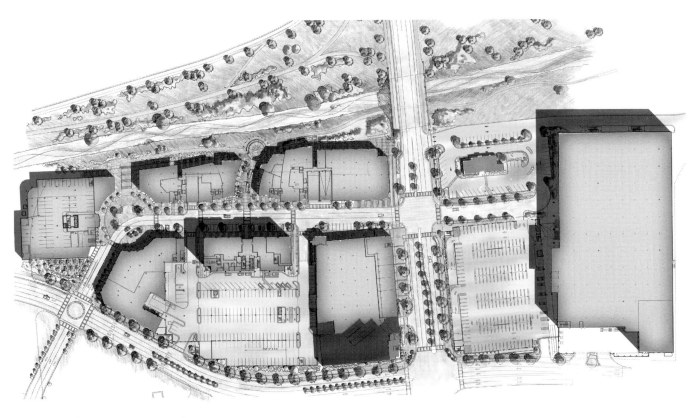

6.7 Metropolitan Avenue, master plan

6.8 Metropolitan Avenue, general view

illustrates what can be achieved when appropriate zoning is in place ahead of the development. Huntersville adopted a New Urbanist design or form-based ordinance in 1996, and the town was proactive in shaping new mixed-use development to its preferred urban village pattern. Like any complex development, Birkdale Village was not without its challenges, but the developers and the town officials collaborated effectively within a regulatory framework that not only permitted the urban village style of development, but required it. In certain instances as the design evolved, the developers and their architects suggested amendments to the zoning code that would allow interesting urban design details to be implemented. In almost all cases, the town agreed and incorporated these changes into its ordinance.

Despite the success of mixed-use developments like Birkdale Village, the most significant factor keeping the town center development trend in check appears to be the fundamental lack of experience with the mixed-use product within the development community. The overwhelming number of developers engage in either residential, or retail, or office; few are involved in all three and far fewer combine them in any one development. Overcoming their concerns of how to plan, finance, and assemble the land, as well as navigate the approval process, can be simply too daunting for many, irrespective of the bounty illustrated by favorable examples currently in the marketplace.

Developers who have risen to this challenge have determined the following key points creating a successful design:

- *Demogaphics*: Bringing a major mixed-use development to market requires that the area demographics support such developments. A critical mass of population, employment and affluent income is required.
- *The right mix*: The development plan must ensure that the mix of facilities relates to the need. If the center is primarily shopping, then the type of shopping to be provided, e.g. a major shopping center with desirable anchors and high-end shops or a neighborhood shopping center, must be defined carefully.
- *Be aggressive*: If the market is hot, then the greater the density, the greater the opportunity to create a strong epicenter of growth irrespective of other sub-market performance. A design that is too tepid may never create the demand for later higher density phases.
- *Know where your strengths lie*: Many developers may not have the experience in retail or housing if their expertise is primarily office. Hubris can ring the death knell for mixed-use projects if the primary players do not understand the critical nuances needed to bring successful products to market.
- *Act quickly*: Secure the entitlements and other municipal entitlements as soon as possible. Time delays normally mean money wasted and potential opportunities lost to bring something unique to market ahead of competitors.
- *Differentiate the product*: In several markets the uniqueness of simply bringing a new town center or walkable village may not be that distinctive in itself. Therefore, the need for a differentiator is critical. This differentiator may be in the type of retail or housing provided and not currently in the market, or amenities and events that may give rise to greater appeal outside of the immediate area, i.e. a farmers' market, extensive festival programming and the like.

The continued success of urban villages and suburban town centers will really come down to numbers and overall, the numbers look extremely bright. Office tenants seem willing to pay a premium – sometimes a substantial premium – to be part of something different, especially something that offers the promise of a tangible connection with a community. This trend is creating improved value for everyone from the developer to the municipality while also improving the quality of life for the office worker. Therefore, we should continue to see this developing trend reshape our suburban communities from the fragmented, disconnected office parks and shopping centers of the past into the more forward-looking, sustainable, livable developments that will hopefully be much more resilient to obsolescence and momentary trends.

New Office, New Community

G.B. Arrington and Craig Briner

Editor's introduction

David Walters

The city *is* the office for any networked organization, and the changing shape of office work has major implications on the changing shape of the city. The revolution in information technology, the massive changes in office design, the dissolution of the workplace into a multifaceted, multi-tiered operation integrated with other aspects of our lives will inevitably change the shape of the city. It is already doing so. The "knowledge worker" uses his or her city like a tourist, not simply as a resident. A tourist needs and expects the facilities of the city on demand 18, even 24 hours a day, and that has major implications for infrastructure, for the design of public space, for the content of buildings, for the adaptive life of buildings, and many other considerations.

Those are some of the themes that are brought to the surface here, first, by G.B. Arrington, Principal Practice Leader for Parsons Brinckerhoff PlaceMaking, who has worked with the public sector and the private sector in many cities worldwide on a host of transit-related issues. He examines the integration of transit planning and land-use planning, noting how the shape of the city is changing. Then, by Craig Briner, of Cherokee Investment Partners, who has extensive experience in the development industry, trying to do things that not all developers are bold enough to attempt, particularly in relation to cleaning up brownfield sites for new, mixed-use urban development. He provides perspectives on these issues from the viewpoint of the private sector.

Places between the Buildings

G.B. Arrington

I want to talk about the places between the buildings. Architects typically talk about buildings, and from my perspective, it is the space between the buildings that matters. It's what creates the real value, what creates the places we want to spend our time in. In the infrastructure business, we can't do our job unless we recognize the intersection where transportation and land use come together. I will look at a variety of different transit-oriented development projects.

There is transit-oriented development (TOD) and then there is its evil brother TAD, transit adjacent development. In the majority of places in the United States, there are more TADs than TODs. In most of the United States, TOD is illegal, not because we chose to make it illegal, but because our existing zoning codes require suburban-scale developments. It's not enough to develop and be next to transit, the developments need to be shaped by transit.

One of the best examples of integrating transportation with land use is the Rosslyn–Ballston corridor in suburban Washington, DC. It's one of the best because it's one of the most mature. Planning started before the rail line opened, and the planned rail line was moved out of the freeway corridor and into suburban areas. The line was buried, and the stations located close together. This strategy captured a tremendous amount of development. In total, 25 percent of all the housing and 37 percent of all the jobs in the county are within walking distance of five stations of the Rosslyn–Ballston corridor. This started as a suburban place and has become an urban place; a different kind of environment was created by integrating transportation with land use. This is an example of the ability to change the future and to make development happen in a different way by integrating these two planning concepts.

Mockingbird Lane in Dallas is an example of creating an 18-hour place around transit, and integrating transit and land use. It is a place that was originally next to the freeway and the transit accessibility changed the nature of this place; the developer was able to create a wonderful place that takes advantage of the proximity of the transit. Unfortunately, TOD is not legal in the city of Dallas; they refuse to change their zoning codes to allow for the presence of transit. So, the developer has $6 million in unneeded structured parking in this project because he was not allowed to reduce his codes to take advantage of the presence of the transit. So sometimes it is not enough to have good development and good transit, you also have to have good planning to go along with it, and that did not exist here.

The Lindberg Center in Atlanta is a project driven in large part by congestion. Bell South did not know how to get their employees to work in a predictable manner because

the freeway system in Atlanta is so congested and unreliable. They decided to combine all their offices in one location on the MARTA rail line, and provide annual transit passes so that employees could get to work on time. This project is partially complete, the offices are finished but the retail hasn't happened yet and will follow. It is an interesting example of a partnership between the public sector and the private sector.

The last example is Orenco Station in Portland. This is a greenfield example; it is located 16 miles from downtown. It was master-planned on 194 acres (78.5 hectares) around the coming of light rail, which now serves the project. It incorporates over 1800 homes, and has a mixed-use town center, with retail on the ground floor, offices above on the street side, and residential above on the interior side. The zoning requires it to be transit-oriented. The other interesting thing is that 45 percent of the people who will live in the single family housing in Orenco Station will likely work for Intel in their nearby research and manufacturing facility, arguably the most sophisticated in the world. It's a $4.8 million facility. This is a great place to live and work; the transit system is good and people use it.

Next, I would like to highlight some important issues regarding planning spaces for the integration of transit and land use. The first point is to understand the market. Clearly, many cities are experiencing a great deal of urban growth, and residential development is being driven by the changing demographics we are seeing here in the United States.

The second point is that it is important to think about this integrated planning early. The planning needs to be done ahead of the engineering so we can plan for that integration. We need to have the right tools; getting the right kind of zoning in place can make this type of development legal and assist in the process of land assembly.

Third, density really matters. Essentially, the more density that can be created around transit, the more successful the development. It is not enough to have just transit, it is necessary to renew and create places to come back to, not just places to leave from. That means we need to design development in such a way that it deserves to have transit next to it, and we need to design the transit itself in a different way. At the end of the day, that means designing for the pedestrian, so there is much of this we can do without the transit being there initially. We can create PODs, pedestrian oriented developments, that can turn into

TODs later. It is important to have a mix of uses but they do not all have to be at one station, they can be between stations and we can think of the train and bus as "elevators" that move between the buildings and between the stations.

Fourth, we have to get the parking right. If we want to create these wonderful, active, walking places, people will drive to them and how we deal with the car is important. The other dimension of transit is we can get away with less parking in terms of how we park these projects.

Finally, if you are successful, those spaces and active places between the buildings create an environment where the future office can be successful because we will create the kinds of places that people want to spend their time.

The Meadowlands, New Jersey, and Magnolia, South Carolina

Craig Briner

I want to just touch on one Cherokee Investment Partners' project in New Jersey, and then focus in on a project in Charleston, South Carolina. First is a very ambitious project in the New Jersey Meadowlands, about 5 miles (8 km) from midtown Manhattan and 3 miles (4.8 km) from Newark. The goal is to remediate existing environmental impairment and redevelop the site to maximize urban space, thus creating plausible communities. Mass transit is the key factor.

There are basically two phases of this project; it's huge and will have a significant impact on that market place (Figure 7.1). The golf courses are actually part of the remediation process because there are significant landfills here that are being capped and remediated. We are getting better in the utilization of former landfills; not everything in the future will be as passive a use as a golf course. The engineering for remediation is improving and there are increased legal protections for non-polluting uses that come to these sites at a later date.

The Meadowlands is very important because the project has a lot of support. The state of New Jersey is one of the most polluted states in the nation. They have assisted our work through tax increment financing. One of the reasons, of course, that they want this done is the development of unrealized

7.1 Master plan for New Jersey Meadowlands

contaminated property which then turns back into tax dollars, and New Jersey is very keen on tying this redevelopment to existing mass transit stations and those stations along the line.

In Charleston, we are working on about 400 acres (162 hectares) in the north end of the peninsula on the site of a decommissioned naval base. This project, called Magnolia (Figure 7.2), is very complex to put together, and we wouldn't be able to do this alone out of Raleigh. We had to have some local champions in order to get this done. Probably the foremost is Mayor Joe Riley, he's been mayor since 1975. He understands density, which was a key issue for us to be able to tackle a project like this.

Our second champion was Tim Keane, the city's planning director. Tim is a graduate of the University of North Carolina at Charlotte's College of Architecture, and was the planning director of Davidson for several years before moving to Charleston. Before we began our project, Tim agreed to run charrettes for this entire area, not just for our site, but also for sites on the other side of Interstate 26. The existing residents on and around the site were very important participants in this process. There is a residential community called Rosemont, where newly freed African-Americans were allowed to live after the Civil War.

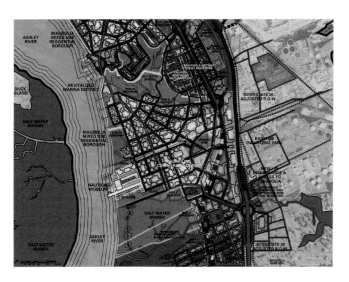

7.2 Master plan for Magnolia, Charleston, South Carolina

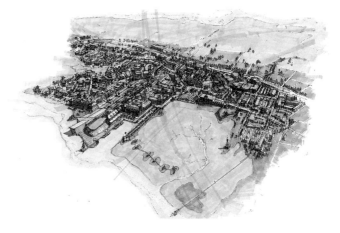

7.3 Artist's impression of Magnolia, Charleston, South Carolina

It is an interesting neighborhood, except that federal planners bisected it when they constructed Interstate 26 coming down through the peninsula (Figure 7.3). By contrast, before we and our designers, Shook Kelley, went public with this plan, we had lots of meetings with the neighbors, and we listened a lot.

Another important issue is branding; we can clean up an area environmentally, but we also have to change the area's image. One of the reasons we bought such a large area was to assemble enough critical mass so that we could change that image. A branding book set out specific sets of proposals, and these were a tremendous part of the community locking into that plan. In August 2004, the town council voted to rezone this entire section on this side of Interstate 26, to mixed use. It passed 11 to 1.

During this process, one of the things that kept coming up was the nuisance of the interstate coming through the neighborhood. So Tim Keane and the city came up with two different plans of improving the existing interstate, or moving it to other locations. A new sales tax measure is coming up on the ballot again, and if it passes, some of the proceeds for that can be used to help move interstate I-26. It will be a massive project. There's a new bridge over the Cooper River to Mount Pleasant that will be operational in 2007, and should improve all the interchanges in North Charleston and beyond. We took on this charge of seeing whether the interstate could be moved, not because it would necessarily benefit our project, but we wanted to be able to plan more effectively. That project's been moved up in priority, so we will see what happens.

Challenges and Lessons Learned at Arlington Potomac Yard

A Work in Progress

Dan Kohlhepp

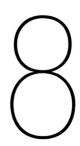

One of the important themes of this volume focuses on "the demand for new kinds of work spaces that can best be met by integrating offices into 'urban villages' that provide housing, retail and transit opportunities." This is exactly what we, the Mid-Atlantic region of Crescent Resources, LLC, have been attempting to do for the last four years at our Potomac Yard development in Northern Virginia on a site directly adjacent to Reagan International Airport. This project comprises 300 acres (121 hectares) at what is a recently decommissioned railroad switching yard that had been used by the RF&P railroad since 1848. With 88 acres (36 hectares) in Arlington County and 212 acres (85 hectares) in the City of Alexandria, Virginia, the land came with conceptual site plans approved in both municipalities, which divided the site into 20 development parcels, totaling approximately 4.5 million sq ft (418,000 sq m) of office space, just under 3,000 residential units, about 200,000 sq ft (18,580 sq m) of retail space, 1,250 hotel rooms, and 92.4 acres (37 hectares) of parks and open space at full build-out (Figure 8.1).

In 1999, Alexandria City Council approved their portion of the plan with 38 development conditions, an additional 17 conditions for a Transportation Management Plan, and other controls contained in a 109-page book comprising the Potomac Yard Urban Design Guidelines. One year later, the Arlington County Board approved plans for the portion of the site within their jurisdiction, with another 47 development conditions and more urban design guidelines contained in their own 82-page publication of the Potomac Yard Design Guidelines.

The development conditions and design guidelines in both municipalities were similar in some respects, but both reflected the essential differences between the two communities. While Alexandria was low density, Arlington was high density; while Alexandria was predominantly residential, Arlington was predominantly office. The Arlington part of the development had to include 28 acres (11 hectares) as a county park, while Alexandria insisted on the construction of a 1.65 mile-long (2.6 km) trunk sewer line. Both municipalities did, however, conceive of the development as a transit-oriented community.

This complex project was brought to a halt by the terrorist attacks of September 11, 2001. On that morning, Crescent Resources had a meeting scheduled on the Yard at 9.00 a.m., and the participants had just entered the office when the

8.1 Master plan for entire 300-acre site at Potomac Yard

hi-jacked jet plane hit the Pentagon. Shortly afterward, the Yard was engulfed in black smoke from the explosion of the jet fuel. The whole area closed down and the dreams of Potomac Yard were put on hold.

However, during 2002, the project revived and plans were approved by Arlington County for new infrastructure construction on and around the site. Construction was begun in May 2003. (The remainder of this chapter accordingly deals mainly with the portion of the project in Arlington County, see Figure 8.2.) The largest component of the new infrastructure was a new sewer pump station, and this was accompanied by nearly 4 miles (6 km) of public and private streets with underground utilities to serve the development.

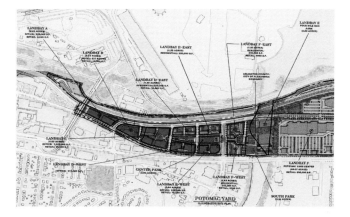

8.2 Master plan for Arlington County site

Conditions attached to the site plan approved by Arlington County in 2000 required that specific site plan approvals be obtained for each separate construction project, and such approvals were obtained for various buildings comprising 648,000 sq ft (60,000 sq m) of office space, 90,120 sq ft (8,370 sq m) of retail, and 873,714 sq ft (81,170 sq m) of residential uses on three parcels totaling 8.62 acres (3.5 hectares) (Figure 8.3). A total of 221 additional conditions were attached to these more detailed site plans. In May 2004, the United States government signed ten-year leases for over 400,000 sq ft (37,161 sq m) of office space in two buildings. To provide incentives for the building design to embrace sustainable design principles, the lease stipulated that if the buildings did not achieve a Silver LEED rating as specified by the US Green Building Council, the *gross* rent would be *reduced* by 10 percent. In anticipation of the lease agreement, Crescent Resources had bid out the building and negotiated the construction contract with the lowest bidder subject to the lease being signed. Accordingly, construction on the first two office towers began in May, 2004, a significant achievement in the face of a series of challenges, first in the process of land development and then in the development of the buildings themselves.

This chapter briefly discusses some of the challenges faced in the development of the land and the buildings, and concludes with a summary of some lessons learned about the process of developing urban mixed-use projects.

Land Development Challenges

The development process at Potomac Yard has had to overcome major challenges in three main areas:

1. Satisfying site plan approval conditions and Urban Design Guidelines.
2. Constructing off-site infrastructure.
3. Reconciling environmental myths and physical realities.

Satisfying conditions and guidelines

The conditions and guidelines that were intended to define clearly the development of Potomac Yard were not as clear

8.3 Aerial perspective of Potomac Yard showing full build-out

as first thought; they were subject to interpretation and re-interpretation caused by changing political and economic realities. The first major clash of priorities came as a result of conflicts between New Urbanist design principles with post-9/11 security concerns. Good urban design requires numerous pedestrian and vehicle access points to city blocks and buildings; security concerns, by contrast, need limited and controlled access. Good urban design promotes street-level retail activity; security issues require strictly limited access to buildings at street level. Good urban design requires buildings to come close to the street to define pedestrian space; new security guidelines require large setbacks of 50–100 ft (15–30 m). Urban design guidelines envisioned many smaller buildings to break down the scale of the development; new security parameters require large, consolidated buildings that are much easier to guard and control.

The reconciliation of these disparate points of view has been the subject of many meetings, seminars and work sessions.

Since the federal government occupies almost 70 percent of the office space in Arlington as a whole, this process of reconciliation will continue for many more years as we dream of "transparent" security systems.

Further negotiation continues to be required regarding the concept of Transit-oriented Development (TOD) as it relates to this project. Both Alexandria and Arlington expected that Potomac Yard would be a transit-oriented community. Alexandria wanted a new METRO station, while Arlington wanted a dedicated transit right-of-way. Ironically, this dedicated transit-way in Arlington won't be able to connect to a transit-way in Alexandria because of its location, and the METRO station in the Alexandria portion of Potomac Yard cannot be justified because it is too close to existing METRO stations in Arlington and Alexandria.

These inter-jurisdictional issues are further complicated by the fact that both municipalities have placed infrastructure restrictions on their own portion based on the level of development in the other jurisdiction. For example, major road construction must be completed in Alexandria before certain thresholds of development are reached in the overall development, including the Arlington portion. Additionally, the layout of one major park that straddles both jurisdictions is tied together through various design guidelines and development conditions from both municipalities. This park also needs separate approvals from the US Army Corps of Engineers and a joint task force including all parties has been appointed to study these potential conflicts. The task force has been given a budget from the US government of $1.5 million but does not expect to produce its final report until 2006.

Constructing off-site infrastructure

Further inter-jurisdictional problems arose in regard to off-site infrastructure projects. A new pump station at the Arlington Water Treatment Plant seemed like a simple project until neighborhood groups objected to the location of the station, the appearance of the pump house, and the landscaping plan. The location, on the site of the existing water treatment plant, was eventually accepted after the citizens understood that no sewage from Alexandria would be pumped there. The pump house was redesigned as an all-brick "colonial-style" structure, which won approval from citizens' groups, as did the revised landscaping plan that is intended to obscure this modest building completely from adjacent streets.

Three road projects also caused unexpected problems. Bridge improvements to US Route 1 were stymied by the conflicting desires by both municipalities for extra turn lanes to suit their own traffic needs in the same enlarged space on the bridge. This impasse was resolved by an ingenious "double taper" solution that was eventually accepted by both parties. Other difficulties involved disputes with property owners regarding road realignment for a transit way and the refusal by the Virginia State Department of Transportation to accept landscaping that was required by Arlington County along certain portions of US Route 1. In this instance, the County finally gave way.

Reconciling environmental myths and physical realities

When the owner of the Washington Redskins announced in 1992 that the new stadium would be built at Potomac Yard, he precipitated a huge public protest. When he withdrew his plan after weeks of heated debate, he announced that the overwhelming environmental problems, along with other reasons, would keep him from building the stadium. While local citizens were ecstatic, Potomac Yard became publicly marred by environmental stigma. Consequently, the development risk that prompted most anxiety at Potomac Yard was the environmental hazards associated with soil contamination.

This turned out to be largely a myth. The site was extensively studied, tested, evaluated by the US Environmental Protection Agency who determined there was no threat to human health except in one particular area, and that area was remediated prior to Crescent's acquisition of the property to the satisfaction of the EPA. Crescent then employed legal and environmental consultants to review these studies, a process that confirmed these facts.

However, there is no such thing as "clean dirt," since all dirt is contaminated to some degree by one constituent or another. Accordingly, Crescent had to develop a "soil management plan" to handle unexpected soil conditions as they were encountered. This plan was then approved by the Virginia Department of Environmental Quality, the same department that had previously issued a letter stating no further action was required to remediate the site. (We learned that "no further action" assumed that the land would not be excavated, and clearly we intended to excavate.)

Building Development Challenges

The challenges encountered in the process of developing the first buildings in the overall project can be summarized under four headings:

1. Obtaining municipal approvals.
2. Reconciling the requirements of the General Services Administration (GSA), the Environmental Protection Agency

(EPA), the US Green Building Council (USGBC), and the Federal Protection Service (FPS).

3. Confronting neighborhood issues.
4. Accepting changing market conditions.

Obtaining municipal approvals

Before beginning construction, building permits must be obtained from the Arlington County zoning officer, who in addition to checking the technical building design in the normal way, also checks the detailed drawings for compliance with the 48 conditions of the original approved conceptual site plan and the 71 additional conditions of the specific site plan approvals, dating from March, 2003. This building permit phase takes 18 months, and can become "double jeopardy" as the zoning officer asks each relevant county staff person to interpret and opine on each regulation for compliance. Eventually building permits for the first two office towers, One and Two Potomac Yard were obtained at the end of August, 2004.

Fortunately, the Chairperson of Arlington County recognized the complexity of the site plan and building permit process, and the multiple, overlapping, and conflicting conditions resulting from this complexity. Consequently, the Chairperson assigned the Assistant County Manager to watch over the Potomac Yard development process, and this individual holds monthly meetings to bring together Crescent and all relevant County parties to systematically review the various issues and challenges facing the land and building development on the project. These monthly meetings have been a godsend, as the Potomac Yard team and the County departments are actively collaborating to solve problems.

Reconciling the requirements of the GSA, EPA, the USGBC and the FPS

The General Services Administration acts as the landlord for the federal government and then releases, subleases or assigns the lease to other federal agencies for occupation. As the landlord agency, it requires compliance with a volume of conditions. The actual tenant, the Environmental Protection Agency, then has its own Program of Requirements, a 143-page document outlining what the EPA would like to have in the building. If these requirements are different from those of the GSA, then the EPA pays for changes or additions.

In addition, since the GSA requires that the buildings obtain a Silver rating from the USGBC, based on the Leadership in Energy Efficient Development (LEED) scorecard, other GSA and EPA requirements must conform to the USGBC requirements for Silver rating (33 points). The newness of the USGBC scorecard requires many interpretations and judgments, and the outcome of this endeavor won't be known until the final rating at the end of construction.

In addition to these regulatory hurdles, the Federal Protection Service (FPS) is reviewing the building development and will recommend what security enhancements, improvements, and/or changes that need to be made for occupancy by the EPA. At the time of writing, Crescent will undertake the following security enhancements:

- parking controls and cameras;
- lobby security equipment and cameras;
- security interrogation and guard rooms;
- concrete bollards around the buildings.

Number Two Potomac Yard will only be partially occupied by the EPA, so the majority of the tenants will be from the private sector. The accommodation of these two groups with different security expectations will present further challenges in the future. Overall, the challenge for Crescent Resources is to reconcile the requirements of the GSA, the EPA, the USGBC, and the FPS while still meeting the numerous requirements and conditions attached by Arlington County to the overall site plan and the specific site plans for each building. The impossibility of this challenge is compounded by staff changes at GSA, EPA and Arlington County.

Confronting neighborhood issues

By definition, an urban infill location has a number of closely located neighbors. At One and Two Potomac Yard our adjacent neighbors include the CSX rail line, a federally-funded but state-owned bridge, and the Crystal City Hyatt Regency and vacant land, both owned by an investment group. This group also owns the land under the adjacent Crystal Drive, which is on an easement. Issues that had to be negotiated with these neighbors were:

Stability of excavation work

Because of the proximity of the neighbors, the excavation of One and Two Potomac Yard was done with a sheeting and shoring system on all four sides. This system is secured to the unexcavated earth through a series of tie-backs, 60-ft-long cables which are drilled and grouted into the earth. These tie-backs extended under the railroad tracks and the bridge, with the agreement of the relevant parties. To avoid drilling into the parking structure under the street and hotel, these tie-backs were replaced in those locations by a raker and bracing system. Securing tie-back agreements with the neighbors was critical to starting excavation.

Tower crane swings

The construction cranes are restricted in their swings because of the railroad tracks and the adjacent hotel. Consequently four cranes rather than two are employed. With other construction beginning on an adjacent lot, two additional cranes (six in total) will be swinging materials around in a very tight, overlapping area. A crane swing agreement with our neighbor was thus very important.

Water connections

The Metropolitan Washington Airport Authority (MWAA), the neighbor to the east, planned to extend its water line to tie into the Potomac Yard water system. Construction began at the same time as the excavation for One and Two Potomac Yard commenced, along with other site infrastructure projects. The timing and location of the extension could not have been worse.

The water line extension required MWAA to bore under the CSX rail tracks. When the boring was half-completed, voids were discovered under the tracks. The boring was stopped and extensive and protracted negotiations took place to resolve this problem. All in all, what should have been a one-week project took two-and-a-half months at the most critical location on Potomac Yard with consequent disruptions and problems to the construction program.

Noise, traffic and parking

Luckily, CSX and MWAA were not impacted by the noise from pile driving and the traffic from 1500 truckloads of dirt leaving the site plus parking for 400 construction workers, but our hotel and office neighbors were. Our neighborhood outreach program has attempted to maintain a dialogue with our neighbors and prepare them ahead of time for the next phase of construction challenges. Good fences may make good neighbors, but talking to neighbors is more important.

Accepting changing market conditions

Any mixed-use project is confounded by the changing market conditions for each use. At Potomac Yard, the residential market, especially for condominiums, improved dramatically. The office market deteriorated, and the hospitality market evaporated since Crescent Resources acquired the property in 2001. Consequently, hotel plans were put on indefinite hold, office prospects were hard to find (especially as the move by the US Patent and Trademark offices to new accommodation in Alexandria released 2 million sq ft (0.18 million sq m) of space back onto the market in Arlington), and residential builders were standing in line to buy land. Fortunately, a condition in the original site plan approvals allowed Crescent to adjust to the changing market conditions by converting 300,000 sq ft (27,870 sq m) of office space to residential space in some parcels.

Lessons Learned

At the time of writing, the challenges of developing Potomac Yard have consumed the writer for four years. The attempt to provide office space in an urban mixed-use development is a noble one; as the development continues, new challenges are confronted daily. The "Lessons Learned" are thus tentative ones, as they are constantly relearned, and in some cases, unlearned as circumstances change. These lessons can be summarized under four headings:

1. Embrace the complexity of urban mixed-use developments.
2. Accept the cultural differences between the public and private sectors.
3. Appreciate that private developers and municipalities together are struggling with regional issues.
4. Go to work every day.

Embracing complexity

Urban mixed-use projects are exquisitely complicated. There are more variables than equations, and some of the variables are random. This indeterminate system must be embraced, rather than solved. The complexity cannot be controlled or reduced. Embracing this complexity allows us to attempt rational decision-making without getting frustrated by the lack of resolutions. The complexity must be worked with, danced with, and ultimately – embraced.

Accept cultural differences

Recognizing and accepting the different cultural values and mores between the public and private sectors can help us deal more effectively with municipal staff and elected officials. For example, private sector participants expect to treat discussions and negotiations confidentially until an agreement is reached. However, participants in the public sector are limited by and subject to freedom of information regulations and the public decision-making process. Consequently, they are expected to disclose discussions and negotiations before an agreement is reached.

Another example is the value of private property rights. In the private sector, private property is sacred and is a commodity that's openly traded in the marketplace. But in the public sector, private property rights are the residual rights after the greater public good has been served.

Finally, in the private sector, most participants believe that a "deal is a deal," and a person's integrity is staked on respecting that deal. Conversely, in the public sector, there is enormous pressure to re-open discussions especially when public opinion changes. To the developer this may feel like the deal is never done, and the agreements that were made are really the starting place for the next round of negotiations. However, the public sector may view this as responsive government. Accepting these cultural differences will enable both sides to work together more effectively without feeling frustrated or threatened.

Appreciate that private developers and municipalities are struggling with regional issues

While well-intentioned people in the private and public sectors deal with very complex problems and cultural differences, the really big issues are regional ones, over which neither party has much control. Issues such as traffic congestion, water and air pollution, affordable housing and protection against terrorism are regional issues that require a regional approach across municipal boundaries to be addressed effectively.

Unfortunately, municipalities and private developers are compelled to address these issues at the site plan approval level. Consequently, private developers may feel oppressed when forced to conform to site plan restrictions that are often token first steps towards solving regional problems. However, municipalities feel compelled to make these requirements to show their citizens that these regional issues are being addressed. Thus by appreciating the struggle to solve regional issues at the site plan approval level, we appreciate good intentions for the noble deeds they are meant to be.

Go to work every day

Finally, I have learned to go to work every day with two things: a good night's sleep and a sense of humor. Without a good night's sleep, my sense of humor is compromised, and without a keen sense of humor I cannot enjoy the folly, craziness and irony that are a critical and daily part of the urban, mixed-use development process.

Part II

Technological Integration

Enthusiastic Pragmatism

Christoph Ingenhoven

Challenges

When I think of the main issues that face architects in the coming decades I believe very strongly that they must confront these challenges head-on. The most pressing objectives that I would like Ingenhoven Architects to focus on in the coming years are: future-oriented, environmentally-friendly sustainable building; mass housing; integrated infrastructure and high quality public space. If I were to summarize our practice's approach to architecture in one phrase, it would be enthusiastic pragmatism. This chapter is an attempt to explain what we mean by enthusiastic pragmatism and how we have started to implement this approach.

We see the process of enthusiastic pragmatism as a search for, and a struggle to create, the best possible solutions by means of intensive collaboration between the many consultants engaged in building projects. We find that success is only possible through a humanistic approach to architecture that allows us to enter into a more detailed understanding of people's needs, the city fabric and the climate. As a practice we strive to make the cities in which we live and work the most sophisticated cultural product that mankind can create. We work to make our small blue planet a better place by helping to save our resources; by reducing energy consumption; by making life easier, healthier, and more joyful. We feel that it is important for us to look after this planet; as parents we want to hand over this planet to future generations in a better condition than we inherited it. We feel that all architects should bear responsibility for these issues. We believe that every architect has an obligation to design buildings, whether they are office blocks or railway stations, that will affect the well-being of users by improving the quality of the city and the environment.

Form Follows Evolution

Architecture's primary task is to provide shelter. The vernacular architecture of every locality, including ours, demonstrates that it serves all the basic needs of human beings. Form does not follow a simple functionality or fashionable aphorism; form follows evolution. The best, most beautiful, most elegant and most sophisticated solutions in nature developed through a process of evolution. Evolution provides a temporary, best answer to a given set of problems. We planned to design the same "best answer" in our proposal for Stuttgart's principal railway station, due for completion in 2013 (Figure 9.1). It is an ingenious construction; a poetic space; a place for people. The solution itself emerged from an evolution-like engineering/ design process. Our philosophy is to look for regional responses to global problems; we believe that different local conditions require different solutions. Building in the USA, for example, presents different challenges and therefore different solutions to building in Japan or in Germany. We do not design projects that are stylish, homogenous solutions no matter where

in the world they are sited. Our buildings are characteristic, singular and specific to their sites. We are constantly looking for newer, better and more efficient solutions. We investigate ways of underpinning our approach, not just theoretically or philosophically, but through a particular concern for technical possibilities and practicality.

We have adopted our own approach to teamwork: we believe that the more difficult a task gets, the more important teamwork is. The computer is only one tool that we use to resolve complex issues. Although we use hundreds of computers to coordinate our work, the act of design takes place in our minds and through our hands. The creative process requires

9.1 Stuttgart station, model showing new ground level

acts of dreaming, talking, visiting, modelling and discussion to name just a few; human processes are much more important than the processes we can expect from computers.

Ecology

We believe strongly in ecology: our primary aim is the invention of environmentally friendly buildings. When we were young, "green" seemed to be the logical alternative to the conventional systems that were destroying our environment so we tried to change things by voting for the Green Party; in our professional lives we seized opportunities to carry out ecologically oriented work on sustainable sites. We have projected these ideas into our current work and look forward to applying them to our future work by insisting on sensitivity to the environment. We attempt to do this primarily through the consideration of building life cycles as this can have great influence on the world's natural resources.

Mending the City

Just as architectural practices in the USA must conform to the relevant codes and standards applicable in their area, in Germany we too must abide by similar sets of standards. In addition, we have to address codes derived from the particular morphology of medieval European cities that relate to population densities and therefore also to energy use. These codes make it essential to consider the redevelopment of urban and brownfield sites to achieve the required densities. Again, in Stuttgart, we have been able to double the city center density by sinking the main railway station below ground (Figure 9.2); this strategy has allowed us to gain approximately 29 million sq ft (2.7 million sq m) of gross floor area in the very heart of the city. The resulting increase in development values and the transformation of the urban fabric give this project an unusual significance.

In our opinion, the maximization of open space and the minimization of land development should be one of the foremost considerations in high-rise development. We put this idea into practice in the case of the 31-storey high-rise RWE Tower in

9.2 Stuttgart station, perspective showing new below ground platforms

Essen. In this case, we did not just create a landmark building for our client (Figures 9.3 and 9.4); by gathering the development around the perimeter of the site, and by placing the most density around the perimeter where it should be located from an urban perspective, we were able to free up the land at the center of the site to create a public park which has become a very popular feature. In addition to the park, the open plan entrance hall and the sky gardens on the roof have returned almost the equivalent area of the entire site to the public. This approach has been advantageous to the client because it gives the building a special quality seldom experienced in high-rise development.

The 146 m (450 ft) high Uptown München Tower situated adjacent to the landmark 1972 Olympic Stadium is Munich's tallest high-rise to date (Figure 9.5). In addition to the 38-storey tower, there are also four, seven-storey, campus-type buildings. With Uptown München providing 84,000 sq m (840,00 sq ft) of office space, the area known as Mittlerer Ring has achieved new focus and new life as a result of the increased density.

9.3 RWE
Tower, general
view of exterior

9.4 RWE Tower, site plan.
1. Opernplatz; 2 Forecourt;
3 Tower; 4 Lake; 5 RWE Park

9.5 Uptown München Tower, general view of exterior

Transport

We also believe strongly in implementing alternative transportation options because we want to decrease the impact on land use development dictated by the increasing dependence on automobiles and the increased pollution that they cause. We were able to implement this philosophy at the new Hamburg Trade Fair. Since this facility will be located in the very heart of the city we proposed a reduction in the total number of car parking spaces because we created direct access to all the existing public transportation systems, thus decreasing the reliance on private transportation. We also employed sustainable strategies in the construction of the exhibition halls where the design of repetitive structural elements, the timber grid shells over the exhibition spaces, make prefabrication possible and thus reduce site construction time (Figure 9.6). The new gleaming white Trade Fair is being built in phases that will allow uninterrupted use of the extensive fairgrounds throughout the construction period. Completion of the Hamburg Trade Fair complex is due in 2008.

In a similar way, we attempted to reduce the reliance on any additional form of transportation in Stuttgart city centre by combining the previously mentioned railway station, high-density hotel, office and retail developments with direct access to the multi-modal station. All the facilities within the station development are linked together as well as to the city fabric by a system of pedestrian walkways that facilitate direct access between these components.

In the city of Düsseldorf, we have been given the opportunity to examine and create new proposals for the central shopping district. The current configuration of this area is unsatisfactory because it is fragmented by the usual system of busy inner city traffic routes and marred by unsightly elevated highways. Our proposals, which will be adopted over the coming years, will revitalize this district by sinking the traffic below ground. This move will allow some of the newly gained land to be converted into parks and landscaped paths which will reunite the once fragmented and isolated areas. The capital raised by selling off the remaining newly freed land will finance this entire redevelopment project.

In the case of the large corporate headquarters we designed for Lufthansa, even though the gardens or atria are not open to the general public but are instead accessible to all Lufthansa employees, we can still consider these areas as public spaces (Figure 9.7). Here, the comb-like plan of the Aviation Centre encloses landscaped gardens that act as buffer zones, insulating the building against polluting air emissions and noise. Plants chosen from the five continents not only symbolize Lufthansa's global connections but also help to purify and "mend" our natural environment (Figure 9.8). All 1,850 office workspaces in this headquarters building have views onto the glass-roofed gardens and can be naturally ventilated. On completion of the second phase of construction, this group of buildings will accommodate 4,500 employees and will include a total of 28 garden areas.

Adaptive Reuse

Building in the heart of a city also means taking care of and revitalizing the street. After we won the architectural competition for the refurbishment of the existing Stadtsparkasse Düsseldorf headquarters in November 1997, we concentrated our attention on two very important aspects of this project. The first dealt with enhancing the integration of this building into the urban fabric, the second attempted to increase the accessibility and transparency of this building (Figures 9.9 and 9.10). In the process, we refurbished the existing high-rise building and restructured the whole building footprint to include a multifunctional financial department store with conference and public facilities such as atria, restaurants and tropical winter gardens, all linked to a large shopping mall on one of the busiest shopping streets in Düsseldorf. Our approach transformed this building from an uninviting corporate headquarters into a building that has now become an integral part of the city and of the everyday life in Düsseldorf. The new highly transparent glass envelope has created a building in which the street has become part of the building and the manifold activities that are now accommodated within the building are separated by the most transparent glass available. This refurbishment project has given birth to a completely new building type: a financial department store that provides a huge variety of financial services in an accessible multifunctional environment.

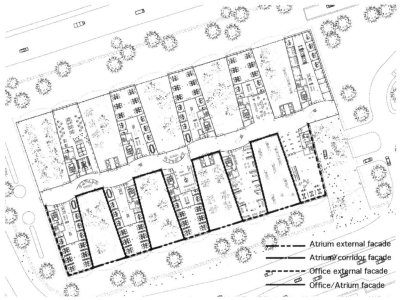

9.6 (above) Hamburg Trade Fair, aerial view showing repetitive wood structure

9.7 (left) Lufthansa Headquarters, ground floor plan showing offices and atria

— · — Atrium external facade

——— Atrium/corridor facade

- - - - Office external facade

——— Office/Atrium facade

Water Management

Our concerns for sustainability cover a variety of scales; the projects described above illustrate many ideas that apply to the macro scale, most of our projects also tackle sustainability on a micro scale. For example, we are interested in issues of indoor air quality and storm water management. Although water is a basic and essential resource it is not unlimited and so we try to conserve it wherever we can. In the case of the Uptown München project, mentioned above, all the rainwater that can be collected is used for the irrigation of a new landscaped

9.10 Stadtsparkasse Düsseldorf Headquarters, internal view showing transparency

garden; this garden includes mature pine trees that are over 30 years old and have been delicately transplanted from a nursery in Northern Germany. At the Burda Media headquarters in Offenburg, Southern Germany, we eliminated heat islands by designing a 100 percent green garden with no impervious areas at all. Where possible, we also include water-efficient landscaping that incorporates storm water retention.

With the Lufthansa project we showed that integrated rainwater collection and used air outlets can be an integral part of the design for atrium buildings because this combination allows for natural ventilation and irrigation of the internal gardens at the same time (Figure 9.11). We have continued to develop and refine this detail in later buildings. It is also important to implement water use reduction by using advanced technology control systems and fixtures such as low consumption toilet flushing facilities.

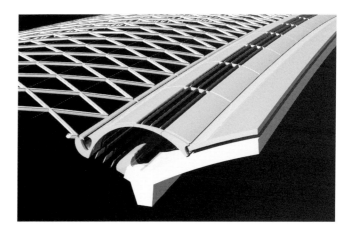

9.11 Lufthansa Headquarters, view of combined rainwater/air outlets

Energy Conservation

Energy conservation is one of our primary concerns. As with nature, our future survival depends on optimizing our energy performance. It is important to note that all our projects achieve standards that are 40 percent better than the requirements of the American Society of Heating, Refrigerating and Air-Conditioning Engineers (ASHRAE); as we refine our skills we hope to achieve a 50 percent improvement on these standards. A high volume-to-surface ratio is an essential requirement for the reduction of heat loss. We strove to achieve such ratios with the simple horizontal glass tube of the European Investment Bank in Luxembourg and the vertical glass cylinder of the RWE Tower in Essen. The proportions of the latter building are: a height of 120 m and a diameter of 32 m. The office spaces which have storey-height clear glazing are arranged around the perimeter of the cylinder (Figure 9.12). The spandrel zone within the double façade, which has a "fish mouth" profile (Figure 9.13) was designed to accommodate a number of environmental control devices: fresh air intake and exhaust; suspended adjustable aluminium louvers provide sun protection; a textile glare screen is installed on the inside face of the glazing. The double-skin façade reduces wind pressure thus allowing openable windows and natural ventilation all the way up to the 31st floor; this access to natural light and ventilation offers new levels of comfort. All offices were designed in accordance with the latest criteria for modern flexible workstations; all employees can control the internal climate of their workspace by using the switching panels in their office.

Effective heat insulation in winter using advanced façade technologies, double-skin façades or atria help to optimize R-values (U-values) and allow significant reductions to code requirements. Adoption of the best glass technology available in combination with external shading systems can achieve results twice as good as ASHRAE standards. To reach these values, it is necessary to develop specific façade concepts. We learned from the Lufthansa project that one way of achieving such results was to consider the performance of both the roofs and the vertical façades together. In this building we developed five different façade systems which worked in combination to provide an integrated strategy towards energy conservation (Figure 9.7). The office/atrium façade uses wood as the framing

9.12 RWE Tower, perimeter office

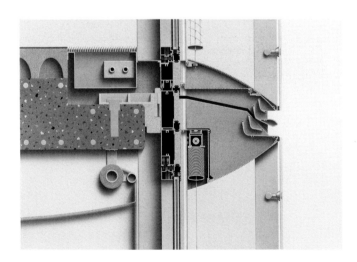

9.13 RWE Tower, detail of "fish mouth" spandrel

elements for the glazing thus providing optimal thermal qualities as well as dramatically reducing the embodied energy of the façade. In the atrium/corridor façade, we used an aluminium rather than wood framing system since the slenderness of the aluminium offered maximum transparency. The four glass layers

9.14 European Investment Bank, general view of exterior

of the external double façade give these areas the same thermal comfort as the atrium façades. The external atrium façade is supported on an almost invisible steel cable-net construction and the fully glazed roof shell construction has been reduced to the absolute minimum to provide a high degree of transparency. In many of our projects we construct large-scale detailed models of up to 1:10 scale that allow us to examine the complexities of a building's high performance specifications as well as its visual characteristics.

The reduction of HVAC equipment through natural ventilation by operable windows should be a fundamental issue for architects all over the world to consider. Natural ventilation now plays a key role in all our projects. In the RWE headquarters, built between 1994 and 1997, we developed the first double façade to be installed on a high-rise building. This strategy allowed us to rely on natural ventilation for about 80 percent of the year. We developed the concept of the double façade even further at the Burda headquarters in Southern Germany where we refurbished their existing small high-rise building with a transparent double-skinned façade that had fully openable windows for summer operation, thus rendering the façade system more efficient. This type of façade allows us to minimize the energy consumption and thus the HVAC unit to about 45 percent of a conventional air-conditioned single façade office building. The benefits can be even greater when an atrium solution is adopted; at both the Lufthansa headquarters and the European Investment Bank (EIB) we were able to ensure that 80 percent of the office areas open onto the atria, thus enhancing

the dialog between the building and its environment. At the EIB, a transparent aerodynamic vaulted glass roof spans over the V-shaped plan of the new office buildings which are bound together by atria and winter gardens. Behind the vertical glass shields separating the atria and offices, the floors are set back to form terraces. The wood framing system incorporates fully operable windows. The atria function as buffer zones between the external environment and the office spaces so that they moderate the climate and form an important part of the building's energy strategy. Building orientation and seasonal climatic conditions can be utilized to assist thermal comfort over a 12-month period; the winter gardens, for example, can be beneficial as thermal buffers in the colder seasons and can also assist natural ventilation during the summer months. In addition to their role as moderators of climate, the atria and winter gardens also provide the psychological benefits mentioned earlier.

The European Investment Bank is the first building in mainland Europe to have been certified as "Very Good"[1] by the British Building Research Establishment's Environmental Assessment Method (BREEAM). This 753,000 sq ft (70,000 sq m) flexibly planned and communication-friendly building integrates all functions of the headquarters and workstations for 750 employees. The building resembles a glazed tube; a continuous glass skin provides shelter for the offices and winter gardens behind (Figure 9.14). The optimized aerodynamic cross-section creates a zone of negative pressure above the apex of the triangular atria. In this way, the warmer used air which rises up the atrium by virtue of its reduced buoyancy is sucked out of the atrium by the wind turbulence created by the building profile. This is just one example of how the building's energy consumption has been reduced.

When designing atria, one of the primary considerations should be the supply of fresh air. This was a particular challenge in the design of the Lufthansa headquarters since the noise pollution at Frankfurt/Main airport was extremely high. Our solution for the Lufthansa Aviation Centre was a comb-like building plan with ten wings of office accommodation separated by enclosed landscaped gardens which acted as buffer zones that insulated the internal environment from air-polluting emissions and noise. The supply air is drawn from the top of a 49 ft (15 m) high air tower (Figure 9.15); it is then taken under the parking garage to the atria where it is let out very slowly. No mechanical equipment is used to move the air; the pressure differences generated by the building's orientation and cross-section are in themselves sufficient. Once this fresh air, which provides the natural ventilation for the offices, has been used, it is drawn through the office windows into the atria and out of the louvers at the apex of each atrium; these louvers are opened wide in the summer to provide maximum ventilation and are adjusted to nearly closed in the winter to minimize energy expenditure during the cold season. It can be seen quite clearly that the ventilation system in the Lufthansa building is integral to the fabric of the building and is not, as we still see

9.15 Lufthansa Headquarters, external view showing air supply tower at right

in so many buildings today, a separate system that has been added to the building.

Daylight

Effective daylight illumination leads to the development of building solutions that can utilize one of the cheapest available natural resources. This means designing buildings with a high degree of transparency and interiors that are finished in light colors. We demonstrated our conviction to this area of design by incorporating high levels of natural lighting in our new architecture studio in the Düsseldorf Media Harbor (Figure 9.16).

We designed this office in 2004 as a team-orientated single volume space in which architects, designers, model-makers and administrative staff can work together effectively. This approach necessarily means optimizing and sometimes restricting the building depth so that practically no artificial lighting is required during daylight hours. Where possible, we use high levels of clear glazing to allow our clients to view the changing light and weather patterns during the day or night; we believe that this is a basic human need. In many cases the perception of these natural phenomena is frequently obscured by the use of body-tinted solar glass; it is precisely because we want our clients to appreciate the ever changing natural environment that we specify clear white glass. In this way we can offer views into as

9.16 Ingenhoven Architects studio, general internal view

well as out of our buildings so that each building can act as a lighthouse and as a showcase.

In 2003, we completed the Gira Production Building in Radevormwald, Germany. Gira produces plastic components for modern electrical installations. The client held an inspired approach to commissioning a new building; they acted as participants in the design process and were intensely interested in reinterpreting the concept of a contemporary production facility in a way that would implement the latest technologies and ideas relating to the social aspects of the work environment. As a result of this dialog, all the production halls were planned to allow complete flexibility of the production process. Throughout the whole of the 111,000 sq ft (10,300 sq m) building all the production and administrative employees share equal working conditions. The façades are fully glazed to provide maximum natural daylight illumination (Figure 9.17); all employees benefit from the spatial qualities of the transparent, brightly lit work environment and the external views to the natural surroundings. The heat produced as a by-product of the production process is recycled, via a heat exchanger, for use within the building. Controllable apertures allow predominantly

natural ventilation. The design of this building provides a high level of thermal comfort combined with individual control while simultaneously reducing the amount of energy consumed.

Effective artificial lighting systems can help wherever needed to optimize the ergonomic performance as well as the energy consumption of a building. Five years ago we established an industrial and product design team within our architectural practice; this group has since developed a number of products such as furniture, fixtures, door handles, lighting and switch systems. In one such design we developed a fitting which included lighting source, acoustical absorption and reflection surfaces and a smoke detector; in addition, sensors linked to this fitting adjust the amount of artificial light required to supplement the available daylight. The inclusion of motion detectors can assist in minimizing the use of artificial lighting when staff are not present. Our office lighting systems use state-of-the-art technologies and are designed to meet all the current regulations.

Thermal Mass

Where possible, we like to utilize the thermal mass inherent in structural concrete; leaving the concrete structural members exposed can help to reduce energy consumption by using the concrete as a thermal flywheel. We made use of this principle at the RWE Tower where we designed fully integrated ceiling components that included a full array of technical functions: three-component lighting, cooling, acoustic insulation, smoke detectors and sprinklers. Although these components were suspended below the concrete ceilings they are perforated to allow air circulation through them to the concrete above thus harnessing the storage capacity of the structure (Figure 9.18).

Passive Solar Energy

The harvesting of passive solar energy can offer huge benefits and is the principal function of an atrium during the winter months. In addition, an atrium can act as a thermal buffer between two extreme environments, thus minimizing heat loss. Double-skinned façades have a comparable effect, however, their reduced depth renders them less effective. For this reason,

9.17 Gira Production Building, general internal view

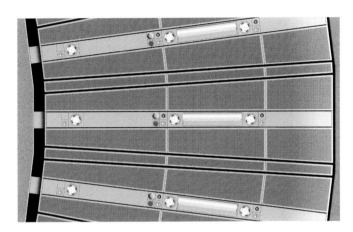

9.18 RWE Tower, ceiling fixtures

double façades can easily become overheated in summer; this can be minimized by using highly effective sun shading and adjustable openings. Atria are also a useful tool for maximizing a building's social qualities as they provide attractive spaces for gatherings or meetings.

The use of renewable energy for at least a part of the building's energy consumption has been an important issue in Germany in the past two decades. The increased use of hydro-electric power stations can help a great deal; photovoltaic or solar thermal equipment are less attractive alternatives. We are very excited at the prospect of designing buildings which would be net collectors of energy so that they generate more energy than they consume. In fact, even in our completed buildings, such as RWE in Essen and the Stadtsparkasse in Düsseldorf, we have included some of the largest photovoltaic arrays yet installed on buildings.

Materials and Resources

The elimination of HCFCs and halons are two other factors we should consider for the protection of the atmosphere. We believe that many countries should be able to guarantee 100 percent clean energy production in the form of water, wind, solar, or geothermal energy.

We have gained valuable experience using some rapidly renewable materials, such as bamboo, which we use extensively for wooden floors. In general, we use only wood which is cer-tified as having been harvested from sustainably managed forests. We used certified wood for the principal façades at the Lufthansa Headquarters and the European Investment Bank. We also used untreated wood for the louvers at the parking garage on the Burda campus; they have now weathered to a beautifully rich natural patina. The building concept for the entire Burda campus was to create buildings that are as friendly and bright as possible so the use of natural materials was central to the design. All materials have been selected for their ecolog-ical sustainability. Where possible, we like to use untreated and non-composite materials in their natural colors; this way we can maximize on the embodied energy efficiency of our buildings.

The biological and ecological qualities of materials offer huge potential for sustainability; just as we can reuse or recycle building materials, building re-use itself offers opportunities to extend the life of a building. We managed this successfully with the refurbishment of the harbor building in Düsseldorf where we converted nearly 100 percent of the old warehouse building into a flexible seven-storey building which now attracts a host of prestigious tenants. In this case we have extended the lifecycle of the building from about 50 to, we hope, as much as 100 years. At the Stadtsparkasse headquarters, mentioned above, we retained approximately 80 percent of the existing structure so that we have extended the 40-year first life of the building by a few decades.

Waste management and resource reuse are a problem all over the world. The use of local materials helps to minimize energy consumption, and also keeps something of a regional character in the buildings.

There are many environmental issues to consider when designing building interiors, however, our primary objective is to create buildings that suit their users' long-term needs just as a perfect suit fits its wearer. Therefore, aside from all our con-cerns regarding sustainability, we endeavor to create buildings that foster communication. Transparency has become the decade's buzz word; it has achieved currency in the field of economics as well as architecture. We believe that architecture of the right spatial qualities can facilitate the collaboration and sharing of knowledge. We call this "the new work spirit";

it enables people to work more efficiently, to be more motivated, to communicate more directly and to be more flexible. Architecturally this means larger floor plates than are usual in Europe; however, it also demands better spatial qualities than are the norm in the USA or even Japan. The new generation of buildings should be designed to facilitate open office landscapes and a variety of other uses such as laboratories, workshops and even production during the lifetime of each building. Equally important, these buildings need to incorporate areas for relaxation such as cafés, atria and winter gardens.

Orientation and Communication

Orientation and communication within buildings are important aspects that can be addressed quite simply by providing interconnecting spaces that allow views to other parts of the building. For example, we approve of exposed or even free-standing elevators as opposed to stair and elevator shafts that are buried deep in the building's fabric. Stairs and elevators are multi-level features that can help the building users to find their way through the building without disorientation or without calling for help. Communication is a critical issue for new buildings. The design of workspaces should provide many opportunities where people can meet and interact informally. We frequently include such meeting areas at the intersections of internal circulation routes such as lift lobbies, stairs, bridges and corridors.

Atria

This chapter has shown a number of different ways in which the inclusion of atria can assist in controlling the air quality within buildings. We typically use the atria as buffer zones not just for temperature modulation but also for controlling air quality by engaging the purifying effect of the vegetation in the atria. In winter, the three warm atria of the European Investment Bank are heated to a temperature of approximately 64°F (18°C), whereas the three cold winter gardens remain unheated, acting as thermal buffers. In summer, the halls will be ventilated by opening various sections of the roof, depending on the wind

direction, to control the air circulation. The adjacent offices are designed to be naturally ventilated from the warm or cold atria or the gardens. To ensure the required comfort level in summer, mechanical ventilation with cooling (when necessary) will be provided to maintain the target temperatures. When outside weather conditions permit, the offices will be naturally ventilated by simply opening the windows.

Natural Ventilation

Appropriate control of systems restores users' dignity by giving them the responsibility for controlling their own internal environment. We have even managed to provide this in high-rise buildings by providing operable windows in a single-layer façade as illustrated in the Uptown München office tower built for the American developer Gerald Hines. The transparency of the tower is achieved by a fully glazed single skin cladding system. Electrically operated circular windows integrated into the façade provide natural ventilation (Figure 9.19). These windows can be controlled automatically by the building's central computer or alternatively they can be operated individually by anyone working in the vicinity. In another of our buildings, the Federal Ministry of Consumer Protection in Food and Agriculture in Bonn, we designed a highly controllable façade with bays of adjustable mid-pane louvers. The installation of user-friendly control panels is critical in facilitating individual work station control. We have been fortunate to be commissioned to design such control panels for many of our clients. Clear control panels are important for what can be complex, multi-layered façade systems that operate sliding doors, sun shades, louvers, and glare screens. It is important to point out that these façade systems can be operated manually, automatically or in a mixed mode.

Flexibility

The facility for flexible planning renders a building lifecycle more efficient and has a significant impact on the geometric configuration of a building. This is especially true in high-rise buildings where the office plan and core design can change over

9.19 Uptown München Tower, view of circular windows

time and from storey to storey. At the European Investment Bank, we devised a modular floorplate that facilitated the transition from single office layout to team areas by using an easily demountable partition system. We also managed to reduce the depth of the typical single office by separating out and grouping together such common functions as departmental storage areas, copying and meeting spaces. The layout of mechanical and electrical systems should also reflect the same degree of flexibility so that it can service the different office layouts during the lifetime of the building.

Innovation and Sustainability

It must be evident that our practice is motivated by innovation in design. We are especially interested in the detailed solutions

manifest by synergistic elements, such as the "fish mouth" component that integrated all the components and functions of the double-skin façade system at the RWE Tower (Figure 9.13); or the multifunctional trough within the roof shells of the Lufthansa headquarters that served simultaneously as storm water drainage elements and ventilation and smoke vents for the atria; or the multi-functional light and cooling ceiling components designed for RWE Tower. These complex building components serve a multiplicity of functions, creating a healthy and welcoming working atmosphere.

Sustainable construction will always be a challenge and remains a personal favorite of mine. In every project we collaborate intensely with our engineers to find methods of construction and solutions that seem inevitable. An excellent example of this collaboration is the innovative membrane structure of Stuttgart Railway Station, designed together with

Frei Otto, and developed through the use of advanced CAD modeling programs. A building is not just a single statement, it embodies many symbols and aspirations that can influence its design as a landmark building.

Conclusion

Buildings demonstrate their value by virtue of the way people interact with them as single artefacts or as elements that fit within the urban fabric. Buildings should therefore make reference to the street and to street life, to the city and the environment; they should be inviting, communicative, animating and motivating; they should be an integral part of our everyday life and they should also be a part of our future. Architecture should not relate to just an aesthetic vision; it must meet basic human needs to create settings that evoke feelings and emotions. As architects, we strive to create buildings that we can be proud of; our vision is to create buildings that have long-lasting social, ecological and spatial qualities; buildings that provide a real, tangible benefit to our environment.

Note

1 The BREEAM rating system is roughly comparable to the US Green Building Council's Leadership in Energy and Environmental Design (LEED) classifications. The BREEAM ratings range from "Pass," "Good," "Very Good" to "Excellent."

Form, Function and Aesthetics in the Design of Tall Buildings

Eugene Kohn

In this chapter, I would like to address some of the aspects that we, at Kohn Pedersen Fox Associates (KPF), consider to be of critical importance in the design of tall buildings; that is, the way that form, function and aesthetics can be combined to create bold yet elegant architectural statements that proudly take their place on a city's skyline. Before I go any further, I would like to stress that great buildings can only be realized through committed teamwork. It is evident at KPF that throughout our practice, from the partners to the technicians, we engage a very talented group of individuals who work extremely well together. We operate from two major offices in New York and London and a smaller office in Shanghai. We appreciate the cultural diversity that these offices bring to our practice.

Iconic tall buildings, like the Chrysler Building in New York (Figure 10.1), that have become great landmarks are truly majestic; they are not only beautiful in form, they also tell us something about their designers as well as the city in which they are located. They, along with their neighbors, create unique skylines that define cities. No wonder then, that in a number of fast-developing Asian cities, tall buildings are being commissioned to play a significant role in establishing those cities' identity. The story is familiar even in the USA; the Sears Tower designed by Skidmore, Owings and Merill when completed in 1976 (Figure 10.2) was the tallest building in the world at 1,458 ft (444 m) and proudly proclaimed Chicago's supremacy as not only the birthplace of the skyscraper but also the home of the tallest building in this category. The Petronas Twin Towers in Kuala Lumpur (1,483 ft, 452 m) designed by Cesar Pelli and completed in 1998 (Figure 10.3) stole the title and held it until 2003. There is no doubt that these twin towers have become the symbol of Kuala Lumpur which demonstrates their success as icons. In 2003, the Petronas Twin Towers were knocked off their pedestal by the Taipei Financial Center (1,670 ft, 509 m), Taipei, China, designed by the Taiwanese architectural practice of C.Y. Lee & Partners (Figure 10.4), so the title of tallest building remained in Asia.

It is impossible to talk about tall buildings without considering aspects of site area and efficiency. One of the early differences between tall buildings in Chicago and New York was that the buildings in Chicago were limited in height due to zoning regulations. Therefore, to take maximum commercial

10.1 Chrysler Building, New York, designed by William Van Alen

Avenue, designed by Mies van der Rohe (Figure 10.7) was the first building to exploit this regulation to astonishing effect; by setting the building to the rear of the site, the architect created an elegant public plaza on Park Avenue that acted as a fore-court to the Seagram Building. Sophisticated as it might be, the Seagram Building set a precedent for the extruded floor plate

benefit of their site, tall buildings in Chicago covered the entire city block and ran tight up to their site boundaries. This approach gave us sturdy-looking buildings such as the Monadnock Building, designed by Burnham and Root and completed in 1891 (Figure 10.5). There were also practical criteria that determined the layout of buildings in Chicago; before the advent of cheap and efficient fluorescent lighting in the 1940s, buildings had to supplement the inefficient incandescent lighting with natural light by incorporating light wells to provide natural light deep into the center of the building footprint.

By contrast, the different zoning requirements that had been implemented in New York forced tall buildings in that city to develop into the elegant, lofty towers that contrasted them with their Mid-Western cousins. The New York City Zoning Ordinance of 1916 required certain minimum set-backs related to the building's height to allow adequate levels of light and ventilation to neighboring buildings. Unlike Chicago, there were no height restrictions in New York, so as long as the building satisfied the set-back requirements, the skyscrapers there could soar elegantly skywards. The Empire State Building completed in 1932 clearly demonstrates the effect of the set-back require-ments in New York (Figure 10.6).

The next significant development came in the 1950s when a new set of codes in New York allowed buildings that occupied 40 percent of their site area to rise without set-backs for their entire, unrestricted height. The Seagram Building on Park

10.2 Sears Tower, Chicago, designed by Skidmore, Owings and Merill

10.3 Petronas Twin Towers, Kuala Lumpur, designed by Cesar Pelli

10.4 Taipei Financial Center, Taipei, China, designed by C.Y. Lee & Partners

10.5 Monadnock Building, Chicago, designed by Burnham and Root

building type that reached its apogee with the twin Towers of the World Trade Center, 1977, designed by Minoru Yamasaki (Figure 10.8) where floor plates of approximately 40,000 sq ft (3,716 sq m) rose up to a height of 110 stories. What we start to see then is the ascendancy of commercial demands over aesthetic decisions; efficiency led to what I call "building by statistics" where the maximization of floor plates became the paramount concern.

There were some changes in the 1980s with the introduction of post-modernism, however, these had more to do with external expression rather than developments to the office as a building type. In the 1990s, we recognized the work of influential architects such as Norman Foster and Christoph Ingenhoven, who were redefining what a contemporary architecture that was concerned with issues of energy and work practices would look like; the results were clear, fresh and modern buildings executed with clarity; although the buildings were concerned with efficiency, they were not banal boxes that ignored their users. Buildings such as Foster's Commerzbank in Frankfurt were fresh because they were well detailed and created exciting

three-dimensional spaces that captivated the public (Figure 10.9).

The most significant changes to occur in recent years have come about through the increased availability of computing power. This technological explosion has allowed architects to design vastly more efficient, better integrated and more comfortable buildings however, in relation to the subject of this chapter, this technological revolution has also been responsible for empowering architects to return to considerations of the sculptural form of architecture.

Up to this point, tall buildings were generally designed on the principle that form followed function, even if function often took the guise of finance or zoning. Carol Willis in her insightful book *Form Follows Finance*,[1] explains how the variations in development economics and building legislation gave rise to a unique vernacular in each major city. However, more recently, the design of tall buildings has been characterized by a certain departure from purely functional logic in favor of greater freedom of expression; as typified by the Office for Metropolitan Architecture's (OMA) proposal for the new Headquarters for

10.6 Empire State Building, New York, designed by Shreve, Lamb and Harmon

10.7 Seagram Building, New York, designed by Mies van der Rohe

10.8 World Trade Center, New York, designed by Minoru Yamasaki

10.9 Commerzbank, Frankfurt, Germany, designed by Foster and Partners

10.10 Headquarters for Central Chinese Television and adjacent Television Cultural Centre, Beijing, China, designed by the Office for Metropolitan Architecture

Central Chinese Television (Figure 10.10) that clearly stakes its claim as a contemporary icon.

This brings me to the Shanghai World Financial Center in China that KPF have been designing for Forest Overseas Co., Ltd. In my view, this building demonstrates a balanced blend of form, function and aesthetics; it satisfies an onerous technical specification and it accommodates a multiplicity of uses within a logical yet sculptural form. One of the toughest challenges we faced with this building was the accommodation of structural and life-safety features that have become necessary in the aftermath of the September 11, 2001, tragedy (although required by Chinese codes prior to 9/11), without compromising the building's elegance.

The World Financial Center is located in the Pudong district of Shanghai that the Chinese government has designated as a center for international banking and commercial interests. The rapid development of this area of Shanghai has resulted in a fragmented urban fabric (Figure 10.11); our reaction was to contrast this apparent chaos with a tower of monolithic simplicity (Figure 10.12). The 101-storey (1,614 ft, 492 m) high tower takes the form of a square prism measuring 184 ft (56 m) along each elevation; as the tower rises, it is sliced away by two shallow arcs until it is reduced to a slender bar at the apex. The gradual reduction in plan occurs for both aesthetic and functional reasons: the lower levels are devoted to retail use which is ideally suited to the deep floor plates. Above the retail, the larger floor plates (34,000 sq ft, 3,995 sq m) are ideally suited for office use, the narrower floors further up the building are better suited to hotel layout and finally at the very top (5,000 sq ft, 465 sq m floor plate) is an entertainment center that also includes a museum. The tapered office section also provides a variety of floor plates such that American or Japanese tenants can rent the deeper plates and European firms that are accustomed to shallower plans (from core to exterior wall), with greater levels of natural light and ventilation, can be located higher up in the building. Figure 10.13 illustrates the gradually changing floor plans. The diagonal orientation of the upper portion of the tower is a gesture of acknowledgement to the Oriental Pearl TV Tower, the area's dominant landmark, which is a fifth of a mile away.

10.11 Pudong skyline, Shanghai, China

10.12 General view, Shanghai World Financial Center, Shanghai, China

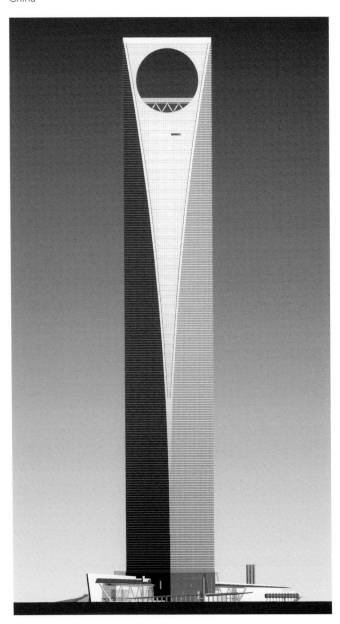

To relieve wind pressure, a 164 ft (50 m) diameter cylinder was carved out of the upper section of the building. Equal in diameter to the sphere of the television tower, this void connects the two structures across the urban landscape. Our original plans were to include a giant ferris wheel in the circular cut-out. It would have been appropriate to locate this at the center of the entertainment area. Ferris wheels have enjoyed a comeback in recent years as demonstrated by the popularity of the London Eye. This one would have had 28 cars, each with a capacity of ten people per car, circulating every 15 minutes around that opening. This wheel, 1,535 ft above ground, would have been quite spectacular. We also designed an observation deck that spanned across the opening like a bridge.

The structure also includes a number of novel features that have been included to avoid the type of catastrophic failure we witnessed in the collapse of the Twin Towers of the World Trade Center in New York. We worked very closely with Les Robertson, a pioneering structural engineer who has advised us on many

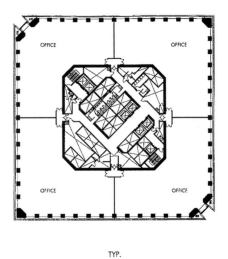

TYP.

FLOOR PLANS

10.13 Typical office floor plan, Shanghai World Financial Center, Shanghai, China

projects, to develop a sophisticated structural system. Since the building codes in Shanghai stipulate the use of refuge floors every 12 or 13 stories, we included these and used structure in these floors as outrigger trusses that brace the building at regular intervals. The structural members that make up these trusses are 17-inch (375 mm) square tubes filled with concrete. The theory is that these trusses are designed to withstand the forces produced by the collapse of the floors above, thus preventing cumulative collapse.

Another aspect that we wanted to avoid was the type of lightweight core construction used in the Twin Towers. Since these towers were designed to be lightweight buildings, and the New York codes allowed the use of gypsum board walls in the stair and elevator cores, that is what was used. As we know, these proved vulnerable to impact (by the airplane engines) and absorption of fuel oil. Fortunately the requirements of the Chinese building codes coincided with our desire to build our cores of more durable construction; at the base of the building they are solid concrete with steel reinforcement 4 ft (1.22 m) thick and transition to steel at the top of the tower.

The last item I would like to mention with regard to enhanced life-safety systems are the fireman's lifts. In the USA we do not currently have a requirement to install fireman's lifts, however, they are mandatory throughout Europe and Asia. These are lifts or elevators that are purely dedicated to use by firemen in case of an emergency; they allow quick access to the upper floors of a building without having to access any public circulation routes. These lifts also allow firemen to evacuate disabled or injured people from the building. As an added precaution, they are also enclosed in fireproof shafts. Needless to say, if such fireman's lifts had been built into the Twin Towers, hundreds of lives might have been saved. We have included about six of these lifts in the Shanghai World Financial Center. While it is practically impossible to design tall buildings that will be unaffected by the impact of aircraft, we have acknowledged the threat that such events pose and have, we hope, dealt effectively with the related life-safety issues primarily again within Chinese building code requirements to allow for the complete evacuation of all the people in the building during an emergency in an orderly and safe manner.

In summary, I argue that although form and aesthetics are important components in the design of tall buildings, they are of little value if they cannot serve the primary functions of a building. The changing profile of the Shanghai World Financial Center provides visual interest and neatly accommodates a variety of uses; the two square, vertical corners act as a foil for the gentle arcs of the two main elevations as well as harboring the vertical circulation systems; the dramatic circular cut-out relieves wind loads and acknowledges existing buildings in the area. By developing a simple yet elegant profile, the Shanghai World Financial Center will make its own contribution to the Pudong skyline.

Green Design

Kenneth Yeang

11

I have spent the last 30 years of my work as an architect developing the idea of sustainable practice in its broadest sense. Sustainable design takes many forms. In this chapter, I shall outline some propositions that address the idea of green design.

The *need to* save our environment for future generations is one of the greatest challenges that mankind must address today; this task is fuelled by the growing realization that if we maintain our current rate of growth and consumption this may be our last millennium on Earth. Therefore the compelling question for any designer is: how do we design for a sustainable future? This is a question that concerns industry just as much as it concerns the design professions; many corporations now anxiously seek to understand the environmental consequences of their current activities and attempt to envision what their impact might be if their business were sustainable. The most committed businesses also seek ways to realize their vision through ecologically benign strategies, new business models, production systems, materials and processes. An ecologically responsive built environment will undoubtedly change the way we work and will significantly influence the ecologically profligate way of life pursued by many of us in developed and developing countries.

The most effective ecological approach to business practice, as well as design, will develop through environmental integration. If we integrate everything we do or make in our built environment (which, by definition, consists of our buildings, facilities, infrastructure, products, refrigerators, toys, etc.) with the natural environment in a seamless and benign way, there will be no detrimental environmental impact whatsoever. Simply stated, ecodesign is design for bio-integration; this can be regarded as having three facets: physical, systemic and temporal. Addressing each of these facets successfully is, of course, easier said than done; but herein lies our challenge as designers.

We can start by looking at nature. Nature without humans exists in stasis. Can our businesses and our built environment imitate nature's processes, structures, and functions? Ecosystems have no waste; everything is recycled within the system. Thus by imitating the ecosystem, our built environment should produce no waste; all emissions and products would be continuously reused or recycled and eventually reintegrated with the natural environment. Designing to imitate ecosystems is *ecomimesis*. This is the fundamental premise for ecodesign: our built environment must imitate ecosystems in all respects.

Nature regards humans as just one of its many species. What differentiates humans from other natural organisms is their ability to force large-scale devastative change on the environment. Such changes are often the consequence of rapacious (manufacturing, construction) or superficially benign (recreation and transportation) activities.

Our built forms are essentially enclosures erected to protect us from inclement weather and enable activities (whether residential, office, manufacturing, warehousing, etc.) to take place. Ecologically, a building is just a high concentration of materials extracted and manufactured, often using non-renewable energy resources, from some distant place in the biosphere and transported to a particular location and assembled into a built form or an infrastructure (road, bridge, sewer, etc.) whose subsequent operations create further environmental consequences and whose eventual after-life must also be accommodated.

There is a great deal of confusion and misperception as to what exactly constitutes ecological design. It is easy to be misled or seduced by technology and to think that if we assemble enough eco-gadgetry such as solar collectors, photovoltaic cells, biological recycling systems, building automation systems and double-skin façades in one single building that this can automatically be considered ecological architecture. Although these technologies are commendable applications of low energy systems, they are merely useful components leading towards ecological architecture; they represent some of the means of achieving an ecological end product. Ecological design is not just about low energy systems; to be fully effective, these technologies need to be thoroughly integrated into the building fabric; they will also be influenced by the physical and climatic conditions of the site. The nature of the problem is therefore site-specific, there will never be a standard "one size fits all" solution.

The other misperception is that if a building achieves a high score on a green rating scale, then all is well. Of course, nothing could be further from the truth; this attitude can engender self-complacency, whereupon no further action is taken to improve environmental degradation. Green rating systems are useful in publicizing certain goals, however, they should be considered as threshold standards that designers should aim at achieving and exceeding.

In a nutshell, ecodesign should be viewed as the design of the built environment as just one system within the natural environment. The system's existence has ecological consequences; the way it functions and interacts with other systems over its entire life cycle must be benignly integrated with the natural environment. In this way it is the life-cycle analysis of the system, rather than its value at any one particular point in time, that gives a better idea of its cumulative effect on its neighboring systems.

Ecosystems are definable units in a biosphere; as such, they should contain both biotic (living) and abiotic (non-life-supporting) constituents acting together as a whole (Figure 11.1). Following this model our businesses and our built environment should be designed analogously to the ecosystem's physical content, composition and processes. For instance, besides regarding buildings as we do currently, as artistic endeavors or as serviced enclosures, we should regard them as artifacts that need to be operationally integrated with nature. It should be self-evident that the material composition of our built environment is almost entirely inorganic, whereas ecosystems contain a complement of both biotic and abiotic constituents, i.e. organic and inorganic components. The enormous number of existing buildings as well as our current manufacturing and processing activities are making the biosphere more and more inorganic and increasingly simplified biologically. To continue doing what we have always done without balancing the abiotic with the biotic content means simply adding to the biosphere's artificiality, thereby making it increasingly inorganic and reducing its complexity and diversity. We must first reverse this trend by starting to balance our built environment with greater levels of biomass; by ameliorating biodiversity and ecological connectivity in the built forms and by complementing their inorganic content with appropriate organic biomass.

We should improve the ecological linkages between our activities, be they design or business processes, with the surrounding landscape in ways that connect them both horizontally and vertically. Achieving these linkages ensures a wider level of species connectivity, interaction, mobility and sharing of resources across boundaries. Such real improvements in connectivity enhance biodiversity and further increase habitat

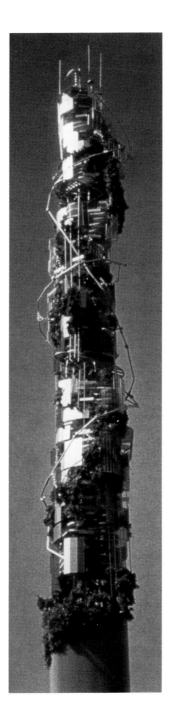

11.1 Integration of biomass with inorganic mass in built system, Tokyo-Nard Tower

resilience and species survival. An obvious demonstration of horizontal connectivity is the provision of ecological corridors and linkages in regional planning which are crucial in making urban patterns more biologically viable. Besides improved horizontal connectivity, vertical connectivity within the built form is also necessary since most buildings are not single-storey but multi-storey. Design must extend ecological linkages vertically from the foundations to the rooftops.

More important than the enhancement of ecological linkages is the biological integration of the inorganic products inherent in the built environment with the landscape so that the two become mutually ecosystemic. In this way we can create "human-made ecosystems" compatible with nature's ecosystems and by doing so we will enhance the ability of human-made ecosystems to sustain life in the biosphere.

Ecodesign is also about the discernment of the ecology of the site; any design or business activity should take place with the objective of integrating benignly with an ecosystem. In the case of site planning we must first understand the properties of the locality's ecosystem before imposing any intended human activity upon it. Every site has an ecology with a limited capacity to withstand the stresses imposed upon it; if stressed beyond this capacity, the ecology will be damaged irrevocably. Stress can be caused just as much by minimal localized impact (such as the clearing of a small land area for access) as by the total devastation of the entire landscape (such as the clearing of all trees and vegetation, leveling the topography and the diversion of existing waterways).

To identify the capacity of a site to withstand human intervention, an analysis of the existing ecology should be carried out; we must ascertain, for example, the structure of the site's ecosystems, energy flow and species diversity. Then we must identify which parts of the site, if any, have different ecosystems and which parts are particularly sensitive. Finally, we must consider the likely impact of the intended construction and use. This is, of course, a major undertaking, however, it needs to be done to better understand and appreciate the nature of a site. To be thorough and effective, this type of detailed analysis should be carried out diurnally and seasonally over a period of a year or more. To reduce this lengthy process landscape, architects have developed the "layer-cake" method; this sieve-mapping technique enables designers to map the landscape as a series of separate layers that provide a simplified matrix for the investigation of a site's ecology. As the layers are mapped, they can be overlaid and the interaction of the layers can be evaluated in relation to the proposed land use. The final product of this study is a composite map that can be used to guide the proposed site planning (e.g. the disposition of the access roads, water management, drainage patterns and shaping of the built forms). It is important to understand that the sieve-mapping method generally treats the site's ecosystems statically and may ignore the dynamic forces taking place between the layers within an ecosystem. As mentioned above, the separation of the layers is a convenient intellectual construct that simplifies the complex natural interactions between layers. Therefore the comprehensive analysis of an ecosystem requires more than sieve-mapping – the inter-layer relationships should also be examined.

As designers, we should also look into ways of configuring built forms, the operational systems for our built environment and our businesses as low-energy systems. In addressing these systems we need to look into ways of improving the internal comfort conditions of our buildings. There are essentially five ways of doing this: *Passive Mode*, *Mixed Mode*, *Full Mode*, *Productive Mode* and *Composite Mode*, the latter being a composite of all the preceding modes.

The practice of sustainable design requires that we look first at Passive Mode (or bioclimatic) design strategies, then we can move on to Mixed Mode, Full Mode, Productive Mode and Composite Mode, all the while adopting progressive strategies to improve comfort conditions relative to external conditions.

Meeting contemporary expectations for office environment comfort conditions cannot generally be achieved by Passive Mode or by Mixed Mode alone. The internal environment often needs to be supplemented by the use of external sources of energy, as in Full Mode. Full Mode uses electro-mechanical systems often powered by external energy sources – whether from fossil fuel-derived sources or from local ambient sources such as wind or solar power.

Passive Mode means designing for improved internal comfort conditions over external conditions without the use of any electro-mechanical systems. Examples of Passive Mode strategies include the adoption of suitable building orientation and configuration in relation to the local climate as well as the selection of appropriate building materials. When considering the design of the façade, issues of solid-to-glazed area ratios, thermal insulation values, the incorporation of natural ventilation and the use of vegetation are also important.

Building design strategy must start with Passive Mode or bioclimatic design as this can significantly influence the configuration of the built form and its enclosure systems. Passive Mode requires an understanding of the climatic conditions of the locality; the designer should not merely synchronize the building design with the local meteorological conditions but should optimize the ambient energy of the locality to create improved internal comfort conditions without the use of any electro-mechanical systems. The fundamental nature of these decisions clearly dictates that once the building configuration, orientation and enclosure have been considered, the further refinement of a design should lead to the adoption of choices that will enhance its energy efficiency. If, as an alternative, a design solution is developed that has not previously optimized the Passive Mode options, then these non-energy-efficient design decisions will need to be corrected by supplementary Full Mode systems. Such a remedy would make a nonsense of low-energy design. Furthermore, if the design optimizes a building's Passive Modes, it remains at an improved level of comfort during any electrical power failure. If the Passive Modes have not been optimized, then whenever there is no electricity or external energy source, the building may become intolerable to occupy.

In Mixed Mode, buildings use some electro-mechanical systems such as ceiling fans, double façades, flue atria and evaporative cooling.

Full Mode relies entirely on the use of electro-mechanical systems to create suitable internal comfort conditions. This is the option chosen for most conventional buildings. If clients and users insist on having consistent comfort conditions throughout the year, the result will inevitably lead to Full Mode design. It must be clear now that low-energy design is essentially a user-driven condition and a life-style issue. We must appreciate that Passive Mode and Mixed Mode design can never compete with the comfort levels of the high-energy, Full Mode conditions.

Productive Mode is where a building generates its own energy (Figure 11.2). Common examples of this today can be seen in the generation of electricity through the use of

Cultural Plaza View

11.2 Productive Mode, Chongqing Tower

photovoltaic panels that are powered by solar power and wind turbines that harness wind energy. Ecosystems use solar energy that is transformed into chemical energy by the photosynthesis of green plants which in turn drives the ecological cycle. If ecodesign is to be ecomimetic, we should seek to do the same, however, we will need to do so on a much larger scale.

The inclusion of systems that create Productive Modes inevitably leads to sophisticated technological systems that in turn increase the use of material resources, the inorganic content of the built form, the embodied energy content and the attendant impact on the environment.

Composite Mode is a combination of all the above modes in proportions that vary over the seasons of the year.

Ecodesign also requires the designer to use materials and assemblies that facilitate reuse, recycling and their eventual reintegration with ecological systems. Here again we need to be ecomimetic in our use of materials in the built environment: in ecosystems, all living organisms feed on continual flows of matter and energy from their environment to stay alive, and all living organisms continually produce "waste." However, ecosystems do not actually generate waste since one species' waste is really another species' food. Thus matter cycles continually through the web of life. To be truly ecomimetic, the materials we produce should also take their place within the closed loop where waste becomes food (Figure 11.3).

Currently we regard everything produced by humans as eventual garbage or waste material that is either burned or ends up in landfill sites. The new question for designers, manufacturers and businesses is: how can we use this waste material? If our materials are readily biodegradable, they can return into the environment through decomposition. If we want to be ecomimetic, we should think, at the very early design stages, how a building, its components and its outputs can be reused and recycled. These design considerations will determine the materials to be used, the ways in which the building fabric is to be assembled, how the building can be adapted over time and how the materials can be reused after the building has reached the limits of its useful life.

If we consider the last point, reuse, in a little more detail we come to an increasingly important conclusion. To facilitate the reuse of, let us say, a structural component, the connection between the components should be mechanical, i.e. bolted rather than welded so that the joint can be released easily. If, in addition to being easily demountable, the components were modular, then the structure could easily be demounted and reassembled elsewhere. This leads to the concept of Design for Disassembly (DfD) which has its roots in sustainable design.

Another major design issue is the systemic integration of our built forms, operational systems and internal processes with the natural ecosystems that surround us. Such integration is crucial

11.3 Recycling of water and waste, EDITT Tower, Singapore

because without it these systems will remain disparate artificial items that could be potential pollutants. Unfortunately many of today's buildings only achieve eventual integration through biodegradation that requires a long-term process of natural decomposition.

If manufacture and design for recycling and reuse relieve the problem of deposition of waste, we should integrate both organic waste (e.g. sewage, rainwater runoff, wastewater, food wastes, etc.) and inorganic waste.

There is a very appropriate analogy between ecodesign and surgical prosthetics. Ecodesign is essentially design that integrates man-made systems, both mechanically and organically, with the natural host system – the ecosystems. A surgical prosthetic device also has to integrate with its organic host being – the human body. Failure to integrate will result in dislocation in both cases. These are the exemplars for what our buildings and our businesses should achieve: the total physical, systemic and temporal integration of our human-made, built environment with our organic host in a benign and positive way. There are, of course, a large number of theoretical and technical problems to be solved before we have a truly ecological built environment, however, we should take encouragement from the fact that our intellect has allowed us to create prosthetic organs that can integrate with the human body. The next challenge will be to integrate our buildings, our cities and all human activities with the natural ecosystems that surround us.

Best Practice

A Developer's Perspective

Michael Harrison

12

I graduated in architectural engineering, but I spent my first year trying to be an architect before realizing that I needed to do something differently. As a result of this brief experience, I can appreciate more fully the architect's role in the design and construction of buildings and I consider it an honor to be able to work with the architects on the projects we commission.

Gerald Hines has been in the business of real estate development for nearly 50 years and the major reason I went to work for him straight out of graduate school was because of his reputation as someone who was regarded as the first national developer to recognize the value of architectural design in the marketing of office space. Initially with the development of One Shell Plaza, Shell's Headquarters in downtown Houston, and more notably with Philip Johnson and John Burgee's design for Pennzoil Place Towers, Gerald Hines set the tone for the way he intended to develop his portfolio as an office developer; he has also maintained a consistently high standard for the past three decades.

It is important to preface my comments by making the point that as a developer I have a different perspective of office building from most architects. I will focus on the aspects of best practice as seen by a developer. This generally means that what architects look at as a design issue, I look at as a *process* issue. The best way to explain this is to go through a few examples; to demonstrate the benefit of seeing how developers think about the procurement of office buildings as they try to balance the architectural integrity of a project with economics and profitability.

The impetus behind establishing a focus on best practice took place in 1999 when Gerald Hines convened a group of about 15 key players from Hines' various offices around the world for a three-day retreat in Aspen, Colorado. The purpose of this gathering was to recognize how office design had changed over the previous decade and to attempt to forecast what the main directions would be over the next 20 years. By doing this we attempted to assess how we might best reshape our development process to continue being at the leading edge of office development. One of the clearest demonstrations of how the market had changed was the fact that the scale of development had changed: office buildings were generally getting smaller. We realized that this was happening because it was taking a much higher pre-leasing requirement to kick off an office development so developers were initiating smaller buildings with fewer tenants. Another indicator of change was the different attitude towards the quality of fit out: it was evident that corporate America, as well as many professional service firms, were developing different ideas about what they saw as appropriate office environments; we were heading away from the 1980s-style granite-clad lobbies with fancy chandeliers to more sober, less opulent interiors. We wanted to acknowledge these changes and still be able to create world-class architecture.

Since we were going to brainstorm some new ideas, we realized that we shouldn't go about this merely as an internal exercise; we sought input from a selection of consultants and advisers who had a closer relationship with the end user than we did. We also wanted to send the message that *everything* was on the table for re-examination and discussion; we wanted to be open to, and take advantage of, any innovation in office design once we had assessed its practicability.

One of the organizations we invited to join us in Aspen was the Rocky Mountain Institute which we considered to be one of the front-runners in sustainable development and environmental sensitivity that is so important today. We also invited Art Gensler to participate because we thought that it was important to consult an architect who was well practiced in architecture and interior design and because we felt that he would be able to offer us his extensive experience and knowledge of working with an enormous diversity of users. On the engineering side we invited representatives form Flack and Kurtz to join us because we believed they had designed some of the most innovative mechanical and electrical systems in office buildings. Another participant was John Cushman whose experience as a global real estate advisor would be crucial since so many of Hines' end users are tenants who are represented by brokers.

One of the most important, and lively, discussions that we generated at our Aspen gathering was related to the question of what best practice actually meant to us. We decided that our goal would not be to say simply that we would incorporate operable windows or light shelves into our next buildings. Instead we took a step back and realized that best practice shouldn't be about just bricks and mortar; we needed to look at best practice in terms of the way we would execute our development process. There were certainly aspects of best practice that related to technology but there were broader issues that

related to benchmark analysis. An important component of benchmark analysis is the greater understanding of our end-users' requirements and their decision-making criteria.

On reflection, it is clear that even before 1999 we engaged in benchmarking, however, it was carried out on an *ad hoc* basis; we never produced any documentation that really helped us see in black and white the differences between our competitors' criteria and what it was that we were supposed to be creating. Today we prepare a comprehensive benchmark study for every project we embark on, whether it is residential or mixed-use, an individual office building or community master plan. In the case of office buildings, for example, we benchmark the competition: in some cases this could mean benchmarking an individual sub-market, such as South Park, or it could be the whole of Charlotte. We do this to understand what options a prospective client might have in terms of the standard of office development in a locality. In this way we can address specifically those parameters that we believe are important for that sub-market. For example if one considers floor plate size and configuration, it is surprising how widely this varies from market to market. For example, a new office building in the central-perimeter sub-market of Atlanta would require a floor plate average of between 25,000–27,000 sq ft (2,322–2,510 sq m). If you consider Buckhead (70 miles east of Atlanta), which represents a typical small town market, it would be 15,000–20,000 sq ft (1,393–1,858 sq m). The requirements even vary within cities based on the tenant mix of that particular sub-market.

We also benchmark project amenities. We deliberately put this category high on the list since an increasing number of office users focus on the amenities provided in a building. The amenities available in the locality are also important; people are interested if there is a Starbucks or supermarket close by; or whether their office building is close to a mass transit stop. These issues become very important when pricing is very competitive and the proximity of one amenity could easily influence a tenant's final decision.

We also recognize that there are two quite separate markets: one for speculative and the other for build-to-suit projects. In the second category a client will usually be represented by facilities groups and will therefore have more sophisticated demands. The benchmark for the build-to-suit client will typically be dictated by their current facilities or those of a competitor. In either case, whether the client is the end user or a broker, we have to work hard to understand their true needs and there is one inherent problem here: clients can't always articulate what their requirements are. It is always easier to express what they don't want, based on what hasn't worked for them. At this point, the architect's skill of being able to visualize three-dimensional environments becomes vital in assisting a client to understand a new environment and in making important decisions about it.

The benchmark analysis also has great value as a marketing tool since we can use this information to speak intelligently about our own buildings as well as being able to differentiate between our buildings and the competition when we come to lease our property.

Another important outcome of the Aspen gathering was the consideration of an alternative systems matrix. The word "systems" is used here in a global sense to refer to architectural systems such as the structural system; curtain walling system; mechanical, electrical and power systems, and life-safety systems. We now engage in a comprehensive evaluation of all the different options available so we create a method for the comparison of price, functionality and maintenance for each system. To do this effectively we consider the first cost and the life-cycle costs and then determine the impact of each option on the other building systems. For example, if we choose a curtain walling system that incorporates external sun-shading, we would like to have an idea of its impact on our energy systems; whether it helps us meet energy codes and/or whether it helps us reduce total energy consumption. We then synthesize all this information and the result becomes the primary design focus for that particular project.

What we have done, since 1999, is to evaluate, on a project-by-project basis, the use of certain technologies that we think are at the leading edge of office development. The first and probably the most important of these technologies is the use of raised floor HVAC systems. The first raised floor we ever installed was at the Owens Corning headquarters in 1994. At that time we tried to benchmark other similar-sized raised floor office environments in the US, however other than a couple of 5,000–7,000 sq ft (465–650 sq m) installations, we didn't find anything comparable; similar-sized installations could only be found in Canada or Europe.

The beauty of an underfloor air delivery system is the simplicity of the concept; in many ways it is more straightforward than a conventional system and it is definitely more efficient. It consists of an access floor, which is raised about a foot above the floor slab, that acts as a plenum (Figure 12.1); instead of a network of ducts under the floor a stub runs from the service core into the plenum where it discharges the supply air. Carpet squares are laid over the access floor but are offset so that the carpet seals the joint between adjacent floor tiles. Vents are cut into the raised floor wherever supply air is required.

What we didn't realize when we started looking at this system were the collateral benefits of delivering air through a floor plenum. In conventional systems the fresh air is supplied at high level through the ceiling plenum. As warm air is more buoyant than the cooler (supply) air, the stale warm air floats upwards so that as the fresh air is blown down to the breathing zone it inevitably mixes with the stale air; to get the right quantity of cool fresh air the amount of air has to be increased to compensate for this contamination. The air is exhausted through the light fixtures and some of the fresh air inevitably short-circuits from the ceiling level supply to the extract zone. A much smarter way of delivering fresh air more effectively to the breathing zone is to supply it at low level, through the floor, and upwards, so that as it rises it picks up pollution and heat and is then exhausted into the ceiling plenum through the light fixtures. The raised floor allows exactly this to happen and because 100 percent of the fresh air is being delivered to the breathing zone before it can be contaminated, it provides a much more efficient delivery system. Better still, the fresh air is not being forced through a warm zone so it does not need to be supplied at temperatures as low as in a conventional system which results in greater comfort and less energy consumption. In addition, the heat from the light fittings is exhausted immediately into the ceiling plenum. Although the amount of cooling required to counteract the effect of computers is about the same, the more natural air circulation route allows for a reduction in fan sizes and therefore reduced energy costs.

The raised floor delivery system also allows almost total flexibility. It is also important to consider churn and the related costs of churn to a client. Some businesses such as law firms don't generally have to deal with churn, however, I have had experience of some clients whose churn rates (the number of

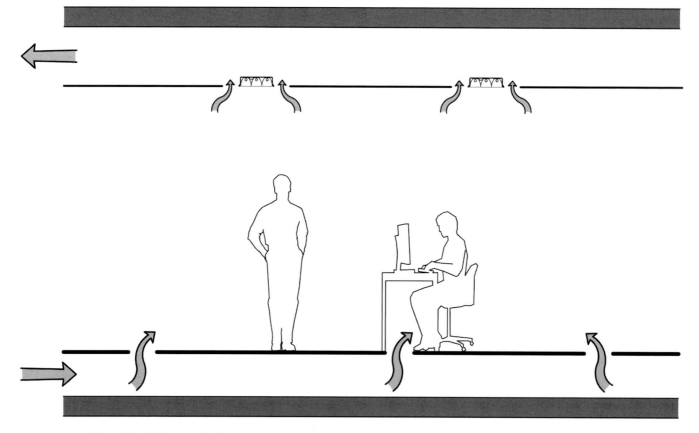

12.1 Diagram of typical underfloor air distribution system

employees being moved versus the total number of employees) exceed 100 percent per year. Furthermore, I predict that with advances in technology and with the increasing ability to design more efficient workplaces, the 100 percent churn rate could be exceeded by many clients.

As we were doing our research, one of our biggest concerns was whether the low-level supply air would create drafts and be uncomfortable. We were able to address our worries quite easily when we visited an installation in Canada; by asking the people working there we found out that they were very comfortable. In fact, we realized another positive facet of underfloor air delivery systems. In many conventional situations we rely on thermostats to control the temperature in a room. The beauty of a raised floor air delivery system is that each worker has a diffuser in their area and each diffuser can be controlled simply and individually. So as long as there are a sufficient number of outlets in the common areas such as hallways and corridors to provide the minimum amount of fresh air, the rest can be controlled separately.

One little incident convinced me of the effectiveness of this system. I was waiting for an opportunity to meet the CEO of the corporation we were visiting in Canada and, as he was involved in a conference call, I took the opportunity to walk around and ask people what they thought about the raised floor HVAC system. I even asked the CEO's assistant, who was wearing a skirt, and had been working in this building since it opened, whether she felt comfortable. She replied that she didn't think that the air diffusers had been installed in her area. So I asked if

I could look around; we started looking for the diffuser and couldn't find one under her desk until she eventually pushed back her chair to reveal that the diffuser was located directly below it. That little investigation told me all I needed to know about the comfort of underfloor air delivery systems.

Back at the Owens Corning project, we continued our research; as there weren't many US installations we tried to develop our own system; we wanted the flexibility to be able to deal with a number of different situations but didn't want to have six different types of access panel or carpet tile – we just wanted a simple kit of parts. Hines has a long-standing relationship with Titus, one of the leading diffuser manufacturers in the US, so we got together with them and developed an efficient 6-inch diameter diffuser that was simple to adjust (Figures 12.2 and 12.3). We decided to locate the diffuser in the corner of the tile so that by rotating the tile you had some adjustment as to where the diffuser would be located. This way we needed only two tiles: a solid one with no diffuser and one with a hole in the corner. We also added a basket below the diffuser that would hold up to 15 oz. (0.45 liters) of liquid so that in the event that someone spilled a can of soda, it would not leak into the underfloor area.

The swirl pattern is very important because it spins the air stream as it comes out of the diffuser and this helps it to distribute effectively. The air is distributed at a comfortable temperature around 63° F with the result that our HVAC hot and cold calls in our raised office environments are about a tenth of what they are in our conventional air delivery environments, diffuser to shut off some of the cooler supply air. When they warm up, they slide it off the diffuser. The convenient thing about individual control is that it doesn't affect the system's performance.

Likewise if you're going to implement a system that incorporates a raised floor to provide your air delivery systems, it makes perfect sense to use that same space for the delivery of power, voice and data. So again we set about devising a customized power distribution box that allowed connections to power, data and voice through a 6-inch circular cut-out with a similar spin top.

I mentioned earlier that first cost premiums don't always translate into rental rate premiums; the following example is a good illustration of that. Hines commissioned an office building in the suburbs of Chicago about three years ago, and to the best of our knowledge, it was the first speculative office building in that marketplace that used an all raised floor environment in an office building. We delivered the HVAC and power through the floor rather than through the ceiling. The estimated first-cost premium for the underfloor delivery system was about $5.00 per square foot increased construction cost, however, we didn't assume that we would receive a rental rate that was equivalent to that $5.00 premium. We realized that this was a technology-driven sub-market of Chicago, where a number of the tenants were technology or software companies; we therefore thought (and were proved correct) that although we didn't achieve the $5.00 per square foot rental rate premium, we did lease the space a lot faster than our competitors. As it turned out, the technology users flocked to the building when they were presented with an underfloor delivery system.

We have recently started incorporating operable windows into our office designs. We were skeptical at first because we didn't think we could use operable windows on a high-rise building without having papers blown out of the windows. Well, we managed this in Frankfurt, Germany, and we have since incorporated high-level hopper and low-level awning windows in a couple of build-to-suit projects in the mid-West. We have also evaluated a new technology known as rotating vents that we used on the Uptown München Tower (see p. 93), however, we haven't yet included them in a project in the US. These vents allow us to introduce natural ventilation to high-rise buildings without the disruptive effects of unwanted drafts.

which is a very good indication of how effective this system is. I believe that the main reason why we get so few complaints is that the diffusers are so easy to control; I would think that in 90 percent of cases someone can just reach down and control their own environment. My favorite temperature control technique is the "notebook method"; I've seen folks when they get too cool take a notebook off their desk and drop it on their

One of the most beneficial, yet most understated innovations, we have made use of is the use of increased ceiling heights. Wherever we have provided ceiling heights greater than the 9-foot standard, this is without doubt the single most noticeable feature that the users have commented on. The increased ceiling heights don't just add space and volume, they add grandeur and provide additional daylight penetration. Even when we take into consideration the increased cost of adding an extra foot to the ceiling heights, we believe that there are a number of benefits that still make it viable. In fact, we have found a way to increase the ceiling height by a foot and only take the floor-to-floor height up 9 inches by reorganizing the mechanical, electrical and fire protection systems. We now consider this to be one of the better features to be incorporated into a new office building. In fact, we are now doing this for the first time in a speculative 40-storey office building in Atlanta.

The move to increased ceiling heights also favors indirect lighting as a means of achieving uniform lighting levels. We have done some work in evaluating the use of light shelves; ceiling heights of 9 feet restrict the penetration of daylight and therefore make them less cost effective. With 10-foot ceiling heights, the benefits of using light shelves increase dramatically and so we have begun to incorporate light shelves into the design of some of our office buildings. We have also included automatically operated sunshades that are controlled by the Building Management System. We use a variety of shading devices depending on the task that needs to be performed, i.e. solid louvers that block direct sunlight and perforated blinds that still allow some vision yet cut glare and heat gain.

Lighting is another very important architectural system that we are very interested in. Historically, Hines has been a good guinea pig for the lighting industry; our headquarters in Houston is a good example of a number of different lighting experiments. Many years ago we were one of the first developers to incorporate deep cell parabolic louvers. One of the problems associated with the parabolic fixtures is that they create dark spots on the ceiling and this isn't desirable from an aesthetic perspective. More recently we have installed a combination of recessed and pendant fixtures that give a combination of direct and indirect light. This, however, may not suit clients with high churn rates as the pendant indirect light fittings restrict the positioning of partitions. With today's fast-improving lighting technology and increased ceiling heights there are a multitude of lighting solutions that can address our increasingly technology-driven office environments where people may now have two or even three VDU screens on their desk.

Another aspect of daylighting that is very important is the design of appropriate structural bay depths to maximize the amount of natural light penetration. In many European countries regulations stipulate maximum distances for office workers from operable windows. In Germany, for example, that distance is 49 ft (15 m) in a new office building. We are actually implementing some of these criteria in the US.

Earlier, when discussing raised floors, I referred to life-cycle cost analysis. We have also carried out similar exercises on other technologies; after looking at external sun shading we found that while it adds high first costs, we had never looked at the life-cycle cost benefits of the reduced air conditioning loads of the building. So as we evaluated them more holistically, we found that the premium of adding them when compared to the aesthetic benefits on the façade design was much less than we thought and as a result we are now starting to incorporate them more and more into our office buildings.

Subjects such as air and water filtration, although they may not have great visibility, are of great importance to developers and building owners because they influence issues of performance, risk and liability and can have drastic financial implications. Hines has over the past decade taken indoor air quality very seriously; in fact, we feel that technology has only recently been able to offer what we have thought necessary for many years. Indoor air quality has a direct impact on performance; it is one of those areas where office workers can detect the difference but can't tell you exactly why they feel better.

We generally use electrostatic filters to get the right air quality because we believe they are the most efficient technology available. They are rather more expensive than conventional filter systems even though the price has gone down dramatically since we first used them. The major challenge with conventional air filtration systems in office buildings, is that the filters are low efficiency when they start, and actually get more efficient as they get dirty, however, at some point they lose their efficiency and dirt begins to pass through them, so the maintenance regime presents something of a challenge to keep them at their optimal efficiency. On the other hand, electrostatic systems operate at 98 or 99 percent starting on day one, and then on throughout their operating life, so it just isn't necessary to worry about inefficiencies over time.

Purified drinking water is another of our favorites; we see no reason why water purification systems shouldn't be considered as standard facilities so that when one goes to a drinking fountain in the hallway one can drink water just as pure as bottled water. We think this facility should become standard in all offices. In fact, it can sometimes be used as a marketing tool when we emphasize to clients that by incorporating purified water drinking fountains, they can eliminate their monthly bills for bottled water.

Since Gerald Hines started out as a mechanical engineer, he has always ensured that the Hines Corporation has placed a premium on the design of mechanical and electrical systems in its buildings. We continue to do this, not just because we want to be leaders in this regard but also to encourage others to raise standards. So recently we focused on the Energy Star and LEED programs and where possible we have been active participants in these initiatives. So much so, that we have had the good fortune of being acclaimed as the Energy Star Partner of the Year by the Department of Energy for the past three years.

Finally, when I think of the "office of the future," I don't have a vision of some new architectural style or a specific energy-efficient system; instead I think that we will see a combination of systems and technologies that will be integrated to provide practical, affordable and comfortable office buildings. In my experience the best examples of the "office of the future" have tended to be corporate headquarters or build-to-suit projects for a single user. I believe that in these cases a client will be focused on issues beyond the rental rate since he/she is taking a longer-term view of their new development and will be considering a multiplicity of objectives. It is precisely in situations like these that employee comfort and access to amenities assume greater importance because a corporate client generally takes more interest in their own employees because it is these people who are their clients.

Conversely, why doesn't this happen in a multi-tenanted building? Generally because the smaller tenants that require, say, 15,000 sq ft (1,394 sq m) cannot afford the time to analyze the ten or more options that are available. They might be represented by a broker but these brokers may have a choice of up to 30 different properties and they don't have the time or the fee to do the extra work of analyzing a Hines project which is different from all the others because it has a raised floor and is going to have a lower life-cycle cost for the tenant. However, I believe that as developers such as Hines encourage willing corporate clients to provide enhanced environments that include the kinds of technologies I have mentioned above, we will gradually be able to set the bar increasingly higher so that all office environments, including multi-tenanted speculative offices, will benefit by being more pleasant and more comfortable places to work in.

The Added Value of Sustainable Design

Chris Hays, Brad Smith and Steven Ott

Editor's Introduction

Chris Grech

Rapidly increasing fuel costs and global warning are forcing architects to think more holistically about the natural and the built environments. Yet, while many architects are keen to investigate opportunities to incorporate sustainable design features in their buildings, they often feel frustrated when clients curb their enthusiasm because of the lack of proof with regard to the tangible benefits of this approach. At the root of this dampening factor is the inbuilt conservatism of the financial institutions on whom a large proportion of building and infrastructure development depends for their start-up funding.

The authors in this Chapter have been chosen to investigate how the gap between these seemingly divergent views can be narrowed. First, Chris Hays of Chris Hays Design Studio, through his work with William McDonough, has designed many innovative and sustainable buildings for corporate and individual clients. Next, Brad Smith, National Sales Performance Executive for Commercial Real Estate Banking at Bank of America, introduces us to the financier's perspective of sustainable practices. Finally, Professor Steven Ott, John Crosland, Sr., Distinguished Professor of Real Estate and Development at the Department of Finance and Business Law at the University of North Carolina at Charlotte, outlines the priorities that concern developers with regard to sustainable development.

The Designer's Perspective

Chris Hays

There is an old joke that runs along the lines that engineers know more and more about less and less and that architects know less and less about more and more. The joke to me is that the opposite seems to be the case; I am finding that the further design professionals delve into issues of sustainability the more they start to see the incredible level of detail needed to understand how they can implement them. Many designers are now researching at a molecular level to better understand how sustainability can be implemented. In the ten years I worked for Bill McDonough I had the good fortune to work with many talented people; one of these was Dr Michael Braungart, who was very involved in examining the chemical composition of the materials we design with. Then, at the other end of the scale we were also dealing with entire communities. Architectural design is an expansive field and this volume gives a good idea of the breadth of issues that I am referring to. I will refer to some projects where McDonough worked with clients who were very keenly interested in the financial as well as the social and environmental benefits of their buildings.

I think that the best way to start thinking about sustainability is to consider some design strategies. I want to distinguish these from design concepts because concepts are a distinct layer of issues which I do not include here. In general, the idea is to work with a series of strategies that reinforce a design concept and which we can use to create an integral design idea.

The first overall strategy is to look at daylighting as a primary energy-saving component. Taking the Gap Corporate Campus in San Bruno, California, as an example, we employed greater floor-to-floor heights, taller windows and clerestories to allow light to penetrate the south elevations and to bounce it around the interior so we could get daylight that is actually pervasive throughout the environment. To assist us in achieving a greater diffusion of daylight we designed the ground floor to have a 15.5 ft (4.7 m) floor-to-floor dimension as opposed to the normal 10–12 ft (3.66 m) (Figure 13.1). The dimension from the second floor to the underside of the clerestory is another 20 feet which means that we have some very tall spaces which facilitate greater daylight penetration.

Figure 13.2 summarizes the simple payback that we estimated for some of the features we included in this project. The payback is based on the additional cost to the project beyond what was estimated to be the norm and looking at the amount of time that the energy savings would actually help it pay for itself. Therefore in the case of the daylighting we divided the figures derived for the additional cost of providing greater floor-to-floor heights and clerestories, etc. by the estimated annual savings and this gave us a payback period of just under six years. Payback periods are very difficult to predict in advance because, first, it is virtually impossible to guess what energy costs are going to be and, second, rebates can also come into

play. We suggest revisiting projects a couple of years down the line to update the actual costs and to build a reliable set of post-occupancy data which can be used to inform future clients.

The second strategy we looked at was the use of a raised floor system. The benefit of using a raised floor is that you are supplying air from a low level (Figure 13.3). There are many advantages to this, first, it is generally closer to the breathing zone than other supply zones; second, as the exhausted air is warmer and therefore less buoyant, it rises, taking the pollutants with it. Therefore, the cooler, cleaner air remains in the breathing zone.

The next strategic move was to consider a grass roof. In the case of the Gap project, this idea germinated, first, from the larger idea of how to work with the context of San Bruno and, second, from a more particular consideration of the existing site which had some very park-like qualities. Grass roofs also offer a range of benefits to the technical performance of roofs: improved thermal and acoustic insulation as well as longer life expectancy for the vital waterproofing membranes. In this particular case, we were able to achieve a roof with an R50 (0.11 W/m²K) insulation value, approximately three times better than conventional roof construction. The improved acoustic insulation of approximately 50 decibels proved very helpful in reducing airborne noise from the nearby airport. Furthermore, as the earth and grass protected the waterproof roofing membrane from degradation due to ultraviolet radiation, the membrane manufacturers estimated that the membrane's performance could be extended from 15 to 20 years. This extended membrane lifetime gave us the potential for much greater energy savings, not to mention less disruption in future years. There was also the added advantage of creating a limited natural habitat on the roof and lessening the heat island effect. The simple payback on the grass roof was estimated to be at about 11 years. The additional benefit (to which it is very difficult to attach a monetary value) can be seen in the way that the grass roof fits into the background of the hills of San Bruno (Figure 13.4).

Another important strategic approach was the inclusion of natural ventilation; in most cases this means the substitution of

13.1 Gap HQ, interior view showing effect of natural daylighting

FEATURE	SIMPLE PAYBACK
GREEN ROOF	8.8 YRS
UNDERFLOOR HVAC	2.9 YRS
DAYLIGHTING	5.9 YRS
COMBINED	*3.3 YRS*

13.2 Gap HQ, table of Cost Benefit Analysis

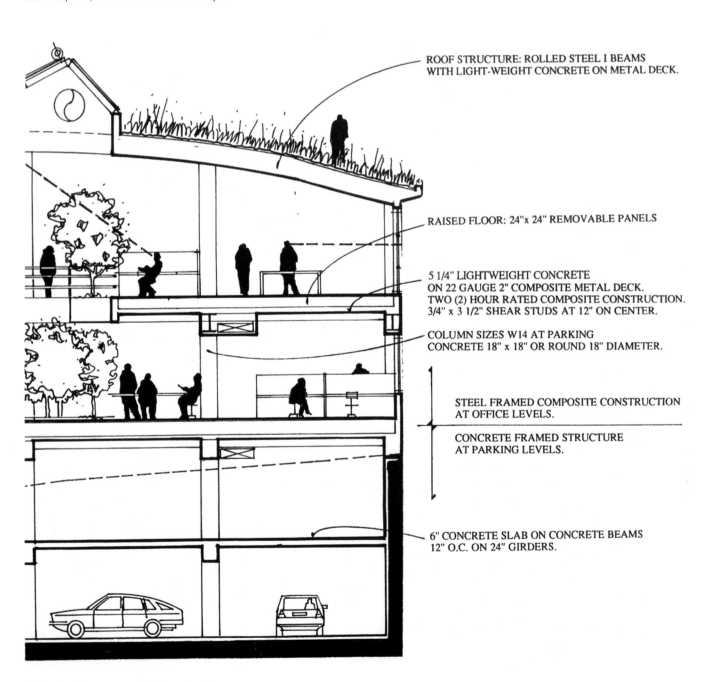

ROOF STRUCTURE: ROLLED STEEL I BEAMS
WITH LIGHT-WEIGHT CONCRETE ON METAL DECK.

RAISED FLOOR: 24"x 24" REMOVABLE PANELS

5 1/4" LIGHTWEIGHT CONCRETE
ON 22 GAUGE 2" COMPOSITE METAL DECK.
TWO (2) HOUR RATED COMPOSITE CONSTRUCTION.
3/4" x 3 1/2" SHEAR STUDS AT 12" ON CENTER.

COLUMN SIZES W14 AT PARKING
CONCRETE 18" x 18" OR ROUND 18" DIAMETER.

STEEL FRAMED COMPOSITE CONSTRUCTION
AT OFFICE LEVELS.

CONCRETE FRAMED STRUCTURE
AT PARKING LEVELS.

6" CONCRETE SLAB ON CONCRETE BEAMS
12" O.C. ON 24" GIRDERS.

13.3 Gap HQ, cross-section through office

sealed windows by openable windows. Natural ventilation offers a number of advantages: employees have a measure of control over their environment; the fresh air is generally healthier than re-circulated air and natural ventilation uses less energy than mechanical ventilation. Openable windows are something that our practice always tries to incorporate; we did this even before all the major power outages in the San Bruno/San Francisco area. In fact, shortly after the Gap building was completed, there were a number of power outages in this area. The Gap also occupied a couple of buildings across the street that had

been constructed with sealed windows and so when the power failed they had no mechanical ventilation and everybody had to leave the office and go home. When this happened, the client who had previously resisted the idea of the openable windows called us and said, "Look, the power's out and we opened the windows; we've got natural light and ventilation and we're fine. From now on I will always support openable windows." After this, he became our strongest advocate; as he put it: "Why is it that we would never build a house in which you could not open a window? So why would you build offices without openable windows? Especially when you consider the amount of time that we spend in our office environment? Natural light and ventilation have such a tremendous impact in a positive way."

The furniture manufacturing plant that we designed for Herman Miller in Holland, Michigan, illustrates a couple of other sustainable strategies (Figure 13.5). The manufacturer started off as a subdivision of Herman Miller and was so successful that it was subsequently absorbed into the parent organization. We have good reason to believe that at least part of the success of this subsidiary was due to the improved working environment created in their new facility.

Some of the strategies employed in this building were similar to those used in the Gap building. Again we used daylight to save energy and create better work spaces; first, the client came to us with the idea that he wanted to create a building which felt like it was in California not Michigan. His vision was for a building that would appear bright and lively. At the same time we started to look at ways of using daylight to provide natural light as well as a component of passive solar gain to reduce heating costs. Our target was a low one of a saving of about 13 cents a square foot for floor area which, although it does not seem much, aggregates to a substantial overall saving. We introduced a series of roof monitors which allowed plenty of the generally overcast Michigan sky to pour light into the production spaces below. When you stand in that space now, there is so much natural light that it feels like there is no roof at all.

A strategy that we use quite frequently is to examine internal finishes such as carpets and paints to see how their chemical composition will affect indoor air quality due to the volatile organic compounds (VOCs) they produce. We take these things very seriously because it has been proven that if people have a sense that they are operating in a healthier environment they

13.4 Gap HQ, green roof

13.5 Herman Miller manufacturing facility, interior view

feel physically better overall and this has a direct result on their output. In fact, to quote directly from our client, Bill Bundy: "We've doubled our productivity in this space in the last five years which means that we're producing twice as much with essentially the same number of people." These comments illustrate a fundamental point about the value of sustainability; even though our objective is to save on energy consumption and maintenance costs these cost differentials are miniscule compared with the potential for the much higher levels of productivity and employee retention in these buildings. A short anecdote illustrates this point quite well: there were a handful of employees working in the Herman Miller plant we designed in Holland, Michigan, who quit their jobs and went to work for one of the competitors down the road thinking that all manufacturing facilities were like this one. They found that this was anything but the case; they worked in a more typical warehouse environment and even though they were paid higher salaries they left and came back to Herman Miller because they could not function properly in a conventional environment.

I am proud of the fact that both the buildings I have shown so far have won *Good Business and Good Design* awards. These are a joint award given by Architectural Record and Business Week magazines with the intention of highlighting buildings that speak to the core mission of a company, that benefit the company, and are at the same time good designs.

These awards also go some way towards underscoring the idea that sustainable design leads to an integrated product that should be supported by the whole community.

The Capital Provider's Perspective

Brad Smith

It is interesting for me as a financier to contribute to this volume; clearly the provision of capital presents developers and architects with a number of challenges as they strive to break the mold by developing and implementing ideas and strategies related to sustainability. My task is to shed some light on how providers of capital see these same issues. The first challenge we have to face as capital providers is that capital, unlike most other resources, is expected to end up with a little bit extra on top – that is, to provide a financial return. It is almost as if at some prearranged point in the construction of a building, the steel is returned to the manufacturer for redeployment. Another feature of capital is that there are different time horizons of capital that must be addressed in the project. I set out here to address these aspects of finance and, more pointedly, the fact that the developer, the architect and the other members of the construction team are often looking at the lifecycle of the building, while the lifecycle of capital does not necessarily match up.

If I had to define capital, I would describe it as three buckets. The first two buckets are, of course, debt. As National Sales Performance Executive for Commercial Real Estate Banking at Bank of America, I represent principally debt. This is typically what financial institutions provide. An alternative bucket is the permanent finance market typically provided by a Life Company, Bank of America Conduit and others. The third bucket is equity. It is, of course, the building owners and the people who share the vision of the real estate who influence the decisions that can lead to sustainable development.

The good news from the debt perspective is that we are not really your enemy. We do not look negatively at sustainable development. Many institutions feel the need to remain neutral, but market perception often has us as the enemy of progress. This is not a plot against the design community; if you look at the short- and long-term buckets of debt capital (the primary source of development funds and the dynamics of the business we operate in), we have certain requirements and certain reasons for getting the money back within a certain time frame. These requirements can impact our analysis when we take into account multiple year payback periods on investments. Sometimes sustainable development returns may not be monetary. They may be expressed in terms of user efficiency or productivity for the occupant. Since we cannot collect a direct return on these phenomena, we cannot reward the people who have in turn invested in us. This is the central dichotomy of the issue.

So how do we deal with change? At the moment we are in a phase of incremental change so the pioneering work – the risk – will need to take place in the equity bucket. As the owners control that bucket, so they control their own destiny and the destiny of sustainable development.

The next phase of the challenge will be to "commoditize" the sustainable technologies and techniques that are being discussed in this volume. Once these technologies are proven to be successful, the more risk-averse capital investors will feel safe entering into that environment because it will feel like a level playing field for all types of development. The model I am talking about is evolutionary. There are also certain steps that can be taken to speed up this evolution. For example,

municipalities may encourage or, going further, stipulate that certain measures must be adopted.

In closing, I would like to qualify my earlier statement that all capital is neutral. This is not always the case. Currently the most aggressive capital that is non-neutral is oriented around socio-economically sustainable development. I have a personal interest in this area, as does Bank of America. The bank is highly regarded for this work both by our communities and our regulators. We take great pride in the work we do to revitalize rather than gentrify the neighborhoods where we serve. Our challenge together is to find out how we can link the socio-economic aspects of development with the environmental benefits and still satisfy the requirements of debt capital.

The Developer's Perspective

Steven Ott

It is important to look at the issue of sustainability from a developer's perspective; a developer's first priority is to satisfy his/her capital providers. Nothing gets done without the flow of money into a project; architects and engineers cannot be paid if there is no capital, so finance is the lifeblood of the business. The largest issue associated with sustainable design is that capital providers want to see the evidence of a development's viability before they commit their money to the project. Justifiably, they want to be convinced that sustainable design will provide benefits; they want to know where those benefits are coming from; they want to know how that will add value to the building, and they want to see how those benefits are measured. Unfortunately, it is sometimes difficult to measure some benefits such as the increased productivity of a workforce. In some cases even the factors that can be measured sometimes take a number of years before the kind of time-series data can be produced that will provide enough evidence for capital providers to feel comfortable with a particular type of development. Therefore, capital providers are generally skeptical and a difficult group to convince to be pioneers or champions of a new methodology.

Although it might not be possible to convince all of the banks all the time, when it comes to implementing cutting edge technologies there are some other strategies that can be adopted to encourage the implementation of sustainable projects. For example, a committed developer might be able to convince the equity holders to take a certain level of risk and to be a pioneer. With enough supportive equity holders, one of the large banks, such as Bank of America, will probably not worry too much about their position because they are always in the first position to get their money back. If the bank has enough equity in a project, they will be comfortable even though the project is unproven.

There are some creative developers and we certainly could do with more of them. Some developers are willing to be pioneers but they generally only do this if they have their own capital. Sometimes developers are wealthy enough to roll the dice on something they really believe in. As Michael Harrison of Hines mentioned in Chapter 12, some corporations have the advantage of a corporate purse to realize their own particular vision in the form of a headquarters building that goes beyond the norm.

Some creative developers would love to have the level playing field that Brad Smith mentioned so that everybody would have to create sustainable buildings. If the market were to be regulated in some way in terms of sustainability, creative developers would become interested in sustainability. Their attitude would be: "I can compete in that market. If everybody has to do what I have to do, I can do it better than they can." At the moment, developers compete at the level of the lowest common denominator because that is the easiest option; it is what the market knows and is ready to finance. However, it is important to realize that even the creative developers who would be willing to work with regulations that promote sustainable design would ask themselves how those regulations will affect their existing portfolio of buildings.

Developers will engage in sustainable design if they know that by its inclusion they will achieve good rental rates. If tenants can be convinced that a building that includes sustainable features is a better building; that the tenant will increase productivity; that they will save operating costs, then the market will demand higher rents. If this happens, then we will eventually see more sustainable buildings being built, however, this will not happen to any great extent until the data confirm the economic benefits of sustainability.

Q&A Discussion

STEVEN OTT: Brad, when a developer approaches a financier like you with a proposal for a cutting edge, sustainable design what is your first reaction?

BRAD SMITH: From my perspective, as a banker or as a provider of capital, it is actually very exciting to be associated with projects that seek to do something innovative for a community. As an example of just such a project in Charlotte, I was delighted to be involved in Gateway Village on Trade Street. This project was a first step in the direction of some of the sustainable approaches that we are talking about today. It was gratifying to be part of the team that put that development together.

The main questions that the banker would ask are: "Will people pay for it? Will it prove itself in the marketplace? Can you convince me that this is a superior product that will attract a superior, or at least equal, return on the investment?"

There are priorities that the first tier provider of capital has to keep in mind. Typically, in a large project, we have a time frame of between three to five years for the return on our debt instrument. We therefore analyze that first risk on a project by asking: "What if it doesn't work as planned?" In a good relationship, we get together with the developer and his design team and examine the project, the schedules and the paybacks in great detail. We try to determine, based on the pre-leasing levels and other market indicators, whether tenants are really interested in leasing the property as designed. A fair amount of analysis and risk evaluation takes place. Then comes the delicate art of assembling all the resources and capital that are required to deliver the project. As a short-term provider of capital, we also monitor the appetites of the long-term providers of debt capital. Although they generally have the luxury of established project history, their views are important because we have projects where their investment interests will be in several years. We have to make sure there is a reasonable progression so our capital can exit and be replaced in an orderly manner.

STEVEN OTT: If at the end of a conversation with a developer or architect you remain skeptical about working with them on a unique or cutting edge project, what would make you feel more comfortable?

BRAD SMITH: It is important to understand their financial capabilities. Ultimately, their practical sponsorship can say the most about a developer. Also, the experience of the design team can provide a good indication of the possible success of a project. However, one must bear in mind the fact that the experience of designing and building sustainable buildings is not currently extensive. But we generally look for a credible track record and financial stability. We may take a calculated risk, but we need to be reassured that we can retrieve our capital from the project in the future. We also need to recognize that there is a possibility that the development economics may not always work out in the future as everyone had anticipated.

Part of the due diligence considerations that we go through in our preparatory work has to do with the contractor–architect team. We need to reassure ourselves that all parties in the team are comfortable with each other and that they are capable of producing what they propose. Finally, three factors (the sponsorship, the teams, and how they are made up) are carefully balanced as we make the decision whether to proceed. We start our work from hard facts, but often it is the experience and integrity of the professional that play a significant role in developing cutting edge projects.

STEVEN OTT: Chris, sustainable design is promoted as offering a number of benefits; could you tell us about those benefits and where they come from?

CHRIS HAYS: This is a very broad subject since there are a huge number of benefits; the various forms of sustainability have been amply demonstrated. The two major benefits are the economic benefits that I mentioned earlier and the psychological benefits that are considerable since they affect the productivity of employees. A productivity study was undertaken for the Herman Miller project referred to above by Judith Heerwagan. She carried out a detailed study that demonstrated a significant increase in productivity as a result of the architectural design solution we implemented.

The psychological benefits work on a number of levels. In our own post-occupancy feedback we hear about a general level of health and well-being; employees feel that their employer cares deeply about them and wants them to be in a safe and healthy place and as a result generally they feel better and perform better. There is generally a reduced level of absenteeism and a high level of staff retention. Gap actually turned their new building into an employee-recruitment tool. Even though their headquarters were in San Francisco, they placed their Human Resources division in San Bruno and used that facility to attract people to come to work for them.

BRAD SMITH: One should remember that investors are cautious people. This was very well demonstrated in the case of mixed-use developments. Twelve or more years ago there were only a small number of developers and capital investors who were prepared to take a risk on mixed-use, high-density development in the United States. The slow accumulation of projects which have held or gained in value over the years has shown the viability of these properties. The successful attraction of second- and third-generation users has convinced today's intermediate and long-term capital providers to be more confident in contemplating mixed-use development. In the last couple of years, we have also seen a renewed interest in Transit Oriented Development. This demonstrates that the gradual exposure and ongoing success of such projects will chip away at the skepticism and reluctance to try new types of development.

There are probably only two ways that the pace of innovation can be accelerated. The first is through continued entrepreneurial and visionary leadership by developers who share the design teams' objectives. These people have the power to make progressive, executive decisions. The second way is through space end-users who have deeper pockets, longer-term perspectives, and appreciate the opportunity to make a philosophical as well as economic statement in the marketplace. The responsibility of the design team and the researchers is to collect and analyze data from the building users and to present it to potential clients in a clear, unambiguous format. This type of evidence is always useful in convincing future space owners/users of the viability of a proposal, especially if it is an innovative one. Data such as operating costs, rents, evaluations, the history of a building, and the returns are all helpful, irrespective of whether they come from Canada or Europe.

The benefits aside, there can be a significant challenge for the long-term equity providers. Even if they believe in the product and its benefits, buy into a development and take on the role of pioneers, there are limited mechanisms for them to maintain their "first move" advantage. In other industries, patents offer some protection and allow a period of exclusivity during which the risk taker can reap the financial benefits of their investment; there are limited protections for real estate and the competition can move quickly to duplicate a successful development.

High Performance Building Envelopes

John Breshears, Christoph Ingenhoven and Kenneth Yeang

14

Editor's Introduction

Chris Grech

The recent dramatic fluctuations in energy prices and the unprecedented large-scale power outages that hit a number of North American and European cities have demonstrated with alarming effect the dependence of our technologically advanced society on a precious resource that many of us habitually take for granted. The geopolitical implications of this dependence are clear to see and worrisome to speculate about. Building construction, use and maintenance generally consume between one half and two-thirds of national energy production in the developed countries. These figures generate a huge responsibility for architects to assume if we are to consider that a large proportion of the energy we consume is non-renewable.

The three architects who participate in this chapter – John Breshears, Christoph Ingenhoven and Kenneth Yeang – take their responsibilities seriously. Christoph Ingenhoven and Kenneth Yeang outline the ways they are addressing themes of energy conservation and sustainable construction in Chapters 9 and 11, respectively. This chapter takes a closer look at the particular issues posed by our climate in the South-east United States. John Breshears is an Associate Partner at the Zimmer Gunsul Frasca Partnership in Portland, Oregon, who has worked for more than 14 years in the design and engineering of buildings. He has pursued lines of research into non-traditional solutions to architectural problems, particularly aspects of bio-mimetic design. Christoph Ingenhoven will bring his well-articulated European perspective to bear on our regional climate. Finally we feature Kenneth Yeang who for the last thirty years has been researching into and designing buildings and master plans that are ecologically sustainable.

Respiration and Transpiration: Building Envelopes in a Humid Environment

John Breshears

This project was initiated in 1994 when I was awarded a research grant established by Ove Arup and Partners to honor the memory of Peter Rice, one of the UK's most inspired structural engineers. Rice died in 1992, the same year that he was awarded the Royal Gold Medal by the Royal Institute of British Architects and this award was intended to promote original thinking and research in building design and engineering.

The basis for my research was to look to biology and medical technology for non-traditional solutions to architectural problems. Once I had received the award and started to discuss my area of interest, I encountered the following reaction: "Because your background is in mechanical engineering, why don't you look for a way to reduce energy consumption in air conditioning systems?" "Fine," I said, not realizing just how difficult this would be to achieve.

I started by thinking about the ways one can deal with moisture in the environment so looked at the way moisture, i.e. humidity, diffuses through the air as well as the ways it can be absorbed or adsorbed by certain solids such as desiccants. Traditionally in building systems we remove water from the air by turning it into a liquid (condensation) and so that it drops out of the mixture. If you think about a typical separation process in the chemical industry you would probably come up with distillation, which is a similar principle. These phase-change separation processes are very energy-intensive, and so I wanted to examine whether there were any low-energy ways of achieving the same ends.

I started by talking to the good people at GORE-TEX®, and asked them, "So what is a breathable fabric anyway?" They weren't about to tell me anything about their proprietary secrets. After a long and fairly futile conversation with a gentleman there, I was about to hang up the phone, when he said: "You know, you should really speak to someone in our surgical implants department." His comment stopped me in my tracks because I thought that their business was outdoor clothing and tent fabrics. Well, if you go to the GORE-TEX® webpage today, you will see that they offer a whole line of medical and surgical products.

Figure 14.1 is a diagrammatic representation of how a GORE-TEX® "breathable" fabric works; it's a micro-porous membrane, meaning that it has tiny holes in it so that a molecule of gas or water vapor, vibrating its way along, could pass through one of those holes whereas liquid water would be blocked. When we are referring to clothing, we can think of perspiration as molecules of vapor, and they would be able to pass through the

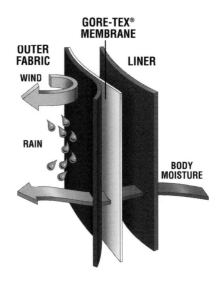

14.1 Micro-porous "breathable" GORE-TEX® fabric

pores in the GORE-TEX® and migrate away from the body. A droplet of rain, by contrast, is a liquid and can form itself into a sphere only so small, as defined by the physics of surface tension. It would be too big to pass through the pores in this "breathable" fabric. So, the first generation of GORE-TEX® was *phase-selective* but not *compound-selective*, meaning that it would separate a liquid from a gas, but it would not separate two gases, i.e. it would not separate air from water vapor.

I got in touch with the surgical implant specialists at GORE-TEX® and found out that they were actually making a series of items that could be implanted into the body. They were making them out of nonporous polymer compounds and they were tailoring them so that certain compounds could actually permeate through them and other compounds could not, which was very interesting. Permeation is a chemical process, as opposed to the mechanical process of the micro-porous membrane described above. I talked with the membrane industry and asked: "Can you develop a membrane that is very highly permeable to water vapor and very impermeable to air?" They said, "Yes, that's possible. We usually get asked to deal with much more exotic and toxic substances. Dealing with air and water is a relatively simple thing."

If you look at the natural world, you will find that nature is ripe with examples of selectively permeable membranes. Plants present excellent examples: they pull moisture through their root systems in the ground and force it up to their leaves where it is transpired through their stomata. At the same time they are extracting the nutrients from the water across selectively permeable membranes into the cells that use them. There is an appropriate natural example of a selectively permeable membrane very close to home: Figure 14.2 shows an artist's rendering of the surface of the human lung. The human lung uses selectively permeable membranes in its surface to exchange oxygen from the air in the lung into the bloodstream and carbon dioxide out of the bloodstream back into the lung, and that is what we know as respiration.

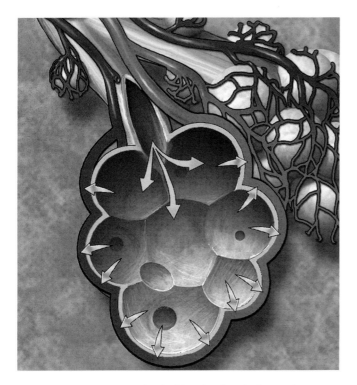

14.2 Gas exchange at the level of the alveoli in the human lung

We worked out a series of equations for the physics that describes two streams of air, one very cool and dry, one very hot and moist, moving in opposite directions on either side of a selectively permeable membrane, to find out how much heat and how much moisture would move between the two streams. This mathematical model showed us, as you might expect, that heat exchange (energy) moves across relatively quickly compared with moisture (mass); in fact, the moisture moves across the membrane very slowly. In the chemical industry, they combat this problem by operating at a very high pressure since pressurizing a gas stream forces the moisture to permeate the membrane very quickly. Of course, in a building application, we generally don't want to do that; you could very quickly use up any potential energy savings due to the extra fan power required to operate at high pressure.

We tried to figure out how to operate at low pressure and still make this work. The answer seemed to be to create a very, very large surface area for exchange so the gas would have plenty of time to get across before it moved away from the surface. The idea that suggested itself was to take an already available, very large surface on the building – the building façade – and make this exchange happen there. That is essentially how this got to be a building envelope project.

Figures 14.3a and 14.3b show two conceptual diagrams. In each case we have a ventilated triple façade; two cavities separated by a selectively permeable membrane. In the first illustration we have a hot and humid supply air stream coming down one of the cavities. This air is then drawn into the underfloor system and mixed with the very cool dry return air system. The air that is then exhausted out of the building goes up the outer cavity before venting to the outside. In the process they exchange their heat and moisture across the membrane.

That was the concept. Being an engineer working at an engineering firm, I wanted to prove this and to determine whether it would really work, and if so, how well? Figures 14.3a and 14.3b show sectional diagrams of our proposal with a computational fluid dynamics analysis overlaid onto it. Computational fluid dynamics is a very sophisticated way of modeling fluids to simulate the way they flow and the way they transfer heat and moisture.

Figure 14.3a shows the temperature distribution in the two airstreams, while Figure 14.3b shows moisture distribution. The

a

STAR
CD
PROSTAR 2.30

08-Jan-97
TEMPERATURE
ABSOLUTE
KELVIN
ITER= 199
LOCAL MX= 307.1
LOCAL MN= 293.2

307.1
306.5
305.8
304.6
303.9
303.3
302.6
302.0
301.4
300.7
300.1
299.4
298.8
298.2

b

STAR
CD
PROSTAR 2.30

08-Jan-97
SC 1-steam

ITER= 199
LOCAL MX= 0.2799E-01
LOCAL MN= 0.1001E-01

0.2799E-01
0.2671E-01
0.2542E-01
0.2414E-01
0.2285E-01
0.2157E-01
0.2028E-01
0.1900E-01
0.1771E-01
0.1643E-01
0.1514E-01
0.1386E-01
0.1257E-01
0.1001E-01

14.3 Computational Fluid Dynamics Study: (a) temperature; (b) humidity

legends on the right indicate the levels of these parameters. Heat exchange between the airstreams is seen in the temperature diagram. The darker arrow at the bottom symbolizes the warm airstream entering into the channel on the left (outer) side of the membrane. It cools as it moves up the channel, and by the time it gets to the top and enters the building it has reached a temperature which is almost equal to the entrance temperature of the relief air stream. The relief air stream, symbolized by the arrow entering the system at the upper right enters the channel on the right (inner) side of the membrane at the upper right. As it moves down the channel, it begins to warm, soaking up the heat from the opposing airstream, and it almost reaches the intake temperature by the time it comes out. The extent to which the temperature of the two airstreams changes within the system suggests that it is a very efficient heat exchanger. Figure 14.3b represents the moisture exchange. You can see that the system is less efficient at exchanging moisture between the two streams because there is not as great a range in each stream as there is in the temperature diagram but nonetheless the streams are exchanging moisture across the membrane.

We constructed a small bench-scale experimental mock-up of the envelope in collaboration with the Department of Mechanical Engineering at University College London; into this model we installed a piece of membrane that had the right permeability and hooked the frame up to a couple of air conditioners and measured what happened. The active layers of these membranes are extremely thin; they consist of polymer coatings deposited on a supporting matrix that, in this case, happens to be opaque.

Figure 14.4 shows that we actually achieved a reasonably good agreement between the analytical measurements and the experimental data. These results gave us confidence that this concept could be made to work. What we also figured out from this test was that we needed to increase the surface area of membrane; we needed to get more transfer happening in this space. If we were just talking about heat, we could have put fins on this membrane to increase the surface area for heat transfer. This would not work in our case because we needed to have gas immediately on either side of the membrane so the vapor could transfer directly across it.

We began looking at the work of fashion designers such as Issey Miyake and his protégés who were coming up with

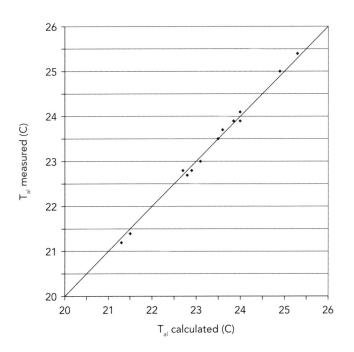

14.4 Graph showing theoretical and actual results of the study

14.5 Fabric from a study for "Pollen Project" by Kei Ito

amazingly beautiful creations using wonderfully pleated surfaces. In fact, what these folded surfaces are doing is creating a very high surface-to-volume ratio (Figure 14.5). We started looking at these fabrics and asked the manufacturers if we could apply the active coating to the thin diaphanous supporting layer instead of this heavy rigid stuff. They said, "Sure, we can do that." We had this idea that we could use very delicate fabrics so we went to a fashion designer in London and worked on different ways to pleat fabrics to create very dense surface-to-volume ratios.

Development of this system has continued since the completion of the original research award. With support from the Charles and Anne Morrow Lindbergh Foundation, we have refined some of the mathematics. We have also been talking with some curtain wall manufacturers and researchers at some of the national laboratories about prototyping and testing a full-scale version of this idea.

In summary, the concept is this: in a humid climate, it may be possible to gain a double benefit from a triple-skin façade

where the middle layer is a very thin, diaphanous lung surface that allows heat and moisture – but not air – to move across it. This could help manage ventilation loads through a sort of enthalpy recovery. At the same time, this system might confer some of the benefits of a traditional double-skin ventilated façade system by decreasing envelope loads, increasing the interior comfort, and allowing greater daylight into the building without the attendant heat gain. There are still many unanswered questions about this idea, and we are anxious to build a full-scale prototype.

Our hope is that this system could offer a way to make our buildings use less energy and still produce the comfort levels that people seem to be demanding. As architects and engineers we are fond of talking about buildings that breathe – that is, buildings that move volumes of air into and out of themselves. We all know that moving air into and out of the lungs is really only a part of the true respiration process. It is a means to the end of actually exchanging carbon dioxide and oxygen into and out of the bloodstream across the lung's surface. We are hopeful that this idea, if it someday comes into practice, could perhaps bring us a step closer to truly breathing and respiring buildings (Figure 14.6).

Alternative Solutions

Christoph Ingenhoven

Whatever we do as an architectural practice, we do it to save energy. When we talk about energy we generally mean energy that is generated from oil or out of waterpower, and that's more or less it. The use of coal is shrinking in most countries. Fossil fuels are not endless; however, waterpower and solar energy are more or less endless. So when we talk about saving energy, we are referring to a drastic reduction in non-renewable energy sources such as oil.

If you look at the total energy used in creating and maintaining buildings in Germany, for example, it is 50 percent of the total energy used in that country. In America, it is more, it is approximately two-thirds. In both cases these are large percentages and the different proportions demonstrate various cultural attitudes to comfort and climate. In the southern states of the USA, there is quite a high level of humidity during the summer months. The climate in Charlotte, North Carolina, is similar to Southern Europe or areas of Asia like Hong Kong, Shanghai, or Malaysia, where the issues of humidity and high temperatures are serious. All the systems I discussed in Chapter 9 and all our practice's experience come from mid-European continental experience. This means that for 80–100 percent of the year we can solve problems with the internal environment by opening a window or providing some shading; when this is not sufficient we can add a little bit of cooling. So, when I visit a region with a different climate, my first thought is to ask whether the climate is a year-round problem. If it is only a problem for part of the year, then the problematic period should not dictate

the solution to be applied throughout the year. A more sustainable approach should lead to a solution for just the problem period.

I am very interested in vernacular architecture; going to a purely technology-driven solution might be interesting, however, if you look back a few years, a few dozen years or a few hundred years, you will find simple passive solutions that have been consistently successful. Take the window, for example: for hundreds of years we have used openable windows, so why should we change that now? If you look at the vernacular architecture of the southern states of the USA, you will not see air conditioning; instead you will see shading systems such as porches and verandas. You will see people employing those features successfully: shading their houses; not having large windows; looking for some wind and using intelligently located openings on opposite sides of the house to let air in from the cooler side of the house allowing light breezes to flow through a house. The same passive systems can be found in Southern Europe. Thus, 100 percent of all vernacular architecture works quite well and people are satisfied with their homes.

The problem occurs when the environment is hot and humid, however, is it right to solve the problem with high-end technology solutions or are there other ways? I would like to suggest some alternatives. The first is the effective use of sun shading. If wind pressure doesn't present a problem, you can do away with a double skin and use a single skin with an external shading system. Openable windows are very important for everybody. They are what we used to do for generations; just open the window and you will feel better. It is very much about the way you feel and not just what you can measure. Experiments show that even if people open a window and let high temperature air in they will feel better. This may seem strange but it's also true; the data show this to be the case.

Another low-energy solution is to use the thermal mass inherent in a structure, which means, for example, no suspended ceilings or raised floors so that the maximum benefit of the structure is achieved through its exposure to the circulating internal air. In this case concrete structures are preferable to steel structures as they have a higher thermal mass. Everybody who lives near a lake knows that the climate near the lake is milder close to the lake than it is 10 km (6.2 miles) away; this is due to the thermal mass of the lake that absorbs the ambient heat. If you have one big thermal mass in every building, i.e. a concrete structure and you cover it behind raised floors and suspended ceilings, it is no longer active, so that is inefficient. The thermal mass will also be more effective if the floor-to-floor heights are reduced since a smaller volume of air will need to be conditioned.

One other thing to think about: if the nights are cooler than the days and the lower the air temperature the less humidity it carries, so it would be very useful to consider night-time cooling. Automated windows and a system of ductwork can draw in the cooler night air to reduce the temperature of the structure and utilize the thermal mass of, say, a concrete structure to reduce the day-time temperatures by absorbing the energy generated during the day.

The next logical step is to activate the thermal mass by casting small air ducts into the concrete slab. This renders the thermal mass of the structure much more efficient and will lead to smaller service cores; this in turn reduces the non-usable floor area which leads to a reduction in the area of centrally planned mechanical rooms. The other great benefit of this strategy results in much healthier cooling and heating systems because it does not use just the air, which is an inefficient medium, it also uses the surface area of the structure. Using this system can lead to reductions from six, seven, eight, or even ten air changes per hour down to about two, which is all that is necessary for healthy breathing. Cooling by forced air requires another six or so air changes because air on its own is an inefficient medium; water, for example, is four times more efficient. The use of water leads naturally to a low-end technology solution for harnessing the inherent temperature of ground water, generally at temperatures around 61–64° F (16–18° C), to act as a heat source in winter and a cooling medium in the summer. Even without groundwater, you can bury the pipes in the ground because the ground itself, if you go down 10–12 m (30–40 ft), has a constant temperature of about 16–18° C.

All these issues and many more show that it is possible to substantially reduce the energy used in buildings without incorporating high-end technologies in the façades. If the problem of humidity remains, it is important to ascertain precisely how long that problem persists. If it exists, for example, for eight weeks I would suggest you introduce a four-week holiday. This is quite normal in Europe; if you look at France and Italy, it's not a joke, they take national holidays for four weeks, generally in the hottest month of August. In these cases, nearly everybody leaves the city and heads for the cooler coasts, and that is a very clever method of reducing energy use in summer. What we tend to do is keep working; no computer could do that, when they get too hot, they quit. A four-week holiday is a healthy step as well as being good for the environment. For the other four weeks, you would close a window; that is acceptable too because ideally one would have a very small and efficient cooling, heating, and ventilating system that would provide adequate working conditions.

This whole issue of saving energy involves two other important issues: the cost of energy, and the cultural expectations of the building users. First, I think that the price of energy in the USA is much too low. In fact, even in Germany, where energy prices are two to three times more than in the States, they are too low to justify the use of the highly efficient technologies that are available today. The second issue is whether it is tolerable to live in a house or work in an office that gets a little bit warmer than the normal average standard. Apart from the issue of comfort I believe that it is unhealthy to occupy spaces in which the temperature difference between inside and outside is greater than, say, 10 ° F (6° C). I think that greater tolerance would make it much easier to deal with internal temperatures and energy saving. We should be adjusting ourselves to greater not less tolerance.

A New Ecological Aesthetic

Kenneth Yeang

I like John Breshear's approach, which is to try to find solutions from nature. His approach is referred to as biomimicry where the use of biological analogies is based on the principle that nature is so much better a designer than we are. If we look into biological systems, we can actually discover a lot of things that could be useful to us as human beings. Essentially John's design is a triple-skin façade in which the middle skin is a membrane and the analogy with the lung, I think, is a great idea. What Christoph is saying in a very polite way is that John might be using a sledgehammer to crack a nut. It doesn't invalidate what he is doing, and it is an interesting experiment that is worth developing. What Christoph means is that having passed the air through the two layers, when it enters the building, it will still need some sort of mechanical system to bring the humidity to an acceptable level. While John is designing a triple-skin façade as a low energy system, Christoph is asking whether it is worthwhile devoting so much technology on a system that covers the entire façade just to reduce the level of humidity. John might want to consider removing the glass and just developing the membrane itself to see what develops in designing a membrane that solves the following: keeping out the rain; letting air through; adding some insulation; reducing humidity and being able to see through it. If all these requirements can be achieved, I believe this would be a viable technology.

In trying to create a comfortable environment we should look at the issue holistically as demonstrated in Chapter 11 of this volume; we should look at the problem not just in terms of enclosure but also in terms of the different modes of creating conditions of comfort. As I mentioned in Chapter 11, there is *Passive Mode* where improved comfort conditions are created without any mechanical or electrical systems; as Christoph Ingenhoven mentioned earlier, examples of these native or vernacular dwellings can be found in any country; *Mixed Mode* includes some mechanical and electrical systems; *Full Mode* would be totally mechanically and/or electrically driven; *Productive Mode* would cover buildings that could generate their own energy, and *Composite Mode* would be a combination of all of the above. It is necessary to work

progressively through each of these modes before completing the design.

Charlotte, North Carolina, at a latitude of about 35 degrees and a longitude of 80 can be categorized as having a "warm-temperate" climate in what is also called the *Overheated Zone*, i.e. the worst of both worlds: cold winters, hot summers and a mid-seasons (Spring and Fall) in between. So, let us consider what action we might have to take to moderate this environment. The *Passive Mode* here would necessitate shaping the building appropriately, thinking about orientation, façade

Editt Tower

14.7 EDITT Tower project, Singapore

design, the use of building color and natural ventilation. By considering these strategies it would be possible to improve the comfort conditions a little bit in the winter and the summer. *Mixed Mode* would entail the moves mentioned above as well as some partial mechanical systems like ceiling fans to improve the comfort conditions further in the summer. However, neither the *Passive Mode* nor *Mixed Mode* could ever compete with *Full Mode*. Thinking that the equivalent comfort conditions could be achieved using only low-energy devices is a dream; I don't think it's possible.

Since our practice is interested in the different options for achieving comfort conditions we have investigated a variety of different *Passive Mode* systems. For instance, the building shape relative to the sun path in that locality, building orientation, building color, the type of façade, the ratio of solid to glass areas, solar control devices can all be helpful passive moves. Early in the design of large buildings we always examine the building shape; when appropriate, we try to use lift cores as buffers between the hot parts of the building and the heat-sensitive areas as a means of reducing energy consumption.

A particularly sustainable strategy is to use vegetation which helps us in three ways: by increasing biodiversity; by creating healthier buildings because vegetation absorbs carbon dioxide and carbon monoxide and gives off oxygen through photosynthesis; through evapo-transpiration which lowers the ambient temperature which in turn lowers the air-conditioning requirements of the building. Figure 14.7 shows a building in which we located the vegetation on the hot parts of the building, i.e. the balconies. This is a concept that I am preoccupied with at the moment. The visual result is unusual, however, it is like a "new" architecture and I believe strongly that by looking at a building's ecosystems we can develop a new value-system of aesthetics; a new ecological aesthetic.

The prevailing winds of a locality can also be used to help cool a building and thus reduce the air conditioning load. We sought to achieve precisely this effect at the recently completed National Library Building in Singapore (Figure 14.8). Here we designed a building that uses 170 kWh/m²/yr (53,923 Btu/ft²/yr), as compared to a typical office building that uses 230 kWh/m²/yr (72,955 Btu/ft²/yr). This is a very favorable comparison when one takes into consideration that the air conditioning in the library is on 24 hours a day, 7 days a week.

14.8 National Library in Singapore, external view

14.9 IBM Plaza, Kuala Lumpur, general view

Low-energy design can also be achieved by considering the building configuration, as mentioned earlier. Figures 14.9 and 14.10 show the second building we designed for IBM, where we looked at the sun path for the locality to determine how this would affect the design. Since this building is on the equator the

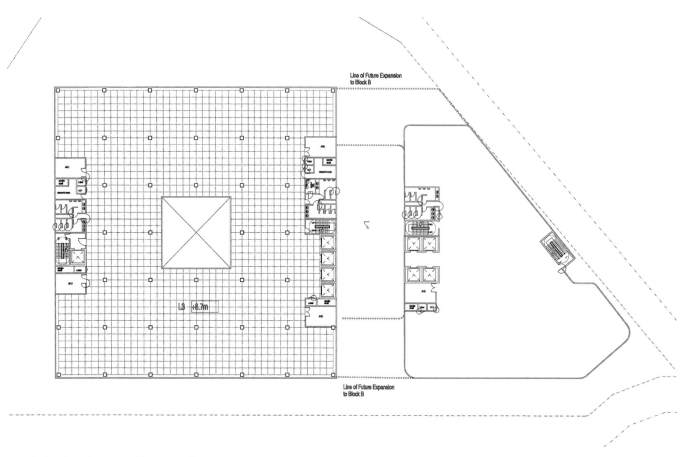

14.10 IBM building, typical floor plan illustrating location of service cores

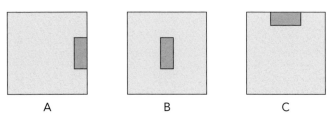

A   B   C

14.11 Service core options

sun-path is almost directly east–west. We used the perimeter lift core as a buffer between the inside and the outside. As a comparative exercise Figure 14.11 shows three possible options: the first one shows the building as built with the lift core on the right-hand side, i.e. between the hot side and east side. Option two is what happens if the cores are in the middle; the third option is what happens when the cores are on the north. We evaluated them using the Overall Thermal Transmission Value (OTTV) as a comparative index. For the first option, the OTTV = 43.3 W/m^2 (13.7 Btu/h/ft^2), the second the OTTV = 47.5 W/m^2, (15 Btu/h/ft^2) and the third the OTTV = 47.6 W/m^2 (15.1 Btu/h/ft^2). Clearly, the first option gives us the best value, which is why we implemented that option. This exercise demonstrates clearly that if you want to design a low-energy building, then the

first stage is to optimize all the *Passive Mode* strategies by designing the most suitable building shape and the most appropriate orientation. If a building isn't configured appropriately in the first instance, then mechanical and/or electrical systems will need to be added to cool it or to heat it which makes total nonsense of low energy design logic. Strategically, the *Passive Mode* design should be optimized before addressing the *Mixed Mode* and then the *Full Mode* design.

It should be clear that both Christoph Ingenhoven and I agree that there are a variety of ways in which tried and tested strategies and passive technologies can be incorporated into building designs to lower the ambient temperature and to create conditions of comfort, however, the degree of acceptance and therefore success of these moves will be determined by the extent to which the building users recognize that it is lifestyle issues that are really the key here. If one is prepared to wear warmer clothes in winter and lighter clothes in summer, then obviously the amount of air conditioning can be reduced and the environmental conditions can be relaxed beyond those recommended by, say, ASHRAE. If folks are prepared to expect hotter summer and cooler winter internal environments, then we can work on extending the mid-seasons which will lead us towards a low energy situation that is, I believe, our ultimate objective.

Information Technology and Building Infrastructure

Wolfgang Wagener, Jupp Gauchel and Matthew Spathas

Editor's Introduction

Chris Grech

We have all heard a great deal about the way that information technology is transforming our lives generally; both at work and during our leisure hours. In many cases this transformation is leading to a convergence of work and leisure that is having a marked effect on the architecture of office buildings; the blurring of these boundaries can generally be witnessed by the increasingly informal work environments that include open plan as opposed to cellular office spaces, and lounge areas or coffee bars that double up as meeting points with facilities for electronic presentations. The technology that facilitates many of these "front of house" transformations has to be accommodated in a discrete and flexible manner behind the scenes; the contributors to this chapter will outline some strategic approaches to the task of integrating emerging information technologies with the building infrastructure in a seamless manner that will provide benefits to both user and owner.

Wolfgang Wagener of Cisco Systems is an architect; his primary area of expertise is working with occupiers, developers and property owners to deliver innovative real estate and technology solutions. Jupp Gauchel is also an architect and he explores how computers can be incorporated into architecture. Matthew Spathas is a Partner at Sentre Partners and is responsible for investment acquisitions and value-added strategies. He has over 20 years of real estate experience, having acquired, developed, managed, or facilitated an excess of $800,000 of real estate transactions.

Building and Technology Integration

Wolfgang Wagener

The integration of technology and buildings is something that, as an architect, I find very stimulating. What brings us three contributors together is that we approach this opportunity from an architectural as well as a business perspective. Therefore we are familiar with the issues related to the entire real estate lifecycle. We are not "techies," or IT experts. We share a passion for technology that is derived from the realization that technology has had a significant impact on our day-to-day lives; in the jobs we do; in how we deliver our services and how we design, build and operate buildings.

We identified four major areas in which technology is having a significant impact on what we do; the first is in the way technology affects our business processes as building and real estate professionals. The second is how the workplace is changing; how the use of space is changing dramatically through the availability of communication technology. Third, how the information technology network is becoming part of the base building infrastructure. The fourth is how technology can increase building performance by making the building safer, more comfortable and more energy-efficient.

As an introduction, I would like to give a very brief overview of Cisco Systems. We are the worldwide leader in networking for the Internet; networks are an essential part of business, education, government and home communications, and Cisco Internet Protocol-based (IP) networking solutions are the foundation of these networks. We are based in San Jose, California, and are operating in 90 countries. Our real estate portfolio includes office, research and development environments for approximately 40,000 people in 16 million sq ft (1.5 million sq m) of space. We occupy about four hundred buildings; about 80 percent of our portfolio is leased. Our core holdings are in the United States. We are a knowledge-based company that looks very carefully at our office space. The culture at Cisco is about innovation, creativity, embracing change, collaboration and working together cross-functionally. As a corporate real estate organization we are in the unique position of being able to treat our entire real estate portfolio as a laboratory for innovative technology and real estate solutions.

Cisco has another focus that is unique for a real estate organization; we partner with Cisco's core business to develop technology solutions for the real estate and construction industries.

My primary message is that we have to re-think building use and the building infrastructure. Most of us use the Internet at work and at home and most of us have broadband high speed connectivity; about half are using it through wireless connection; some of us also use Voice Over Internet Protocol (VOIP) where we can make telephone calls over the Internet. The point I want to make is that the network is already ubiquitous and information technology is evolving very fast which makes it difficult to think too far ahead. Yet we need to bear in mind that this technology is becoming seamless, robust, and most importantly it is becoming increasingly user-friendly. The challenge for us as building professionals is how to incorporate this technology into buildings.

How does technology impact the workplace? The typical North American office is generally laid out in a series of cubicles designed for individual productivity. Some 70 percent of the space is planned for individual work and 30 percent as collaborative space.

We have just completed a "proof of concept" project at Cisco Headquarters in San Jose where we came up with a radical change to our office layout (Figures 15.1 and 15.2). First, we turned the office design on its head by taking advantage of the new user mobility inside and outside our buildings. Then we asked the question: why do we come to the office at all? From a technology infrastructure point of view, it is no longer necessary to go to the office for individual work. However, it is today even more important because work is about people, it is about face-to-face communication, it is about getting together to collaborate. We could work by communicating online, but it wouldn't be as effective as meeting in person and collaborating in groups.

Our workplace solution in San Jose is to do away with individual offices; instead we have created a single space which provides a shared environment. It is not a traditional open plan either; we have provided a variety of settings that are designed to support collaborative work. Private spaces within the shared space facilitate both small and large groups. These areas are selected on a first come first serve basis where people select the space they need to perform certain tasks. Conceptually we have created something very different. We completed this set-up only recently; it is up and running but we have not had the opportunity to evaluate user satisfaction or improvements in productivity.

Historically you came to an office looking for your cubicle; you individualized the space and could say "This is my office." What you get today is a space that looks more like your home; you have a living room, a bedroom, a kitchen, etc. and you can experience the whole space designed for your varying needs.

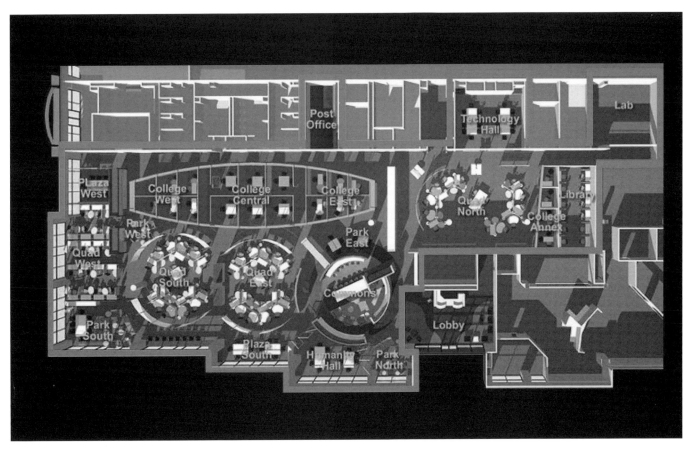

15.1 Connected Workplace layout, Cisco Headquarters, San José

15.2 Connected Workplace interior view, Cisco Headquarters, San José

In addition to the environmental change we have introduced a cultural change; we have instituted change management; we encourage more collaboration and this generally leads to higher productivity and greater satisfaction for the employees. As a result of these changes, we were also able to increase our asset utilization significantly.

The second trend we see is how commercial real estate is changing. The challenge today is that the network infrastructure decisions are being made by the tenants. The comparison with traditional building technologies is that if a tenant wants to install some equipment requiring plumbing it would be necessary to contact the utility provider and say: "Hey, I'm moving into a new office and I need a new water pipe." It does not make much sense calling the utilities every time a new supply is required. The communications infrastructure we suggest is a shared common infrastructure that is provided like any other utility in the building; the infrastructure is designed into the building from the very start. The real estate industry recently started implementing these infrastructural systems in buildings before the tenants moved in. Once this infrastructure is in the building, it utilizes one network to achieve connectivity in a number of realms: telephone, video, fire alarm, security, building management, etc. We believe that this innovation is as radical as the adoption of the steel frame or the elevator in the nineteenth century. It is the deployment of connectivity and building intelligence through the communication infrastructure that can differentiate buildings in the current and future real estate markets.

I believe that Cisco is best positioned to become the industry leader for this type of technological solution and I hope that in the near future you will see a great expansion into this field. So much for the building infrastructure. How would we as users interact with it? Figure 15.3 is a guess at what a typical terminal might look like which incorporated some of the services referred to above. It would look like a telephone because that is the equipment we are all pretty familiar with but it is a networked communications device with multiple functions and services; it would also work with other communication devices like a laptop or a PDA which would also incorporate a little screen and a web cam. There will be many such products that can be plugged into the network and this is just one example of an emerging product type that will impact the physical design of buildings.

15.3 Internet-based communication device

Building Operating Systems

Jupp Gauchel

RaumComputer is a small organization of 16 employees. We are based in Germany and we have a partner organization in California with whom we collaborate. We implement Building Operating Systems.

Before discussing Building Operating Systems in detail, it is important to explain why building automation is becoming increasingly important. Building automation constitutes a small percentage of the overall building budget, generally around 1–1.5 percent. If one installs a smart building automation system, then one can reduce the annual operation costs of a building by approximately 30 percent. Many studies have now

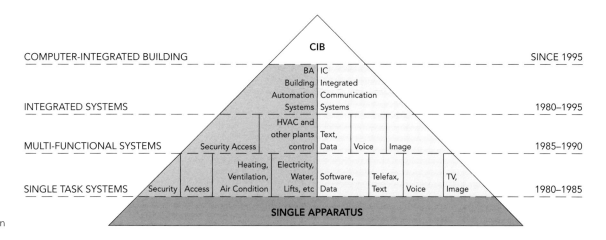

15.4 Intelligent Building: CIB-Vision

been carried out to substantiate this claim. One such study carried out by Luxmate, a very highly regarded Austrian lighting manufacturer, shows that substantial savings can be made just by installing daylight-linked lighting control systems; these measure the amount of natural light available and supplement it with artificial light as necessary.[1]

Another very useful study was carried out by Manfred Riedel who developed a very smart system for separate heating and ventilation control systems in residential buildings. In the past half a dozen years he has managed to build this system into more than 25,000 homes. His results show that energy savings of between 25–30 percent can be achieved in this way. The equipment to facilitate these savings is really quite simple, it is only slightly more complicated than conventional switching systems but overall it remains quite simple.

Turning to the work that I am currently engaged in at RaumComputer, Figure 15.4 shows a diagram which was very influential as our starting point in the early 1990s. It was actually generated by Francis Duffy and illustrates the idea held at the time by specialists in this field, that all the different building operating systems that could be installed in a building should converge into one integrated system. This concept was developed long before its originators knew what the Internet was, let alone what a modern data network could do. Nevertheless, it was a powerful vision of the future. So when we

started our research at RaumComputer we took this idea and tried to realize this vision.

When we started to tackle this problem, we thought: let's take this drawing and use the information technology available to realize this concept in an actual building. Working with organizations like Cisco Systems we succeeded in bringing all the right parts together to formulate an integrated communications approach. If one looks at all the different Building Operating Systems on the market, it is quite obvious that they are not all compatible. We focused our attention on a very simple idea: we took all the technologies that were developed by companies like Cisco and made them compatible and used them to do all the things that these technologies are theoretically capable of doing in terms of servicing the building occupiers and the Building Operating Systems. We have now been working on this idea for just over five years.

The implementation of these ideas necessitates a paradigm shift; we must move away from systems that are based on electricity to systems that are based on data. This transition is facilitated by the idea of moving away from very narrow bandwidths to bandwidths that are so broad that they are very accommodating and allow multiple functions to be carried out simultaneously. This shift inevitably leads to changes in related technologies. Two changes that resulted from these innovations were: a move away from conventional, i.e. dedicated, wiring circuits and the substitution of conventional switches by interactive web pages. RaumComputer believes strongly in the idea of having one IT infrastructure for all services, thus eliminating the proliferation of single task wiring systems common today. We believe this idea saves time and money and brings greater convenience to the occupants.

Even though we are introducing a great deal of new technology it is important to bear one thing in mind: there are people like my 84-year-old mother who will never learn to manage lighting through a web page so the simple light switch will retain its importance because of its simplicity and legibility. However, when functions start to get complex, controls can be better managed through web pages. These web page-based controls may be unfamiliar to a US audience but they are becoming increasingly common features in buildings in Germany as well as in other European countries.

RaumComputer is implementing this vision by using PC and Internet technologies. We are also expanding the functional range of this vision in three important ways; first, the whole approach is heavily rooted in facilities management; second, we are including multimedia and conferencing facilities; and third, we can also offer eCommerce. Very few clients are currently willing to engage in eCommerce but we believe this will change radically in the next few years.

If we consider the conventional building design process, we see that in many cases the decision regarding the incorporation of building automation is made at a relatively late stage in the design. At this point the tenant will decide what kind of IT systems they want. We take a quite different approach; we prefer to introduce, in the very early stages of the design, what we call an Integrated Information Technology Infrastructure. This way the information technology becomes embedded and integrated into the architecture.

Next I would like to say something about the technology we use. RaumComputer is wholly dependent on Intranet and no other system. A very important aspect of our organization is that we develop integrated software tools for management and automation. In the field we can use any device or bus system that talks TCP/IP (standard Local Area Network/Internet Protocol). The interface can be any mix of standard control device, webpage, or Internet Protocol (IP) phone. Wolfgang Wagener mentioned the new generation of IP phones. We

believe that the new telephones will not be real telephones in the sense that we understand them today; they will be small, smart audio computers that will utilize the Internet as a medium for communication. This is something that Wolfgang, Matthew and I all believe in quite strongly as a vision for the future. Although many of the systems that are on the market today need very special devices, the equipment we use is all standard and commercially available.

RaumComputer is geared up to deal with the increasing pace of change in modern work organizations. We feel that this is one of our most important assets. Whenever necessary, we can reconfigure RaumComputer installations online. It is not necessary to have detailed technical knowledge to be able to do this since the changes are not being carried out to the hardware; instead it is the settings that are being adjusted. Our ultimate objective is that these tasks should be carried out by the tenants' own facilities manager.

The next important factor to mention when dealing with the technology is to stress that because we are handling data and because there may be multiple clients in any one building, data security is imperative. We have proved that our installations are very secure and our many clients are quite satisfied with our product.

The way we organize our work is very important: we designed our own management tools based on facilities management systems. Our tools use graphics but they are based entirely on one object-oriented database that allows us to represent any building automation installation as one large data model; so, first we use software that is capable of designing and documenting the entire installation, then we use another type of software that is capable of automatically translating the design into automation functions (automatic commissioning). At the same time our management tool automatically represents each operable device and automation function as a web-based user interface i.e. as a small web page. A significant result of developing this system is that there is no longer a need for any additional documentation of the installation; the model itself is the documentation and it is free. When the automation is successful, the facilities manager can, from his/her computer, check whether a particular light fixture in another building is working or not and take appropriate action. As well as dealing with individual fixtures, we can group them together in rooms or suites of rooms. The installation of this software gives the building owner the option of making these controls available, via web pages, to the facilities managers or the individual user.

A good example of the installation of this kind of technology was a showcase building we worked on for Cisco Systems in Amsterdam (Figures 15.5 and 15.6). This was the first time we had implemented building automation; we were able to link it with many different services and devices in the same system such as audio and video devices to facilitate multimedia presentations and video conferencing. We also installed wireless readers based on Radio Frequency Identification (RFID) for secure access to certain areas. As we get involved in more projects, we are working on broadening the spectrum of devices and services we can offer.

One of our first installations was in the German Headquarters of Microsoft in Unterschleissheim, Munich in 2000 (Figure 15.7). This project presented us with the opportunity to do something new. The Microsoft offices accommodate approximately 1,500 workspaces and we installed a version of our system where the employees could control their workspaces via web pages

15.6 Cisco Systems, European Headquarters, Amsterdam; conference room showing RaumComputer installation and control panels

on their PCs rather than using switches (Figure 15.8). This innovation was very popular with the workforce and the building owner. In addition, this installation proved that this type of technology was absolutely secure.

Building Optical Networks

Matthew Spathas

Sentre Partners is a real estate service and investment company headquartered in San Diego, California. Our core strategy is really to play at the intersection of real estate, technology, and purpose. If we can execute all three of these effectively, then we'll have a successful and hopefully profitable project. I think the real estate speaks for itself although as we know the workplace is constantly changing. When we look at purpose, we think of Disneyland; people pay a lot of money to stand in line to get onto the rides. If people do that for a building, we know we have a successful real estate project. People want to go to Disneyland; we want people to want to come to our projects.

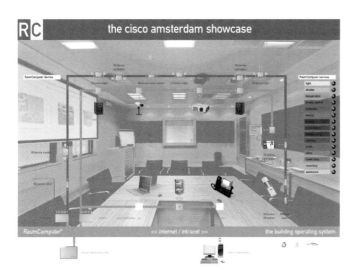

15.5 Cisco Systems, European Headquarters, Amsterdam; conference room showing RaumComputer installation

15.7 Microsoft Headquarters, Germany, external view

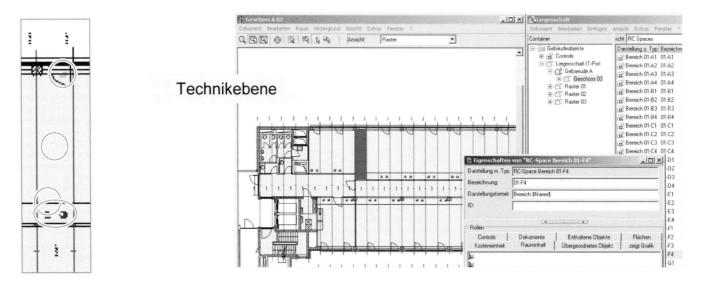

15.8 Microsoft Headquarters, Germany, example of web page control

I wear a second hat as a CEO of a company called Bandwidth Now, which is a next generation utility company that deals with bandwidth and the types of infrastructure we need to put into the buildings that Wolfgang Wagener and Jupp Gauchel were just talking about. I believe that utility companies such as Bandwidth Now will in the near future become as familiar to us as, for example, the traditional electricity utility companies we use today.

One very important way to explain what I do is to address the obstacles to change. The main obstacle is not technology, it is human behavior. Jupp gave the example of his mother; we cannot expect to change her. However, younger generations are growing up with many of these new technologies at their fingertips. Recently, I was talking to Nathan, a student; we were talking about the textbook he had with him; this textbook is a good example of being "stuck in the middle." Nathan was saying that he did not need this textbook since the contents could be web-produced. In fact, I would think that this textbook could become three-dimensional; it could be web-linked and video clipped. If this particular piece of material were web enabled, Nathan could drill down and consult the top experts on that subject and not only read about the topics but hear what they have to say. The technology that allows us to do that starts to change the whole workspace; we don't need this textbook; we don't need the bookstore on campus, if we no longer need to be in our office to work any more that affects the work we do. So, we are now presented with a new set of rules and we need to pay attention to them. We need to bear in mind the new technology and the new generation; these are the people we should be building for; building environments that will provide live–work–play environments.

Another major change that is under way is the notion of the address which locates each of us. The traditional street address was created for the horse and buggy; we have developed beyond that technology. We now need to pay attention to the Internet Protocol (IP) address that is being referred to as part of the new technology. So even an address is a changing paradigm. The next generation of maps may well list your IP address and not your street address. How many addresses do most of us have? A phone address, a street address and an email address. In the future, all we will need will be one IP address; it will direct us and enable us to make calls and locate people. I think of our generation as the Etch-a-Sketch generation and Nathan's generation is the Play Station generation. There are fundamental differences between these generations.

How will the IP address impact the street address? To answer this I would like to outline how we at Sentre Partners tackled this issue. About three years ago we embarked on a one-year pilot scheme with Intel; we said to them: "We have big boxes called buildings, you have little boxes called PCs, they both need processing power. How can we make our buildings smart? How can we brand our buildings the way you brand your PCs?" After a two-year study we invited some market leaders like WFI, Cisco, and Corning to join our team because we wanted the specialists in our area of interest to study the new "eco-system" inside our buildings. As a result of their input, we have been able to complete six "next generation" buildings. We name them in Gs; since there are six of them we call our sixth one 6G, i.e. sixth generation and every generation gets better and more sophisticated. One important innovation is that the networks are "standards-based"; we have created some standards such as the use of fiber optics rather than copper wiring throughout the building. Another idea was the introduction of bandwidth as a utility and Wireless Fidelity (WiFi) as an amenity. We think it is all about the tenants; these innovations improve our buildings' efficiency for our tenants by allowing them to plug into a data port and be on the net wherever they are in our buildings. What is more important is that our infrastructure can be ten times faster and six or seven times cheaper than the one you can get from most service providers.

There are questions and implications here for architects: the new data networks need to be included in the design just like the water, gas and electricity utilities. Clients and architects should be investigating how this new infrastructure can best suit the user. We should be thinking about the optical network in similar terms to the electrical network except that it is much safer since it will not electrocute us. In fact, since the optical network is IP-based, it is a great deal simpler than the electrical system. Our objective is to enable the tenant to plug into any data port just like they plug into an electrical outlet. Building owners should own the pre-optical infrastructure such as the electrical switches, wiring and transformers since they are part of the building, however, the network should be managed by a third party.

As Wolfgang suggested, we believe in multiple carriers in buildings rather than one carrier and one common distribution network we can all plug into. The simplest example of this is a Building Optical Network (BON) installed in the core of a building which would enable the aggregation of bandwidths. Until the real estate community tackles this issue, we will continue to build inefficient buildings.

This Building Optical Network (BON) enables four things inside buildings: it aggregates, automates, integrates and enables. It is quite simple to illustrate the benefits of aggregation over non-aggregation. If individual tenants buy internet connectivity, then they are all paying separately for this service and the unaggregated cost quickly escalates. However, if the building owner installs one common network, as Jupp was demonstrating, then we can treat it like electricity and tenants can plug in whenever they want. As a result the costs are so low that internet connectivity is virtually free. As explained earlier, we can also use the BON to automate our buildings.

The third advantage is integration which allows us to deliver smart services. For example, in my office, my email comes into my inbox as do my voicemail and my faxes. We do not use fax machines any longer; information comes straight to my desktop. In addition we have very few printers. We have eliminated paper; where we once had 99 filing cabinets, we now have one.

The fourth advantage of the BON is enabling, i.e. the enabling that comes about through the introduction of WiFi. Walking into a space which is not WiFi enabled is like walking into a space without electricity; being in a meeting and not being able to flick open your laptop and get connected to the Internet is like not having any light in your office. We have installed WiFi into all six of the buildings that I mentioned earlier so you can double click on Internet Explorer. You have access to the Internet and it is free. In summary, we need to develop a standardized network, we did it for electricity and we can do it again for data.

Wolfgang and Jupp both talked about the "back end" integration of building systems, i.e. the lighting, fire alarms, security, HVAC, access, etc. We call the other side the "front end" which is comprised of a "dumb pipe" and "smart services." Let's not confuse these two; we can separate the dumb pipe (bandwidth as a utility, wireless as an amenity) from the smart services (IP telephony, unified messaging and digital filing). Tenants just want to be able to plug into the Internet when they move in and our tenants plug in the minute they want wireless as an amenity. The smart services can be a little more complicated. We let the market leaders like Cisco Systems provide the smart services.

I would like to address Return on Investment (ROI) briefly. Here is a real estate owner perspective: If we invest $500,000 in a network in a 569,000 sq ft (52,860 sq m) building we would need to get 9 cents a square foot a year in additional rent to get a 10 percent return. Doing this would provide a phenomenal yield in our business. We estimate that we are saving our tenants about $1.56 per sq ft (£10.00 per sq m) a year in rent. Compare this to the 9 cents we need to get; there is a large margin there, and if we can leverage that margin to get better tenants and higher rents, we can create more value inside our buildings.

In closing, I will leave you with some guiding principles that we have come up with. First, as with most things in our business it all starts with a tenant; it is not about technology, it's not about sensors, it's not about VOIP, it's all about how we make our tenants more productive and be more effective in their business and pay us more rent.

Second, install the new technology, i.e. fiber optics. The building owners should also own the infrastructure like they own the elevators. We own elevators; we call Otis or Mitsubishi to manage them. Similarly, we own our Building Optical Network and pick up the phone and call somebody to manage the network for you. Let "best of class" carriers provide you the smart services on the network. We do not see the smart services as an area of revenue share. There is a lot of dialogue about whether owners should be profiting in this area; we do not profit on electricity, we just deliver electricity. We do not think we ought to profit on this as a business. For us, the drivers are higher rents and better tenants.

Note

1 The results of this study are available on Luxmate's web site: www.luxmate.com

Connected Buildings

Wolfgang Wagener

Digital Convergence

Seated on Lufthansa flight 459 – from San Francisco to Munich – I can nowadays switch on my laptop shortly after take-off and via the Lufthansa portal can operate my web browser without needing to plug in. The brand new Airbus A 340s that ply this route are equipped with FlyNet, the first in-flight wireless broadband Internet service offered by any commercial airline. What is more, the bandwidth is very nearly equal to that available on the ground. For a small fee, I can have full Internet access and can even connect remotely to Cisco Systems' secure private intranet, simply by entering my employee password. In flight 37,500 ft (11,430 m) above ground and at a cruising speed of 560 miles (901 km) per hour, I have the same company resources at hand as I would have sitting in Cisco's Silicon Valley headquarters. I can connect with colleagues, business partners, even family and friends, through Internet-based phone calls, instant messaging accompanied by live video, or via e-mail. For personal entertainment, I can mix my favorite live streaming broadcasts from radio stations in Munich and San Francisco. I have the additional ability of watching Web-TV or downloading an online movie. Untethered from my seat, I can roam the aisles with my mobile communication device and be productive from anywhere on the plane during the greater part of my 11-hour flight.

If we stop to think about it, we soon realize that the same infrastructure that facilitates passenger services is simultaneously providing crew communications, airplane operations, onboard retailing, in-flight entertainment, emergency telemedicine, freight, fuel and catering tracking, air traffic control, passenger safety and security, environmental control and energy management services, as well as a host of other applications.

After years of anticipatory tech-talk, my in-flight experience demonstrates that the digital convergence of communication networks, media content and wireless devices has finally entered the mainstream. The communication infrastructure that supports my in-flight connectivity marks the emergence of an integrated wireless communication system. To deliver what we have casually come to call the Internet, four key levels must combine together seamlessly. On the personal level, my headset connects to my laptop via Bluetooth. The airplane environment is defined by my laptop's interface with the cabin's wireless local area network. On a truly spatial level, the cabin links by way of satellite to the terrestrial infrastructure. Finally, on the global scale, the information transmission infrastructure consisting of wired and wireless service providers, public sector enterprise and passengers' home networks, connects in turn to an individual at home or in transit.

Technological advances often offer unforeseen opportunities to streamline existing technologies. For example, the communications infrastructure necessary for a highly complex and mobile airplane environment, presents us with the means of improving the everyday functionality of static building environments. This new technology prompts us to rethink building design to maximize the benefits of technologically enhanced environments. Buildings have the advantage of being inhabited at one's leisure and are not held to an airplane schedule, in addition to offering more legroom. What both mobile and immobile environments have in common is that they can be connected to the same global communication network, a network that is influencing the way we live, work and play (Figure 16.1).

As the communication infrastructure moves out of data-centers and into headquarters, branch offices, transportation venues, mobile devices and virtual spaces, information is being issued to and received by people everywhere and at all times. The growing mobility of employees and the complexity of what work involves are propelling the workplace to evolve into a network of varied physical locations that are complemented by the ubiquitous availability of the virtual workspace. In its final interpretation, the Internet itself is becoming "the workplace"; this changes the role of physical places – the core business of developers, architects, engineers and real estate professionals. Office buildings are currently designed to organize the information-processing activities of businesses and governments with the goal of maximizing worker productivity. Traditionally, office workers have had to go to a fixed physical infrastructure – the office – to be productive. In a world in which the infrastructure is becoming increasingly mobile, information follows the workforce. The emerging real estate pattern of the twenty-first-century workforce is that of self-organizing workers who utilize multiple, diverse workplaces within a single building, a portfolio of buildings or cities at large. The role of real estate is evolving from a predetermined information processing space

into a responsive, smart and effective place for the social interaction of permanent and temporary office users, guests and customers. These new environments should also satisfy the need for face-to-face communication, teamwork, collaboration and informal exchange.

This evolution is one example of how technology is transforming the way we understand real estate. By tradition, we have identified separate vertical retail, industrial, office, education, hospitality and residential markets. The developing technologies are fostering the creation of increasingly distributed activities and increasingly adaptable forms of real estate; the accepted classifications are starting to blur. Horizontal structures with new clusters and development mixes are spanning across various vertical industries and building types. As a result of the growing mobility of people, goods and information, it is now necessary to revisit the production and management of structures for their intended use.[1]

Creating Economic Value

The Internet is the most recent example of a complex network governing modern life. Earlier networks have included the street (as the infrastructure for personal transit), the railroad, the electrical grid and the telephone system. Throughout much of human history, networks were rare and far apart. The speed of their growth was stimulated by events such as the Industrial Revolution, which reduced the costs of manufactured goods to a level that allowed for mass consumption. At the heart of today's network interaction is cheap and plentiful digital bandwidth, this broadband explosion holds the key for the next level of economic value creation.[2] From an economic perspective, the defining feature of a network economy is that the value of the membership increases as the network grows. Each network brings additional sectors of the overall economy into the network economy. Mature industries tend to change slowly; the building industry is no exception. It is also one of the largest segments of the global Gross Domestic Product; however, due to the legacy of a fragmented and localized technological era, it yet has to be brought into the network economy to harvest the potential economic wealth that the network offers.

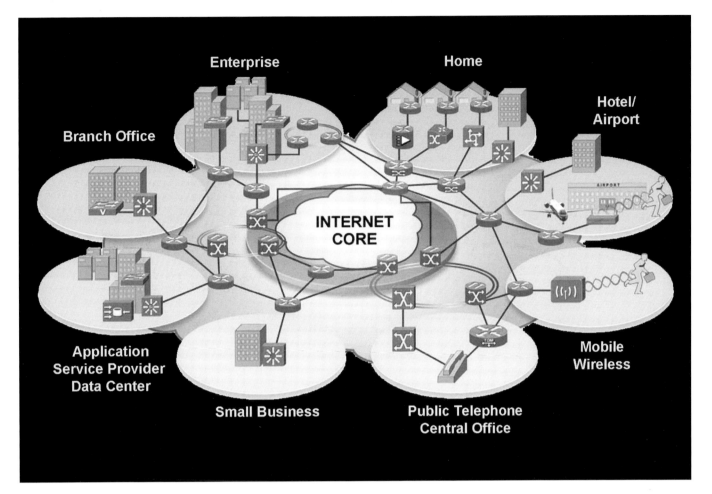

16.1 Places in the global information network

The interaction between real estate, technology, economics, and public policy is a challenge. After all, information technology is not new. The microprocessor was introduced in the 1970s, personal computers date from the 1980s and the Internet evolved in the 1990s from a research tool into an unsurpassed global infrastructure for commerce, entertainment, education, and communication. The placing of a computer on everybody's desk has advanced individual worker productivity to some degree. Yet to reap the full measure of productivity benefits of today's digital network economy, an essential and thoughtful restructuring of the organization of work, the place of work, and the spatial distribution of work should take place.

Stanford historian Paul A. David put this relationship into a historical perspective in his 1990 essay, "The Dynamo and the Computer,"[3] where he studied the relationship of technological innovation and productivity gains characteristic of network industries using electricity as an example. Although electricity was invented around 1870, the big economic payoff from electrification didn't happen until after World War I. The replacement of steam engines with electric motors didn't do much on its own; business owners took advantage of the new technology to reassess what building infrastructure best suited the new technology. Steam-engine-powered factories were compact, multi-storey buildings, the optimal design for power that had to be conveyed via shafts and belts from a steam engine in the basement. When new electric utility companies made cheap electricity available after 1905, manufacturers started to realize the advantage of sprawling, one-storey building structures, where each machine was driven by its own electric motor. The work on the factory floor was untethered from the steam engine and created mobility for people and goods. Machines could now be put anywhere to facilitate efficient operations, not just where belts and shafts could most easily reach them. The implementation of these economic benefits required the design of new buildings that needed a new type of architect, a new type of electrical engineer and contractor that understood electrically powered manufacturing processes.[4]

Technology has always been one of the external factors that shape the economic value of real estate alongside location, market cycles, capital markets, demographics and economics. But it is primarily technology that drives building design and true innovation in the physical fabric of buildings, and therefore cities. Technological developments have liberated buildings and cities from their dependency on site and nature by creating technologically enhanced environments.[5] A few historical examples are quoted below:

• Regional water supply delivery developments and sewage disposal systems in the early 1900s transformed industrialized cities into healthy and sanitary places.

- National electricity and gas systems put into place in the first half of the twentieth century extended the daily hours and the range of human activities by illuminating, heating and cooling places at an affordable rate.
- National telephone and telegraph networks in the early twentieth century allowed communication over long distances, changing the spatial distribution of real estate. Management and industrial production could be separated, thus allowing managers and clerical workers to cluster in central business districts. On an urban scale, noisy, polluted industrial zones were located separately from residential "garden cities."
- International car, train, ship and plane infrastructure developments provided greater speed, safety and economy in transportation. These improvements allowed for true spatial separation between goods and people and resulted in, among other things, urban sprawl.
- Fluorescent lighting and air conditioning were as important for the transformation of the mid-twentieth-century real estate, as the elevator and steel cage were for the late nineteenth century: floor plates became deeper to provide more rentable space; ceiling heights were reduced to provide more stories per building; and space planning favored open plan and flexibility.

One Cable, One Protocol, Plug and Play

The developments mentioned above brought us, in the 1980s, to the doorstep of digital technology. Yet, while the technology itself has become more affordable, ubiquitous, reliable and standardized, hardly any of these advances have yet affected the design of buildings. If we study today's buildings, we see an increase of wired and wireless infrastructures (communications, video, audio, multi-media, digital façade, life safety and environmental control systems) that result in a plethora of separate networks. These networks include physical components and computer intelligence that transport information within and across buildings, i.e. cabling, devices, desktop computers, cameras, access points, displays, servers, routers, racks, antennas, controllers, sensors and operation centers, to name just a few. While the digital communication infrastructure is hardly

understood by today's real estate and building industries, its impact is starting to affect every aspect of the real estate lifecycle. The evolution towards more information technology in buildings, started in the 1980s, was triggered by five major trends:

1   In the mid-1980s, mainframe and personal computers became connected with each other utilizing twisted-pair cables to facilitate the processing of business information.
2   In 1986, the Federal Communications Commission (FCC) deregulated the US telephone industry, permitting the connection of customer-owned devices directly to the public network.
3   By the mid-1990s, the Internet had evolved into a global communications infrastructure.
4   By the turn of the twenty-first century, wireless devices had increased the mobility of people and machines.
5   In 2005, data, voice, video, life safety and building automation systems converged into one intelligent information network platform.

This series of events clearly demonstrates a move towards ever-present information technology in buildings. The role that Internet-based standards are playing has a major impact on the way real estate owners conduct their business. What makes convergence important is that web and communication transmission standards are already incorporated in the information technology infrastructures within major companies, the public sector and across the World Wide Web. The communications infrastructures will eventually carry all the building-related information that real estate owners need to manage and improve both technical building and financial real estate performance. As buildings and their space utilization, services, energy management, multi-media, safety, security, mechanical, electrical, and plumbing systems are increasingly designed to rely on the Internet, the information transmission infrastructure needs to be established as the new 'foundation' of a building. It has to be designed and installed early in the building process, so that other systems can be integrated with a "one cable, one protocol, plug and play" approach. More importantly, utilizing the Internet allows building owners to move from a building-centric to a portfolio-centric approach by means of the centralized

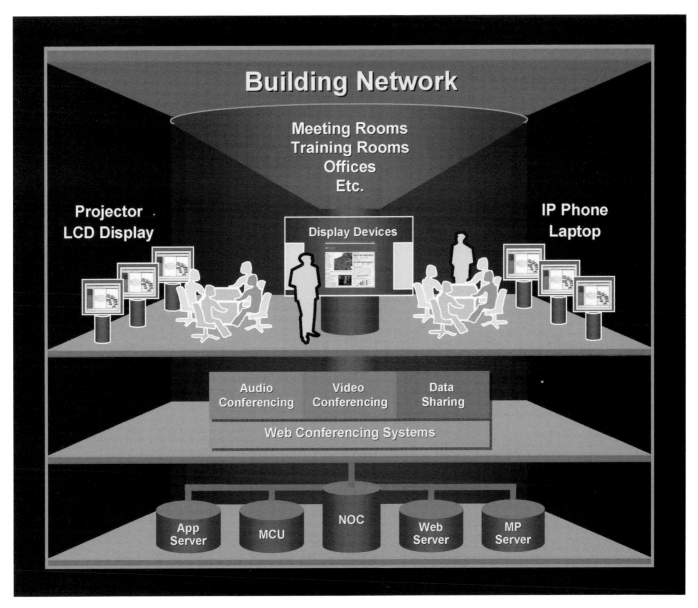

16.2 Building information network

operations and managed services that can now be delivered remotely. The more that buildings get connected to the information network, the higher the economic benefits for real estate owners and operators (Figure 16.2).

Compare today's Information Technology revolution to the advent of mechanical, electrical, and plumbing systems at the turn of the twentieth century to move air, electricity and water within and across buildings.[6] As these systems needed more space and pathways to allow integration into the overall building structure, so the real estate and building industry adapted to these demands. The new technologies forced new types of buildings and professionals to emerge. Architects, mechanical, electrical and plumbing engineers, contractors and property managers understood how to design, build and manage these new systems. Today, these systems account for up to 50 percent of today's building construction costs and their operations are responsible for most of the world's energy consumption.

At the turn of the twenty-first century, the digital convergence of communications, life safety, and automation systems are once again an emerging professional field in the real estate and building industries. Architects, communications and network engineers, contractors and real estate managers who understand how to design, build and manage these technologies are becoming trusted advisors for building owners and developers. Most importantly, they can make the business case of why a technology strategy is needed for new real estate developments as well as for upgrades of existing structures.

Rethinking Design

What do you have when ceilings turn into antennas, signage becomes digital, walls evolve into media-rich surfaces, floors manage comfort and building envelopes develop into programmable surfaces? The answer is: a building, which itself is a computer. This computerized structure is becoming so developed that it senses and responds to climate change, electrical current, air flow, occupant health while simultaneously monitoring the digital design, construction and real estate management process. Time rather than space becomes the principal organizing factor for the activities within and the results are: an intensification of space use; new clusters of adjacencies; enhanced environmental sustainability; and higher levels of amenities and functionality.

The Challenge

In the not too far distant future, we will look back to the present industrial production and transaction-based building types with the same nostalgia we currently reserve for historic agricultural building types, including medieval cities, baroque churches and French châteaux. The acceleration of technology that is enabling new ways of economic and spatial distribution is an invitation to architects to create new building types based on virtual and face-to-face interaction. The question is: can the profession rise to the challenge?

Notes and References

1 For one of the first comprehensive studies on the impact of information technology on real estate, see Dixon, T. *et al.* (2005) *Real Estate and the New Economy*, Oxford: Blackwell Publishing.
2 For an in-depth analysis, see Austin, R.D. and Bradley, S.P. (2005) *The Broadband Explosion*, Boston: Harvard Business School Press.
3 David, P.A. (1990) "The Dynamo and the Computer: An Historical Perspective on the Modern Productivity Paradox," *The American Economic Review*, 80(2): 355–361.
4 One of the key architects was Albert Kahn. See Hawkins Ferry, W. (1987) *The Legacy of Albert Kahn*, Detroit: Wayne State University Press.
5 See William J. Mitchell's trilogy at the turn of the twenty-first century for an in-depth analysis of the relationship of technology, buildings and cities: Mitchell, W.J. (1995) *City of Bits: Space, Place and the Infobahn*, Cambridge, MA: The MIT Press; (1999) *e-topia: 'Urban Life, Jim – But Not As We Know It'*, Cambridge, MA: The MIT Press; (2003) *Me++: The Cyborg Self and the New Networked City*, Cambridge, MA: The MIT Press.
6 Banham, R. (1984) *The Architecture of the Well-Tempered Environment*, London: The Architectural Press.

Part III

The Future

Measurement

The Key to Reinventing the Office

Francis Duffy

Introduction

The first aim of this chapter is to examine why current developments in Information Technology have had so little impact on North American office design with the extraordinary and paradoxical result that a sharp contradiction now exists between the vitality of new office technologies and processes and the inertia of those who design and supply office space. The second aim is to propose a means of bringing supply and demand not just into equilibrium but into a virtuous cycle of continuing improvement.

To a European observer, office design in North America today seems to be largely stuck in a cost-cutting time warp. American office developers in the past two or three decades appear to have reduced their expectations of architectural innovation to cutting first costs and accelerating construction times. The same stereotypical office designs are replicated over and over again, only in cheaper, quicker and, it must be said, generally in ever nastier ways. Unimaginatively standardized floor plates, ever more superficial skins, gas-guzzling environmental systems, formulaic space planning, interiors full of cubicle work stations in the mode of Dilbertville, are the salient features of the vast majority of offices, high or low rise. All of which is very different from the magnificence and inventiveness of the American office buildings of the 1960s and 1970s. While things are somewhat better on the other side of the Atlantic, the fear is that the same could easily happen here for similar underlying, allegedly "economic" reasons.

There are, in fact, two paradoxes in this situation. The first is that, unlike their European equivalents, few American office workers complain about their working conditions. They seem to take the low quality of the office accommodation they are given as inevitable. The second paradox is that during exactly the same period as office accommodation has been degraded, office work, as opposed to office buildings, has been completely revitalized, largely through American technological achievements. The ubiquitous availability of robust, reliable information technology has transformed office processes in ways that are at least as important as the changes stimulated by the huge burst of economic activity and technological invention that led to the invention of the high rise office in Chicago and New York in the decades following the end of the

American Civil War. Indeed, what is happening today in office work may turn out to be as spectacular as the enormous changes in social structure, temporal conventions and urban conditions created by the Industrial Revolution.

The conclusion is that the degenerative condition cited above is certainly not inevitable. Overemphasis on cost-cutting in the supply of office space in North America has been like a temporary medical condition blocking the flow of blood or oxygen to the brain and preventing the body as a whole achieving its full potential. There is far more to office design than economy. Office space can, and indeed must, perform many higher functions for business, especially in the increasingly intellectually demanding knowledge economy. However, in order to harness the power of office design to enhance business performance, two conditions are necessary: (1) users must be prepared to measure office performance against clearly articulated business goals; and (2) developers, architects and other suppliers of office space must listen to the results of such performance measures and be prepared to act accordingly.

An Auspicious Beginning

When Frank Lloyd Wright designed a new office building for the Larkin Company in Buffalo, New York, exactly one hundred years ago, he wasn't working on his own. His clients were pioneers in the rapidly expanding mail order business. They wanted a new office building to enhance their chances of commercial success. They chose Wright as the best architect available to help them reinvent the workplace to take advantage of the latest ideas in technology and management. Wright, despite his notorious ego, played a deftly handled part within a carefully directed and completely self-conscious managerial program. His wonderful building, tiny in relation to the huge expanse of warehouses and manufactories that surrounded it, with its noble atrium, innovative environmental systems, all-round visibility, interconnectedness, and inclusiveness, and above all its sharply directed if somewhat paternalist branding, was at least as much the Larkin Company's achievement as his. Each feature of the architecture of this extraordinary building had a business purpose: to support a commercial strategy, to accommodate innovative work processes, and to broadcast a particular set of business values.

Why aren't all office buildings today in North America, or indeed in Europe, as purposeful as Larkin was in its day? How did we get from this shining example of using architecture as the infrastructure of business achievement to where we are today in the USA, the land of Scott Adams' melancholy comic strip, Dilbert? Adam's visual commentaries are based on his own experience of working in the offices of Pacific Bell, where cubes and labyrinthine interiors have become such powerful metaphors of bureaucratic frustration.

This question was the background to the study commissioned in December 2003 by the Commission for Architecture and the Built Environment (CABE) in liaison with the British Council of Offices (BCO). CABE/BCO's formal objective was a review of the academic and scientific literature that has in the past century attempted to assess the relationship between the design of the workplace and business performance. An important underlying component of CABE/BCO's motive for commissioning the study was the hope that somewhere in the scientific archives must lie a treasure trove of immediately applicable scientific findings, for some reason capriciously neglected, that would throw immediate light on how to make office environments more productive.

Thirty years of experience of both office design and scientific endeavor in this area have made DEGW somewhat skeptical of such an outcome. This field of research is still influenced by the long-term consequences of one of the best-known crises in the development of social science in the first half of the twentieth century, the famous Hawthorn Studies[1] which dashed determinist expectations of finding a simple connection between the working environment and productivity. This disappointment had the unfortunate effect of devaluing for many decades the physical environment as an independent variable worthy of serious scientific consideration by mainstream social scientists.

The CABE/BCO Literature Review

The CABE/BCO study was an ambitious endeavor in a complex and little understood field in which the inadequacies of design research overlap the limits of social science. It is hardly an exaggeration to say that the continuing failure to understand in a scientific way the relationship between the working environment and business purpose puts architects and designers, in this particular field at least, in an analogous position to early nineteenth-century physicians before the science of epidemiology had been firmly established with their limited and erroneous notions about the transmission of disease.

The bulk of the CABE/BCO report consists of an examination of the research literature on the relationship between office design and various aspects of business productivity. Most of the sources quoted are direct attempts to establish such relationships. These studies have generally been initiated by researchers who have started from the examination of office design variables, such as density of occupation, degree of enclosure, lighting levels, presence or absence of external views, in order to establish or test some hypothetical individual or social consequence – such as the holy grail of increased productivity. As the CABE/BCO study progressed, it appeared that one of the principal reasons for the relatively small amount of progress in innovative office design noted above has been that too much has been expected of the wrong scientific model. Given the difficulties inherent in this particularly complex field, treating features of office design as independent variables may very well have been exactly the wrong starting point. An alternative perspective exists, tantalizing but fugitive, expressed occasionally by business writers such as Tom Peters[2] who have looked at office design through the business end of the same telescope.

Such commentators, who tend not to be researchers, start from a business perspective and ask a similar question about the relationship of office design to productivity but in reverse. They are less curious about the consequences of design variables on business but much more interested in the office design implications of business drivers and priorities. This alternative literature was also reviewed but since it stems more from intelligent commentary than from fieldwork it can be used more for its insights than as a database.

Overcoming Failure

There are at least seven very real and practical reasons for the general failure to establish a robust empirical basis on which the design of working environments, and especially offices, can be based:

1   The volatile commercial and economic context within which businesses operate means that they have to continually plan and re-plan the use of the working environment to meet their changing priorities.
2   The inherently complex and multivariate nature of the relationship, even at a single point of time, between the working environment and business processes, organizational structures, and corporate cultures.
3   The large-scale, longitudinal, many layered nature of the physical working environment itself – ranging from urban design to tiny ergonomic details of the adjustment of individual workplaces.
4   The clumsy, fragmented and largely feedback-free ways in which the office building supply chain is managed, from strategic and long-term investment decisions by financial institutions to the tactical, short-term changes continually being made by end users to their immediate working environment.
5   The rapid rate at which office organizations and office technology are changing and developing compared with the sluggish pace at which office buildings are planned, procured, erected and refitted.
6   The plural and highly political nature not only of businesses, which by definition are directed and purposeful, but also of office buildings and interiors, which are used, usually in a less than fully conscious way by various constituencies as a medium to express their culture and values.
7   The largely unexploited potential of the workplace environment, especially in the context of the processes by which such environments are acquired, designed and modified, to accelerate business and cultural change.

Given such a wide canvas of constituencies and interests and the huge variety of physical and temporal scales within which businesses operate, it is not surprising that conventional social science methods have not worked. They have excluded too many variables. They have relied too much on data from individual respondents. Perversely and pointlessly they have aspired to be value-free. This line of attack will never be rich, agile or subtle enough to draw a complete picture of the ever-changing and politically charged relationship between people and the working environment.

The seven problems listed above can be transformed into advantages. Looking coolly at the data surveyed in the CABE/ BCO study, there is certainly a distressing absence of relevance to business performance in most office workplace research. An opposite approach, founded on an insistence of relevance, should cumulatively lead to much more useful results. However, before practical recommendations can be made confidently to developers, designers and researchers, design needs to be linked systematically to business purpose. The best way to do this is by creating two complementary evaluative frameworks.

The Value of Evaluative Frameworks

The absence of such a theoretical approach is the principal reason why management has given up on trying to understand a series of relationships that come into the "too difficult to solve" category, thus opening the way to a simplistic over-emphasis on cost-cutting. No one discipline can provide a complete set of answers to such a wide range of inherently interdisciplinary questions. An alternative, integrated research approach is essential because research in this complex and changing field must depend on the experience, judgment and commitment of all the key constituencies actually involved in office work processes. A much more sophisticated economic dimension of the contribution of design initiatives to business performance is obviously critical to both sides of the supply and demand equation, i.e. research must be conducted in ways that demonstrate to corporate real estate managers and to senior management the contribution that workspace can make, not just to cost-cutting, but also to stimulating and sustaining business success. Similarly, research must demonstrably help institutions and developers to make more profitable and less risk-prone investment decisions.

DEGW's recent work has resulted in two complementary evaluative frameworks that have proved to be useful guides to the measurement of the performance of many aspects of office space in relation to a wide range of business goals; their value may well be because they are both simple and memorable enough to keep the big picture of business purpose in everyone's mind.

The first of these frameworks, now often called "the three e's," is about measuring what the work environment can do for business. The framework distinguishes between three very different contributions that the working environment can make to business – greater *efficiency*, greater *effectiveness* and more powerful and better directed *expression*. The framework has been developed in the past ten years, initially as the result of a very fruitful period of collaboration between DEGW and Steelcase Inc. in the late 1980s and early 1990s.[3] Initially, only two e's were involved, borrowed from the management writer, Peter Drucker who famously distinguished between *efficiency*, i.e. "doing things right" and *effectiveness*, "doing the right things."[4] What Drucker was referring to, in the widest business sense, was in the first case the lower-order business decisions, the effect of which can only be measured within their own narrow terms, i.e. efficiency; the most obvious examples of which are cost-cutting design features and more intensive space use. Second, he was referring to higher-order business initiatives which cross conventional barriers in order to create value, as it were, out of nothing through sheer cleverness and imagination, i.e. effectiveness, examples of which in office design are environments that make possible greater interdepartmental interaction or are stimulating enough to help bright people collaborate more closely.

What Jack Tanis of Steelcase and Francis Duffy of DEGW contributed to Peter Drucker's neatly encapsulated insight was to apply the distinction between efficiency and effectiveness to office design, i.e. to measuring the business benefits of design features that save money and add value. By putting office design into the general context of business, they asserted that the benefits of office design were measurable.

In 2000, Duffy, within the context of DEGW's continuing interest in measuring the contribution of office design to business performance, added a third dimension of measurement: the capacity of office design to express business values and aspirations, internally and externally. The office environment, it was argued, should be seen by management as a powerful and extremely persistent medium of communication. This third dimension was firmly and operationally established as part of DEGW's evaluative framework devised for the financial institution Capital One early in 2002 and has been used extensively ever since.

Within this framework, the performance of the working environment is measured in terms of its success in contributing to three kinds of business objectives:

1   cutting occupancy costs and other business costs – measures of *efficiency*;
2   value added by design to business performance – measures of *effectiveness*;
3   success in broadcasting business values externally and internally – measures of *expression*.

It will be obvious that such measures also provide the basis for setting targets for business performance. Both targets and measures, of course, must be expressed operationally in the same terms – a powerful way of connecting office design and business purpose.

The second framework has the function of relating these specific measures of business performance directly to a wide range of business goals. The pre-existing framework that DEGW (in collaboration with HOK, Gensler and other consultants working together from late 2003 for the Federal General Services Administration and for other US clients) has found most useful for doing this is the "Balanced Scorecard"[5] widely used today in business circles to encourage management to think more strategically and systemically about targets and measures of business performance that go beyond the achievement of purely financial goals. The Balanced Scorecard framework not only takes account of measures of financial success but also three other ranges of measures of business performance that must command the attention of all well-run businesses. The four quadrants of the framework are:

1   the design and conduct of business processes – *Process*;
2   maintaining good relations with customers – *Customers*;

3   maintaining good human relations within the business – *People*;
4   achieving desired levels of financial performance – *Finance*.

Within each of the quadrants, appropriate targets and measures, based on environmental terms upon the three e's, can be organized and displayed. For example, in the CABE/BCO study, the two frameworks were used together to provide the rationale for reviewing the contributions of the working environment to business performance that have been recorded in the empirical literature.

It is important to note that the objective of the Balanced Scorecard is not to insist on any pre-ordained hierarchy of attainment in any of the four quadrants of the model. Nor do the three e's in themselves set automatic targets. Instead, the objective of both frameworks is to help each particular business establish and maintain its own systemic balance between targets and performance measures. All businesses must work out their own priorities for achieving success within their own unique environments and circumstances. The chief value of the Balanced Scorecard is to ensure that none of the four quadrants either totally dominates or is entirely omitted from management's agenda.

Some Practical Lessons

The main lessons that architects and designers may derive from the approach described above when they are seeking to help clients use office space in more powerful and better-directed ways can be summarized as:

1   Always relate measurement to business purpose. Both the workplace and contemporary organizations are complex entities operating within at least four highly volatile environments: physical, technological, social and economic. The workplace does very little on its own. It is only when it is harnessed to business strategy and specific business targets that measurement of workplace performance becomes practical.
2   Recognize that business priorities vary between sectors and, within businesses, even between departments. Moreover,

business priorities change over time. Consequently, diversity and flexibility in the working environment are not just good things in the abstract but are vitally necessary to achieve business objectives.

3   Avoid, in order to prevent the dire consequences so evident in contemporary North American office design noted above, too great an emphasis on measures of cost-cutting. Measures of effectiveness and expression are generally even more important than efficiency.

4   Respect, in the measurement process, the complexity of workplace design, one dimension of which is the varying longevity of different components of the working environment, some aspects of which are measured in decades and some in months. Another increasingly important dimension of the complexity of workplace design is the shifting relationship between real and virtual environments as global networks and distributed working become more important.

5   Take into account the relationship between supply and demand in office design, i.e. understand the relationship between the workplace design and work processes in the context of a full (and critical) understanding of the various ways in which clients and users articulate their requirements, of how buildings are procured and delivered, of how the design and construction processes are carried out, of how facilities management is best conducted. All these processes have an impact on the quality of the workplace (and hence on workplace performance) and must therefore also be evaluated in the context of business purpose. In particular, two parallel kinds of data must be distinguished but also brought together: (a) measures of the performance of office buildings from the point of view of the supply side (investors, developers, letting agents, etc.); and (b) measures of performance of office space from the perspective of the consumers and users of office space.

6   Recognize the existence of different constituencies of interest in the performance of the working environment. The views and priorities of the Boardroom, both long-term and strategic, are likely to be very different from the shorter-term and target-driven needs of department heads, which in turn are certain to be different from the expectations of staff at other levels. Different reporting mechanisms, different targets and different time horizons can be expected. All are legitimate.

7   Realize that the best is the enemy of the good. Not everything can be done at once. Not only is it impossible to measure everything about the relationship between the workplace and business performance simultaneously on every front, it is totally unnecessary. Prioritization is absolutely essential. To make progress in any business context, a relatively small number of highly important and achievable objectives should be the basis on which practical targets can be derived and performance measured.

In the CABE/BCO study, the Harvard Business School Case Study approach is strongly recommended as a potentially effective way of communicating complex, longitudinal, systemically related data involving many interests in a coherent and rigorous way. It is not surprising that this model should be attractive both for research and teaching purposes since there are so many similarities between the kind of data that are useful in the context of a business school and the richness and complexity of the data that are necessary to explain the context, the objectives, the interplay of disciplines and interests, the timeline, the co-ordination, and the consequences that are the stuff of attempts to make the design of office buildings and workspaces actually work for business purposes.

Conclusion: Reinventing the Office

The deterioration of the North American office design has been caused by a classic example of sub-optimization, i.e. too strong a focus on cost-cutting efficiency at the expense of other more important potential contributions of office design to business performance. Given the legacy of Taylorism which encouraged most businesses in the twentieth century to focus on too narrow and too rigid a set of goals, it takes a conscious effort to widen the range of business targets to obtain continuous feedback on a wider range of issues.

Office design has been a neglected resource for too long. Given the opportunities opening up in office design because of the amazing transforming potential of information technology, the first decade of the twenty-first century could see the revival of every aspect of working life, not least the reinvention of the office. However, this possible return to the kind of imaginative grasp of what architecture can achieve exemplified by Frank Lloyd Wright's great Larkin Building depends absolutely upon the systematic measurement of office design against business goals that transcend the short term, the narrow and the purely utilitarian.

Notes and References

1　Mayo, E. (1933) *The Human Problems of an Industrial Civilization*, New York: Macmillan Co.; also Roethlisberger, F.J. and Dickson, W.J. (1939) *Management and the Worker*, Cambridge, MA: Harvard University Press.
2　Peters, T. (2003) *Re-imagine*, London: Dorling Kindersley.
3　Duffy, F. and Tanis, J. (1993) "A Vision of the New Workplace," *Site Selection and Industrial Development*, 38(2): 427.
4　Drucker, P.F. (1964) *The Concept of the Corporation*, New York: New American Library.
5　Kaplan, R. and Nolan, D. (1996) *The Balanced Scorecard; Translating Strategy into Action*, Boston: Harvard Business School Press.

Index

Illustration Credits

The authors and publishers would like to thank the following individuals and institutions for giving permission to reproduce illustrations. We have made every effort to contact copyright holders, but if any errors have been made we would be happy to correct them at a later printing.

Archivision Inc.: 10.1, 10.2, 10.5, 10.6, 10.7, 10.8

Peter Brentlinger: 4.1, 4.2

John E. Breshears: 14.3a+b; 14.6

Tim Buchman: 4.8

Burgess Design Studio: 5.10, 5.11

Cisco Systems: 15.1, 15.2, 15.3, 16.1, 16.2

Center for Building Perfomance and Diagnostics, School of Architecture, Carnegie Mellon University: 2.1

Crescent Resources, LLC: 8.1, 8.2, 8.3

Crosland Inc. & Shook Kelly: 5.7, 5.8

H. G. Esch: 9.3, 9.5, 9.9, 9.10, 9.16, 9.17, 9.19

W. L. Gore & Associates Inc.: 14.1

T. R. Hamzah & Yeang International: 11.1; 11.2; 11.3, 14.7, 14.8, 14.9, 14.10

Hinson Ltd. Public Relations: 6.3

Ingenhoven Architekten GmbH: 9.4, 9.7, 9.8, 9.11, 9.15

Kei Ito: 14.5

Holger Knauf: 9.1, 9.12

Peter Krämer: 9.13, 9.18

Ian Lambot: 10.9

Little (www.littleonline.com): 4.3, 4.7, 4.9

LS3P Associates Ltd.: 6.5, 6.6

Peter Mauss/Esto: 4.4, 4.5, 4.6

Kohn Pedersen Fox Associates: 10.11, 10.12, 10.13

Walter Pieper: 9.6

Maxwell MacKenzie: 6.1, 6.2

Nucleus Medical Art: 14.2

Office for Metropolitan Architecture (OMA): 10.10

Pappas Properties: 6.7, 6.8

RaumComputer: 15.7

Robert A. M. Stern Architects for Cherokee Northeast, LLC: 7.1, 7.2, 7.3

RTKL Associates Inc.: 6.1

Brian Sytnyk/Masterfile: 10.3

The Laurence Group: 5.9

Taurus of Texas, GP, LLC: 6.4

Titus: 12.2, 12.3

William McDonough & Partners: 13.1, 13.3, 13.4, 13.5

Peter Wels: 9.2, 9.14

Jeremy Woodhouse/Masterfile: 10.4